morality

morality:
the why and
the what of it

JAMES P. STERBA

WITH

GERALD F. GAUS

ALLAN F. GIBBARD

TIBOR R. MACHAN

CHARLES W. MILLS

RUSS SHAFER-LANDAU

ANITA M. SUPERSON

CANDACE A. VOGLER

WESTVIEW
PRESS

A Member of the Perseus Books Group

Westview Press was founded in 1975 in Boulder, Colorado, by notable publisher and intellectual Fred Praeger. Westview Press continues to publish scholarly titles and high-quality undergraduate- and graduate-level textbooks in core social science disciplines. With books developed, written, and edited with the needs of serious nonfiction readers, professors, and students in mind, Westview Press honors its long history of publishing books that matter.

Find us on the World Wide Web at www.westviewpress.com.

Every effort has been made to secure required permissions for all text, images, maps, and other art reprinted in this volume.

Westview Press books are available at special discounts for bulk purchases in the United States by corporations, institutions, and other organizations. For more information, please contact the Special Markets Department at the Perseus Books Group, 2300 Chestnut Street, Suite 200, Philadelphia, PA 19103, or call (800) 810-4145, ext. 5000, or e-mail special.markets@perseusbooks.com.

Designed by Trish Wilkinson
Set in 11.5 point Goudy by the Perseus Books Group

Library of Congress Cataloging-in-Publication Data

Morality : the why and the what of it / [edited by] James P. Sterba.
      p.   cm.
    Includes bibliographical references (p.) and index.
      ISBN 978-0-8133-4681-6 (paperback : alk. paper) — ISBN 978-0-8133-4682-3
(e-book) 1. Ethics. I. Sterba, James P.
BJ1012.M6358 2012
170—dc23   2011033192

10 9 8 7 6 5 4 3 2 1

CONTENTS

PART III: RESPONSES TO THE CRITIQUES

PREFACE

Moral and political philosophy has always been a collective endeavor. It is something we work out together in an ongoing discussion. Although some of us are more engaged in that discussion than others, we are all engaged in it because its two central questions, Why be moral? and What does morality require? are inescapable. Even the moral skeptic or the egoist (or the moral skeptic or the egoist in each one of us) has to engage these questions, if only to try to show that we are not really required to be moral because morality is not really rationally binding on us. Accordingly, my own work on these central questions is itself a product of a long historical discussion that goes back at least to Plato and to discussions that I myself have had over the years with other philosophers, students, and people from all walks of life.

The initial essay in this volume presents my current answers to these two central questions. My answer to the why-be-moral question is that morality is in no way optional because we are rationally required to be moral. My answer to the what-does-morality-require question is that morality is very demanding indeed and requires considerable self-sacrifice.

I have written my essay in a way that I hope is accessible and engaging to a wide audience, given that the questions my essay addresses are inescapable for that same audience. My essay is designed to invite both agreement and disagreement with regard to the answers that I give to these two questions.

To facilitate discussion of the answers that I give to these questions, seven distinguished moral and political philosophers have written critical responses to my essay. These critical responses were then discussed and revised in light of my initial replies to them, to which I now have added a revised reply.

In the end, I still endorse roughly the same answers I initially gave to these two central questions. However, to meet the challenges raised by my fellow contributors to this book, I had to uncover and construct additional reasons and arguments for supporting those answers. Mistaken though I may still be, there is no doubt that my own answers to these questions have grown and developed through the critical discussion that is displayed in this book.

So, the hope that I share with my coauthors is that our readers, particularly in discussion with other readers and in discussion with a still-wider audience, will thereby be able to grow and develop in formulating their own answers to these two normative questions, a goal that is shared by students and teachers alike everywhere. Or to change the message from one of hope to one of recommendation, why not use this book to best address these two central questions of moral and political philosophy given the inescapable nature of the questions it addresses?

INTRODUCTION

Philosophers at least since the time of Plato have been searching for an argument that shows that morality is rationally required. At present, the general consensus is that all previous attempts have failed to deliver just such an argument. My American Philosophical Association presidential address, "From Rationality to Equality," which is significantly expanded in Chapter 1 of this volume, is one of the few contemporary attempts to provide an argument of this sort. Thus, I belong to a relatively small group of contemporary moral philosophers that includes Stephen Darwall, Christine Korsgaard, Allen Wood, and some others, who think that it is possible to argue from rationality to morality. I also argue that the conception of morality so justified can be shown to lead to a demand for substantial equality, thereby linking myself to a much larger group of moral and political philosophers, including Ronald Dworkin, Alison Jaggar, Will Kymlicka, Thomas Pogge, and Larry Temkin, who think that a commitment to even a minimal libertarian morality leads to broadly egalitarian requirements, although the view I defend is more egalitarian than the views defended by most of these other philosophers. Nevertheless, my approach is unique in that it attempts to combine these two arguments: an argument from rationality to morality and an argument from (libertarian) morality to substantial equality. By way of introduction, let me briefly say something about each of these arguments in turn.

THE ARGUMENT FROM
RATIONALITY TO MORALITY

My justification of morality is based on the claim that the principle of non-question-beggingness, a principle that must be satisfied by good arguments, favors morality over egoism, where morality is understood to be a nonarbitrary compromise between self-interested and altruistic reasons. A crucial step in this argument for morality is to cast the basic conflict with egoism not as a conflict between morality and self-interest, but rather as a conflict between altruism and self-interest. I argue that although previous defenders of morality understood correctly that moral reasons could not be compromised with self-interested reasons, they failed to recognize that this is because moral reasons are already the result of a purportedly nonarbitrary compromise between self-interested and altruistic reasons. Thus, while previous defenders of morality intuitively knew that moral reasons could not be compromised with self-interested reasons, they were unable to conceptually back up and see how morality itself can be represented as a compromise between altruism and self-interest, and, for that reason, they failed to recognize my approach to defending morality.

THE ARGUMENT FROM
MORALITY TO EQUALITY

The conception of morality that I am non-question-beggingly defending against egoism is anything but complete. This is because its requirements seem to be open to a libertarian, or a welfare liberal, or even a socialist interpretation. While I argue that this conception of morality is quite useful because it succeeds in showing the superiority of morality over egoism, it needs to be completed to determine when its requirements are enforceable. Here, I claim, it behooves us to start with the assumptions of the libertarian perspective, the view that appears to endorse the least enforcement of morality, given that I propose to show that this view requires a right to welfare, and that further, this right to welfare, which is also endorsed by a welfare liberal perspective, leads to the substantial equality of a socialist perspective. My strategy is to find conflicts of (negative) liberty within the libertarian perspective, and then argue that when these conflicts are appropriately resolved, they favor an allocation of liberty that supports a right to welfare. Since fundamental rights are universal rights for libertarians, I then argue that extending this right to welfare to distant peoples, and, particularly, to future generations, leads to the egalitarian requirement that we use up no more resources than are necessary for meeting our own basic needs, thus securing for ourselves a decent life but no more. In effect, recognizing a right to welfare, applicable to all existing and future people, leads to an equal utilization of resources over place and time.

Combining these two arguments together, we get an argument from rationality to (substantial) equality. Now, given the past history of philosophy with respect to such arguments, it seems very likely that there must be something wrong with the particular arguments that I develop in my essay. But just how do these arguments fail? The contributors to this volume have provided the following critiques.

CRITIQUES OF THE ARGUMENT

Charles W. Mills

At the heart of Charles Mills's critique of my argument from rationality to morality justification is his claim to have discovered a new type of egoism—scalar egoism—that is immune from my argument. Mills distinguishes his scalar egoist from a lexical egoist, who always puts her interests first and gives no weight at all to the interests of others. Although the scalar egoist also puts his interests first, what distinguishes him from the lexical egoist is that he gives some weight, albeit considerably lesser weight, to the interests of others. Now, Mills thinks that although my appeal to a standard of non-question-beggingness may work against both the lexical egoist and her counterpart, the lexical altruist, it does not work against the scalar egoist, or for that matter his counterpart, the scalar altruist.

Candace A. Vogler

Candace Vogler argues against my justification for morality by claiming that there is no way to analyze or factor moral reasons into self-interested reasons and altruistic reasons. As she sees it, what is first required is a normative standard. Only by first using such a standard can we determine which self-interested reasons and which altruistic reasons are appropriately justified. And this is just what my justification of morality does not provide.

Anita M. Superson

Anita Superson challenges my rationality to morality argument by denying that to defeat egoism (as I claim to do, by getting the egoist, or the "reformed" egoist, to recognize the prima facie status of altruism) would not lead to a defeat of moral skepticism. She claims this is because the moral skeptic denies or is agnostic about moral reasons and hence denies or is also agnostic about the altruistic reasons that are a significant component of such reasons. Thus, without the admission that altruistic reasons have or should have prima facie status, I would have to grant that the moral skeptic couldn't be similarly defeated. Hence, my defense of morality would fail against the moral skeptic.

Russ Shafer-Landau

Russ Shafer-Landau argues that we cannot construct a non-question-begging argument for morality. Nor is the immoralist or egoist any better off. As Shafer-Landau sees the possibilities for argument here, it is question-begging all around. As examples of where this happens in other contexts, Shafer-Landau offers us flat-earthers, skeptics, and those students who think *you* graded them poorly because *you* hate them. Shafer-Landau also maintains that morality as compromise, the conception of morality that I have argued is rationally preferably to egoism and altruism, is defective in various ways as an account of morality.

Allan F. Gibbard

Allan Gibbard claims that the same style of argument that I use to show the rational superiority of morality as compromise over egoism and altruism may be turned against me to show that morality as compromise is an inadequate conception of morality. With respect to my argument from (libertarian) morality to equality, Gibbard notes that I make a right to welfare conditional upon a requirement that the poor engage in mutually beneficial work if they can, and that they repay the aid they received to meet their basic needs once they can consistently do so while satisfying those needs. It is that second requirement to which Gibbard particularly objects.

Gerald F. Gaus

In his critique of my rationality to morality argument, Gerald Gaus concedes that we do need to sometimes favor self-interested reasons and sometimes favor altruistic reasons, but then he argues against my particular resolution of morality as compromise that there are a variety of ways to do this. However, Gaus's main worry is that my view demands too much altruism. He cites results from evolutionary biology as presumably offering a cautionary tale for any ethical theory that would consider coercively demanding significant altruism. Gaus acknowledges that people do face a choice of altruisms. As he sees it, there is the typically voluntary altruism directed at close relatives, and there is the typically forced altruism directed at the poor. He questions, however, the priority my view gives to the latter type of altruism.

Tibor R. Machan

Against my argument from libertarian morality to substantial equality, Tibor Machan argues that in my view, legitimate property ownership restricts the liberty of would-be thieves. Even more important, Machan argues that I fail to recognize that severe conflicts between the rich and the poor are untypical and rare and so cannot justify the legal imposition of welfare rights, from which I ultimately get my requirement of substantial equality. This is because, Machan claims, hard cases made bad law.

WHERE SHOULD YOU GO FROM HERE?

So you now have a sketch of the main critiques of my initial argument of-.fered by the contributors to this volume. Do you think it possible that I can develop good responses to these critiques? To best determine that, you should first read my essay, then read each of the seven critical essays, and only then read my responses to the critiques in the last section of this volume. After that, you should be in the great position to determine whether I have a promising account of morality, the why and the what of it.

PART I

A Sketch of an Argument

CHAPTER 1

FROM RATIONALITY
TO EQUALITY

James P. Sterba

It is generally recognized that in today's society, academic philosophers have very little impact on moral and political decision making. For example, in contrast to members of other disciplines and professions, philosophers have very rarely in our times been called upon to serve as advisers to governors, labor leaders, presidents, prime ministers, or even dictators. To some extent, this is because philosophers have not, until recently, directed their attention at the practical issues that daily concern our moral and political leaders. But just as important, it is because philosophers have done so little to resolve the fundamental conflicts between opposing moral and political ideals of our times. In this essay, I will try to improve the status of our profession just a bit by offering a justification of morality and, further, by showing how morality so justified leads to a demand for substantial equality.

Now, to defend or justify morality, it would be helpful to show that morality is grounded in rationality. This requires not just showing that morality is simply rationally permissible, because that would imply that egoism and immorality were rationally permissible as well.[1] Rather, what needs to be shown is that morality is rationally required, thus excluding egoism and immorality as rationally permissible.[2] Unfortunately, the goal of showing that morality is rationally required has been abandoned by most contemporary moral philosophers, who seem content to show that morality is simply rationally permissible.[3] No doubt most contemporary moral philosophers would like to have an argument showing that morality is rationally required, but given the history of past failures to provide a convincing argument of this sort, most contemporary moral philosophers have simply given up any hope of defending morality in this way.[4] Here, in contrast, I hope—maybe foolishly—to provide just such a defense of morality and to show further how morality so justified leads to a demand for substantial equality.

OTHER ATTEMPTS TO JUSTIFY MORALITY

The most ambitious attempts to justify morality have tried to show that endorsing egoism or immorality is somehow inconsistent. In one version of this argument, our desires for the freedom and well-being necessary to achieve our purposes, when universalized, as consistency requires, are said to lead to our endorsing a moral right to freedom and well-being, which in turn requires us to reject egoism and immorality.[5] But this version of the argument fails to recognize that when we universalize a prudential claim, we only get another prudential claim, albeit a universal one. Accordingly, when I say that I ought, prudentially, to pursue my freedom and well-being, I have to grant that others, similarly situated, ought to do so as well—that everyone has the same justification as I have for behaving self-interestedly—but I don't have to grant that I should help or not interfere with their pursuit of freedom and well-being or that they should help or not interfere with my pursuit of freedom and well-being, as a symmetrically action-guiding moral right to freedom and well-being would require.

The prudential "oughts" at issue here are analogous to the "oughts" found in most ordinary examples of competitive games. For instance, in football a defensive player may think that the opposing team's quarterback ought to pass on a third down with five yards to go, while not wanting the quarterback to do so and indeed hoping to foil any such attempt the quarterback makes. Or, to adapt an example of Jesse Kalin's, if you and I are playing chess, at a certain point in the game I may judge that you ought to move your bishop and put my king in check, but this judgment is not action-guiding for me. What I in fact should do is sit quietly and hope that you do not move, as you ought. If you fail to make the appropriate move, and later, I judge that I ought to put your king in check, that judgment, by contrast, would be action-guiding for me. So, prudential or self-interested oughts are asymmetrically action-guiding, just as the oughts of competitive games are asymmetrically action-guiding. Universalizing prudential or self-interested oughts, therefore, as consistency demands, only leads to generalized asymmetrically action-guiding oughts; it does not lead to the symmetrically action-guiding oughts that constitute morality.

Something similar obtains with respect to Immanuel Kant's categorical imperative. The egoist, in particular, is not required by consistency alone to abide by maxims that can meet the test of the categorical imperative in any of its formulations. So whether or not Kant's categorical imperative actually succeeds in capturing the requirements of morality, no argument has been given that all rational agents, including egoists, must, in consistency, abide by those requirements.[6]

Still, another version of the argument to justify morality by consistency alone maintains that our reasons for action must be public in the way that languages are public and that this publicity requirement is inconsistent with egoism and immorality.[7] According to this argument, egoism is, in fact, a myth, no more possible than private languages are possible. Although it is surely the case that any normative ideal must be public in the sense that it is communicable to others, egoistic and immoral ideals have no difficulty satisfying this requirement.

Consider the egoistic ideal in its general form, according to which everyone ought to do what best serves his or her overall self-interest.[8] From Plato to the present, we find numerous attempts to defend the consistency and reasonableness of this ideal. So there really is no question about whether philosophers have discussed this egoistic ideal and communicated with one another about it. Moreover, in practice, egoists would also be willing to communicate their reasons or interests to others who have overlapping or compatible reasons or interests in order to secure for themselves the benefits of coordination in joint endeavors.

But what about those occasions when the reasons of egoists conflict with the reasons of others? Surely, then, egoists will not want to communicate their reasons to those with whom they are in conflict so as not to lose out. It is just here that egoists will want their reasons to be kept private. In this respect, egoists differ sharply from those who are committed to morality. Those committed to morality usually want to communicate their reasons to those with whom they are in conflict in the hope that a morally acceptable resolution of the conflict can be achieved.[9] So we can agree that egoistic reasons have a private dimension to them that moral reasons lack. Nevertheless, even when egoists are striving to keep their reasons private, those reasons still remain public in the sense that they are communicable to others. In such cases, their reasons can be found out even when egoists are striving to conceal them.

In this respect, egoistic reasons are again analogous to the reasons found in competitive games. Players in football are usually trying to conceal the particular reasons they have for being in certain formations, just as players in chess are usually trying to disguise the particular reasons they have for making certain moves. Nevertheless, in such cases, the players can be found out, as when an offensive lineman in football inadvertently signals a running play by the way he lines up to block.

It might be objected that the "oughts" of competitive games, unlike the "oughts" of egoism, are contained within a higher normative structure that is itself governed by the symmetrically action-guiding "oughts" of morality. This is true. But for an analogy to be useful, the analogues need not be identical in every respect. However, for an even closer analogue to the asymmetrically action-guiding "oughts" of egoism, think about the asymmetrically action-guiding "oughts" used by players who systematically and successfully cheat to win games they would otherwise lose.

This shows that egoism meets the reasonable demand of being consistent with the publicity requirement of languages and competitive games by being communicable to others, even though it does not meet the stronger publicity requirement of morality of usually wanting its recommendations to be communicable to others.[10] Meeting the stronger publicity requirement of morality would render the practice of egoism self-defeating in just the same way that it would render the practice of many competitive games self-defeating. But this fact could only count against the practice of egoism if it also counts against the practice of competitive games, and it does not count against the practice of competitive games. If we are to defeat the egoist or immoralist, therefore, we need to base our argument on more than consistency alone.

MORE THAN CONSISTENCY ALONE

So let us begin by imagining that each of us is capable of entertaining and acting upon both self-interested and moral reasons and that the question we are seeking to answer is what reasons for action it would be rational for us to accept.[11] This question is not about what reasons we should publicly affirm, because people will sometimes publicly affirm reasons that are quite different from those they are prepared to act upon. Rather, it is a question about what reasons it would be rational for us to accept at the deepest level—in our heart of hearts—because we are trying to answer this question as far as possible without self-deception or hypocrisy.

Of course, there are people who are incapable, by nature, of acting upon moral reasons. For such people, there is no question about their being required to act morally or altruistically. Yet the interesting philosophical question is not about such people but about people, like ourselves, who are capable of acting morally as well as self-interestedly, and who further, let us assume (usefully idealizing a bit), are aware of all the relevant moral and self-interested reasons they are capable of acting upon and are seeking a rational justification for following a particular course of action.

It is important for my argument later that we also include knowledge of one's relevant altruistic reasons here, many of which are also moral reasons anyway. It should also be noted that not all the reasons that people are capable of acting upon are relevant to an assessment of the reasonableness of their conduct. First, reasons that are evocable only from some merely logically possible set of opportunities are not relevant; they must be evocable from the opportunities people actually possessed. Second, reasons that radically different people could have acquired are also not relevant. Instead, they must be reasons that people could have acquired without radical changes in their developing identities.

In trying to determine how we should act, let us assume that we would like to be able to construct a good argument favoring morality over egoism, and given that good arguments are non-question-begging, we accordingly would like to construct an argument that does not beg the question. So instead of trying to justify morality on grounds of consistency alone, I propose that we also appeal to the principle of non-question-beggingness. This principle requires that we not argue in such a way that *only* someone who already knew or believed the conclusion of our argument would accept its premises, or put more succinctly, that we not assume what we are trying to prove or justify.

Now, the question at issue here is what reasons each of us should take as supreme, and this question would be begged against egoism if we proposed to answer it simply by assuming from the start that moral reasons are the reasons that each of us should take as supreme. But the question would be begged against morality as well if we proposed to answer the question simply by assuming from the start that self-interested reasons are the reasons that each of us should take as supreme. This means, of course, that we cannot answer the question of what reasons we should take as supreme simply by assuming the general principle of egoism:

Each person ought to do what best serves his or her overall self-interest.

We can no more argue for egoism simply by denying the relevance of moral reasons to rational choice than we can argue for altruism simply by denying the relevance of self-interested reasons to rational choice and assuming the following general principle of altruism:

Each person ought to do what best serves the overall interest of others.[12]

Consequently, in order not to beg the question, we have no alternative but to grant the prima facie relevance of both self-interested and moral or altruistic reasons to rational choice and then try to determine which reasons we would be rationally required to act upon, all things considered. Notice that in order not to beg the question, it is necessary to back off both from the general principle of egoism and from the general principle of altruism, thus granting the prima facie relevance of both self-interested and altruistic reasons to rational choice. From this standpoint, it is still an open question whether either egoism or altruism will be rationally preferable, all things considered.

MORE ON A
NON-QUESTION-BEGGING STRATEGY

Of course, this is only one strategy to avoid begging the question. Another is to assume the premises that one's opponent actually accepts and argue from those premises. A variant of the second strategy is to put the best construction on one's opponent's view and then determine what follows from the view so construed. Which strategy is appropriate is determined by the context. In this debate with the egoist, requiring both egoist and the altruist to "back up" is appropriate because it permits a debate-settling resolution.[13] By contrast, the strategy of starting with the premises acceptable to one's opponent works well, I hope to show, in the debate among libertarians, welfare liberals, and socialists. This is because each of these three moral/political conceptions represents a different compromise of self-interested and altruistic reasons, so the best way to carry out a debate among them is, in fact, to work internally with one of those conceptions, specifically the libertarian conception, to effect a different weighing of the self-interested and altruistic reasons within it and thereby bring that conception more in line with the requirements of the other two. Nor would the "backup" strategy work well for this particular debate because it turns out that all plausible backup positions seemingly neutral enough to be acceptable to libertarians, welfare liberals, and socialists are too general to support any particular resolution. Of course, we could "force" libertarians, welfare liberals, and socialists to take the backup strategy more seriously. We could have them back up to the basic self-interested and altruistic reasons in their views and work from there. However, we can also just start with the libertarian view and work internally to show how a reevaluation of conflicts of liberty in that view that correspond to conflicts between self-interested and altruistic reasons leads to different practical requirements from those that libertarians usually endorse, thereby helping to reconcile the libertarian view with both welfare liberalism and socialism.

Moreover, whether a view is question-begging or not depends, in part, on the audience one is addressing. Thus, arguing for a particular conclusion, say, the need to pray daily, may not be question-begging in a particular argumentative context, for example, when directed at Christians and (religious) Jews, but that same argument may be question-begging in a broader argumentative context, for example, one that includes atheists and agnostics. Here, the argumentative context requires us to address the defenders of egoism and their opponents.[14]

Now, it might be objected that we do have non-question-begging grounds for favoring self-interested reasons over moral reasons, if not egoism over altruism. From observing ourselves and others, don't we find that self-interested reasons are better motivators than are moral reasons, as evidenced by the fact that there seem to be more egoistically inclined people in the world than there are altruistically inclined people? It might be argued that because of this difference in motivational capacity, self-interested and moral or altruistic reasons should not both be regarded as prima facie relevant to rational choice.

But is there really this difference in motivational capacity? Do human beings really have a greater capacity for self-interested behavior than for altruistic behavior? If we focus for a change on the behavior of women, I think we are likely to observe considerably more altruism than egoism among women, particularly with respect to the care of their families.[15] Of course, if we look to men, given still-dominant patriarchal social practices, we may tend to find more egoism than altruism.[16] But most likely, any relevant differences between men and women in this regard, irrespective of whether we consider them to be good or bad, are primarily due to the dominant patterns of socialization/nurture rather than nature.[17] In any case, it is beyond dispute that we humans are capable of both self-interested and altruistic behavior, and given that we have these capabilities, it seems reasonable to ask which ones should have priority.

This is not to deny that we usually have greater knowledge and certainty about what is in our own self-interest than about what is in the interest of others, and that this difference in our knowledge and certainty can have a practical effect on what good we should do in particular contexts. It is just that, as I will point out shortly, the debate between egoism and morality gets started at the theoretical level where no assumption is made about this difference in our knowledge and certainty, because we can, and frequently do, have adequate knowledge and certainty about both what is in our own self-interest and what is in the interest of others.

Our situation is that we find ourselves with some capacity to move along a spectrum from egoism to pure altruism, with someone like Mother Teresa of Calcutta representing the paradigm of pure altruism and someone like Thrasymachus of Plato's *Republic* representing the paradigm of egoism.[18] Obviously, our ability to move along this spectrum will depend on our starting point, the strength of our habits, and the social circumstances under which we happen to be living. But at the outset, it is reasonable to abstract from these individual variations and simply to focus on the general capacity virtually all of us have to act on both self-interested and altruistic reasons. From this, we should conclude that both sorts of reasons are relevant to rational choice and then ask which reasons should have priority. Later, with this question answered, we can take into account individual differences and the effects of socialization to adjust our expectations and requirements for particular individuals and groups. Initially, however, all we need to recognize is the relevance of both self-interested and altruistic reasons to rational choice.

In this regard, there are two kinds of cases that must be considered: cases in which there is a conflict between the relevant self-interested and moral or altruistic reasons, and cases in which there is no such conflict.

NO-CONFLICT CASES

It seems obvious that where there is no conflict and both reasons are conclusive reasons of their kind recommending the same course of action, both reasons should be acted upon. In such contexts, we should do what is favored both by morality or altruism and by self-interest.

Sometimes self-interested and moral reasons will not conflict in a particular context because only one or the other reason is relevant. In that case, we should act on that relevant reason, whether it be self-interested or moral, when it is conclusive.

Still, it might be objected that even when self-interested and moral reasons do not conflict, there will frequently be other reasons significantly opposed to the moral reasons—reasons that we are or were able to acquire. Such reasons will be either malevolent reasons seeking to bring about the suffering and death of other human beings, benevolent reasons concerned with promoting nonhuman welfare even at the expense of human welfare, or aesthetic reasons concerned with preserving and promoting objects of aesthetic value even if those objects will not be appreciated by any living being. But assuming that malevolent reasons are ultimately rooted in some conception of what is good for oneself or others, these reasons would already have been taken into account, and, in the best construal of both egoism and altruism, presumably outweighed by other relevant reasons in each case. And although benevolent reasons concerned with promoting nonhuman welfare also need to be taken into account, such reasons are not directly relevant to justifying morality over egoism. Finally, although aesthetic reasons concerned with preserving and promoting aesthetic objects, even when those objects will not be appreciated by any living being, might theoretically weigh against human interests, for all practical purposes, the value of such objects will tend to correlate with the value of the aesthetic experiences they provide to humans. Even the famous prehistoric artwork in the cave at Lascaux, France, which has been closed to public viewing since 1963, seems to be valued because of the significance it has for us.

CONFLICT CASES

Now, when we rationally assess the relevant reasons in conflict cases, it is best to cast the conflict not as a conflict between self-interested reasons and moral reasons, but instead as a conflict between self-interested reasons and altruistic reasons.[19] The grounds for this shift will become apparent later.[20] Viewed in this way, three solutions are possible. First, we could say that self-interested reasons always have priority over conflicting altruistic reasons. Second, we could say just the opposite, that altruistic reasons always have priority over conflicting self-interested reasons. Third, we could say that some kind of compromise is rationally required. In this compromise, sometimes self-interested reasons have priority over conflicting altruistic reasons, and sometimes altruistic reasons have priority over conflicting self-interested reasons.

Once the conflict is described in this manner, the third solution can be seen to be the one that is rationally required. This is because the first and second solutions give exclusive priority to one class of relevant reasons over the other, and only a question-begging justification can be given for such an exclusive priority. Only by employing the third solution, and sometimes giving priority to self-interested reasons, and sometimes giving priority to altruistic reasons, can we avoid a question-begging resolution.

PSYCHOLOGICAL EGOISM

Of course, there are arguments for only taking self-interested reasons into account that simply assume psychological egoism, which maintains that despite appearances to the contrary, we actually behave self-interestedly all the time. This may seem to be a surprising claim. Of course, we are well aware that some people we assumed were acting primarily for the good of others later turn out to be significantly motivated by self-interest. For example, a number of years ago, many people were surprised and dismayed to learn of the very large salary being paid to William Aramony, then president of United Way of America. After Aramony was pressured to resign and later convicted of fraud, a significant drop in giving to United Way persisted for some time, with some people thinking United Way was no longer the type of public service organization they had once thought it to be.[21]

Psychological egoism, however, does not maintain that despite appearances to the contrary, some of us are significantly motivated by self-interest. Rather, the view maintains that all of us are ultimately motivated by self-interest all the time. Moreover, if we are to credit the following story reported in the *Springfield Monitor,* Abraham Lincoln at one period of his life seems to have held the very same view.

> Mr. Lincoln once remarked to a fellow-passenger on an old-time mud-coach that all men were prompted by [self-interest] in doing good. His fellow-passenger was antagonizing this position when they were passing over a corduroy bridge that spanned a [muddy stream]. As they crossed this bridge they espied an old razorback sow on the bank making a terrible noise because her pigs had got into the [muddy stream] and were in danger of drowning. As the old coach began to climb the hill, Mr. Lincoln called out, "Driver, can't you stop just a moment?" Then Mr. Lincoln jumped out, ran back and lifted the little pigs out of the mud and water and placed them on the bank. When he returned, his companion remarked: "Now Abe, where does [self-interest] come in on this little episode?" "Why, bless your soul, Ed, that was the very essence of [self-interest]. I should have had no peace of mind all day had I gone on and left that suffering old sow worrying over those pigs. I did it to get peace of mind, don't you see?"[22]

As we can see, Lincoln held that there was no difference between his behavior and that of Ed, his fellow passenger. They both acted self-interestedly and presumably they both wanted peace of mind. Yet Lincoln, not Ed, was motivated to prevent the piglets from drowning and secure his peace of mind in that particular way. So if we just say that both men acted self-interested, as psychological egoism would have us do, we lose an interesting difference between the way the two of them were, in fact, motivated.

When Lincoln decided to save the piglets and Ed decided to remain in the coach, they both were presumably satisfied with what they did. Yet the satisfaction that each experienced does not explain why they acted differently. Rather, Lincoln's action is explained by his concern for the well-being of the piglets and their mother, while Ed's is explained by his greater concern for himself, otherwise he could have helped Lincoln save the piglets. Lincoln, too, could conceivably have behaved more self-interestedly. After he got to the muddy stream, he could have reflected on how wet and muddy he was going to have to get to save the piglets and changed his mind. But he didn't.

So the interesting question here is: To what degree should people be motivated by altruism, like Lincoln, or by self-interest, like Ed, in these and other such circumstances? Psychological egoism, because it espouses an empty, trivial thesis that is true no matter what people do, does not even try to answer this question. In contrast, ethical egoism does try to give an answer to just that question.

That is why I began my argument for the justification of morality with the assumption that we have the capacity to act upon both self-interested and altruistic reasons. Moreover, it is difficult to see how one could attempt to give a non-question-begging argument for the exclusive priority of self-interested or altruistic reasons without proceeding as I have been doing here.

NOT JUST ANY COMPROMISE

Notice also that this standard of rationality will not support just any compromise between the relevant self-interested and altruistic reasons. The compromise must be a nonarbitrary one, for otherwise it would beg the question with respect to the opposing egoistic and altruistic perspectives.[23] Such a compromise would have to respect the rankings of self-interested and altruistic reasons imposed by the egoistic and altruistic perspectives, respectively. Accordingly, any nonarbitrary compromise among such reasons in seeking not to beg the question against either egoism or altruism would have to give priority to those reasons that rank highest in each category. Failure to give priority to the highest-ranking altruistic or self-interested reasons would, other things being equal, be contrary to reason.

Now, it might be objected here that my argument just assumes that we can provide an objective ranking of both a person's self-interested and altruistic reasons.[24] This is correct. But it is difficult to see how any defender of egoism could deny this assumption. Egoism claims that each person ought to do what best serves his or her overall self-interest, and this clearly assumes that each person can know what that is. Nor is it plausible to interpret egoism as maintaining that although we can each know what best serves our own self-interest, we cannot know what best serves the interest of others, and that is why we should be egoists. Rather, the standard defense of egoism assumes that we can each know what is good for ourselves and what is good for others and then claims that, even with this knowledge, we still always ought to do what is good for ourselves. Nor is the idea of providing a relatively precise ranking of one's self-interested reasons from an egoistic perspective or a relatively precise ranking of one's altruistic reasons from an altruistic perspective something to which an egoist would reasonably object.[25] Thus, we are imagining that we are getting a true and accurate ranking of a person's self-interested reasons from an egoistic perspective—one that may be different from what a person thinks is his or her true and accurate ranking of such reasons, and the same holds true of a person's altruistic reasons as seen from an altruistic perspective.

Nor would the egoist reasonably object to the interpersonal comparability of these rankings. Difficult though such rankings may be to arrive at in practice, the egoist's objection is that even when such relatively precise rankings of our self-interested and altruistic reasons are known, and even when it is known that acting on high-ranking altruistic reasons is comparably more beneficial to others than acting on conflicting low-ranking self-interested reasons is beneficial to ourselves, we should still always favor self-interested reasons over altruistic ones.

Accordingly, the egoist's objection to morality must be distinguished from the relativist's or the skeptic's objection. Although it is important to defeat each of these foes of morality, it seems best to take them one at a time.[26] Here, we are simply concerned with the egoist, who does not deny what I have assumed for the sake of argument—a relatively precise ranking of one's self-interested reasons from an egoistic perspective and a relatively precise ranking of one's altruistic reasons from an altruistic perspective, and the interpersonal comparability of these two rankings.

LIFEBOAT CASES

Of course, there will be cases in which the only way to avoid being required or forced to do what is contrary to your highest-ranking reasons is by requiring or forcing someone else to do what is contrary to her highest-ranking reasons. Some of these cases will be "lifeboat cases," as, for example, where you and someone else are stranded in a lifeboat that has only enough resources for one of you to survive. But although such cases are surely difficult to resolve (maybe only a chance mechanism, like flipping a coin, can offer a reasonable resolution), they surely do not appear to reflect the typical conflicts between the relevant self-interested and altruistic reasons that we are capable of acting upon.[27] At least for humans, it would appear that typically one or the other of the conflicting reasons would rank significantly higher on its respective scale, thus permitting a clear resolution.[28]

Now we can see how morality can be viewed as just such a nonarbitrary compromise between self-interested and altruistic reasons. First, a certain amount of self-regard is morally required, and sometimes, if not morally required, at least morally acceptable. Where this is the case, high-ranking self-interested reasons have priority over conflicting low-ranking altruistic reasons, other things being equal.[29] Second, morality obviously places limits on the extent to which people should pursue their own self-interest. Where this is the case, high-ranking altruistic reasons have priority over conflicting low-ranking self-interested reasons, other things being equal. In this way, morality can be seen to be a nonarbitrary compromise between self-interested and altruistic reasons, and the "moral reasons" that constitute that compromise can be seen as having a priority over the self-interested or altruistic reasons that conflict with them, other things being equal.

It is also important to see how this compromise view is supported by a two-step argument that is not question-begging at all. In the first step, our goal is to determine what reasons for action it would be rational for us to accept on the basis of a good argument, and this requires a non-question-begging starting point. Noting that both egoism, which favors exclusively self-interested reasons, and altruism, which favors exclusively altruistic reasons, offer only question-begging starting points, we took as our non-question-begging starting point the prima facie relevance of both self-interested and altruistic reasons to rational choice. The logical inference here is somewhat analogous to the inference of equal probability sanctioned in decision theory when we have no evidence that one alternative is more likely than another.[30] Here, we have no non-question-begging justification for excluding either self-interested or altruistic reasons as relevant to rational choice, so we accept both kinds of reasons as prima facie relevant to rational choice. The conclusion of this first step of the argument for the compromise view does not beg the question against either egoism or altruism because if defenders of either view had any hope of providing a good, that is, a non-question-begging argument for their view, they, too, would have to grant this very conclusion as the only option open to them. In accepting this step of the argument, therefore, the compromise view does not beg the question against a possible defense of either of these other two perspectives, and that is all that should concern us.

Once, however, both self-interested and altruistic reasons are recognized as prima facie relevant to rational choice, the second step of the argument for the compromise view offers a nonarbitrary ordering of those reasons on the basis of the rankings of self-interested and altruistic reasons imposed by the egoistic and altruistic perspectives, respectively. According to that ordering, high-ranking self-interested reasons have priority over conflicting low-ranking altruistic reasons, other things being equal, and high-ranking altruistic reasons have priority over conflicting low-ranking self-interested reasons, other things being equal. There is no other plausible nonarbitrary ordering of these reasons. Hence, it certainly does not beg the question against either the egoistic or altruistic perspective, once we imagine those perspectives (or, more appropriately, their defenders) to be suitably reformed so that they, too, are committed to a standard of non-question-beggingness. In the end, if one is committed to a standard of non-question-beggingness, one has to be concerned only with how one's claims and arguments stake up against others who are also committed to such a standard. If you yourself are committed to the standard of non-question-beggingness, you don't beg the question by simply coming into conflict with the requirements of other perspectives, unless those other perspectives (or better, their defenders) are also committed to the same standard of non-question-beggingness. In arguing for your view, when you come into conflict with those who are arguing prejudicially, you do not beg the question against them unless you are also arguing prejudicially yourself.

According to Bernard Gert, when the notion of rationality is used as a "fundamental normative concept," it does not make sense to ask "Why should I be rational?" or "Can you give me a good (that is, non-question-begging) argument for being rational?" Gert also wants to hold that it does not make sense to ask "Why should I not be irrational?" or "Can you give me a good (non-question-begging) argument for not being irrational?" He then goes on to show that a notion of rationality that he uses in his work meets this condition of being a fundamental normative concept. However, my notion of rationality as non-question-beggingness also satisfies this condition. This is because it also does not make sense to ask "Can you give me a good (non-question-begging) argument for acting in accord with the good (non-question-begging) argument for morality as compromise?" or "Can you give me a good (non-question-begging) argument for acting against the good (non-question-begging) argument for morality as compromise?" or even more generally, "Can you give me a good (non-question-begging) argument for acting in accord with a good (non-question-begging) argument?"[31]

Now, it might be objected that neither the defender of egoism nor the defender of altruism would want to make this move if she were only to take into account where this argument is heading. But if the defender of egoism or altruism were to realize that if she takes a non-question-begging stance, her favored position would turn out to be indefensible and some other position would turn out to be defensible, doesn't that show that she already knows that her own position is indefensible? That is what I argue happens here. A non-question-begging stance requires giving both egoistic and altruistic reasons prima facie status, and this, I will argue, leads in a non-question-begging way to morality (as compromise). Knowing or coming to know this, both the defender of egoism and the defender of altruism either know or come to know that they will lose the argumentative game to the moralist.

OTHER IMMORAL VIEWS

Notice, too, that this defense of morality also works against those forms of immorality that are group based, like racism and sexism, because in the case of these immoralities, there are no non-question-begging grounds for the way those who are dominant favor their interests over the interests of those they dominate. Moreover, with respect to group-based immoralities, unlike the egoistic challenge that we have been envisioning, there is also a group-based epistemic failing—those who dominate use biased, that is, question-begging, information to conceive of their interests as superior to the interests of those they dominate, which they then think entitles them to their privileged status.[32]

Generalizing, then, we can say that all immoralities involve an inappropriate (question-begging) favoring of the interests of self (or a particular group of selves) over the interests of others (or a particular group of others) and in this way run afoul of the defense of morality I have just sketched.[33] Accordingly, when Christine Korsgaard seeks to expose people who adopt and maintain immoral identities as insufficiently reflective, I would suggest that they might better be critiqued for lacking a non-question-begging justification, and hence, a good argument, for adopting and maintaining those identities.[34]

A NEGLECTED DEFENSE

Unfortunately, this approach to defending morality has generally been neglected by previous moral theorists. The reason is that such theorists have tended to cast the basic conflict with egoism as a conflict between morality and self-interest rather than as a conflict between altruism and self-interest. Viewed in this light, it did not seem possible for the defender of morality to be supporting a compromise view, for how could such a defender say that when morality and self-interest conflict, morality should sometimes be sacrificed for the sake of self-interest? Thus, Henry Sidgwick, at the end of his *Methods of Ethics*, unable to find a rational reconciliation between egoism and utilitarian morality, entertained the possibility of an omnipotent and benevolent deity who guaranteed their reconciliation in an afterlife.[35] Although previous theorists, including Sidgwick, understood correctly that moral reasons could not be compromised with self-interested reasons, they failed to recognize that this is because moral reasons, including the reasons that constitute a utilitarian morality, are already the result of a purportedly nonarbitrary compromise between self-interested and altruistic reasons. To ask that moral reasons be weighed against self-interested reasons is, in effect, to count self-interested reasons twice—once in the compromise between egoism and altruism that constitutes a conception of morality, and then again, assuming moral reasons are weighed against self-interested reasons— and this double counting of self-interested reasons would be clearly objectionable from a non-question-begging standpoint. Thus, previous moral theorists intuitively knew that moral reasons could not be compromised with self-interested reasons, but they were still unable to conceptually back up and see how morality itself can be represented as a compromise between altruism and self-interest, and, for that reason, they failed to recognize this approach to defending morality.

This failure to recognize that morality can be represented as a compromise between self-interested and altruistic reasons also helps explain Thomas Nagel's inability to find a solution to the problem of the design of just institutions.[36] According to Nagel, to solve the problem of the design of just institutions, we need a morally acceptable resolution of the conflict between the personal and the impersonal standpoints, which he thinks is unattainable. Although Nagel may be right that a morally acceptable resolution of the conflict between these two standpoints is unattainable, the reason for this is that these two standpoints already represent different resolutions of the conflict between self and others. The personal standpoint represents the personally chosen resolution of this conflict, whereas the impersonal standpoint represents a completely impartial resolution of this conflict, which may not be identical with the personally chosen resolution. Because each of these standpoints already represents a resolution of the conflict between oneself and others, any further resolution of the conflict between the two standpoints would seem to violate the earlier resolutions, either by favoring oneself or others too much or too little in light of the earlier resolutions. It is no wonder, then, that an acceptable resolution of the two standpoints seems unattainable. A compromise between the personal and the impersonal would be judged too much from the personal standpoint if more consideration of others were required than the personal perspective regarded as justified. A compromise between the personal and the impersonal would be judged as too little from the impersonal standpoint if less consideration of others were required than the impersonal perspective regarded as justified. By contrast, if we recast the underlying conflict between oneself and others, as I have suggested, in terms of a conflict between egoism and altruism or self-interested reasons and altruistic reasons, then happily a rationally defensible resolution can be seen to emerge.

Samuel Scheffler holds a view very similar to that of Nagel's.[37] However, Scheffler differs from Nagel in advocating a disproportionate concern for the personal standpoint when it conflicts with the impersonal standpoint. Although Scheffler rightly holds that the impersonal standpoint presents a skewed weighing of the interests of self and others, the appropriate solution is not to disproportionately favor the personal standpoint because that too typically presents a differently skewed weighing of the interests of self and others. Rather, what is needed is a non-question-begging weighing of the interests of self and others, that is, a weighing that is supported by a good argument.

INDIVIDUAL VARIATIONS
IN THE ABILITY TO BE MORAL

In setting out this defense of morality, I assumed that we humans have the capacity to move along a spectrum from egoism to pure altruism. I granted that our ability to move along this spectrum would depend on our starting point, the strength of our habits, and the social circumstances under which we happen to be living. But I argued that, at the outset, it is reasonable to abstract from these individual variations and simply focus on the general capacity virtually all of us have to act on both self-interested and moral or altruistic reasons. Now, however, that I have argued that both self-interested and altruistic reasons are relevant to rational choice and that they will be assigned priorities in cases of conflict, it is appropriate to return to the question of how individual differences and the effects of their socialization should adjust our expectations and requirements for particular individuals and groups.

Notice, too, that if people were capable of only a minimal degree of altruism, then many more lifeboatlike situations would arise because people would not be capable of sacrificing many of their low-ranking self-interested objectives for the sake of conflicting high-ranking altruistic objectives, and for such cases, even a chance mechanism would not seem to provide a reasonable resolution. So it seems more reasonable here to assume a more general capacity for altruism.

Here, two kinds of cases seem particularly relevant. In one case, certain people, owing to their nature, lack, to some degree, the capacity to act on high-ranking altruistic reasons when they conflict with low-ranking self-interested reasons. In the other case, certain people, owing to socialization, lack, to some degree, this same capacity. Obviously, people who have the capacity for altruism and are motivated to act on it will have to try to work around, reform when possible, and, if necessary, protect themselves from those who, to varying degrees, lack this capacity. In cases in which those who lack this capacity are themselves at least partially responsible for this lack, blame and censure would also be appropriate.[38] Nevertheless, as long as the greater majority of people have by nature or by nurture (or by both) the capacity to act on high-ranking altruistic reasons when they conflict with low-ranking self-interested reasons and the capacity to act on high-ranking self-interested reasons when they conflict with low-ranking altruistic reasons and are committed to the principle of non-question-beggingness, then a socialization guided by the previous argument should serve to motivate them to endorse and abide by the basic requirements of morality, other things being equal, thereby exemplifying that common ground toward which the most defensible internalist and externalist views of motivation seem to be gravitating.[39] Similarly, because both ethical realists and ethical anti-realists would endorse the principle of non-question-beggingness, they should also endorse my defense of morality over egoism and altruism, even while they continue to give their competing realist and anti-realist interpretations of the self-interested and altruistic reasons that are employed in that defense.

FURTHER OBJECTIONS

Now, it might be objected that even if morality is required by a standard of non-question-beggingness, that does not provide us with the right kind of reason to be moral.[40] It might be argued that avoiding non-question-beggingness is too formal a reason to be moral and that we need a more substantive reason. Happily, the need for a substantive reason to be moral can be met, because in this case the relatively formal reason to be moral, namely, avoiding non-question-beggingness, itself entails a substantive reason to be moral, namely, to give high-ranking altruistic reasons priority over conflicting lower-ranking self-interested reasons, other things being equal, and to give high-ranking self-interested reasons priority over conflicting lower-ranking altruistic reasons, other things being equal, or to put this same substantive reason somewhat differently, to avoid inflicting basic harm on others for the sake of nonbasic benefit to oneself or others, other things being equal. So, as it turns out, morality as compromise can be shown to provide both relatively formal and substantive reasons to be moral.

It may also be objected that my argument for favoring morality over egoism and altruism would be analogous to naturalists and supernaturalists splitting the difference between their views and counting supernaturalist reasons as valid half of the time, and naturalist reasons as valid the other half of the time.[41] But as I understand the debate between naturalism and supernaturalism, many naturalists claim to have conclusive reasons for rejecting supernaturalism, and some supernaturalists claim to have conclusive reasons for rejecting naturalism. So this example does not parallel the case of egoism and altruism.

But suppose there were equally good reasons for naturalism as for supernaturalism, would we be rationally required to act on naturalism half of the time and supernaturalism the other half of the time? In this case, a far more reasonable resolution would be to continue to lead the life of a naturalist or a supernaturalist while periodically reevaluating the relevant reasons with the hope of someday resolving this issue. This interim solution is preferable because there is no way to compromise the issue between naturalism and supernaturalism that would respect the most important elements of each view. That is why the conflict between naturalism and supernaturalism, even assuming that there are equally good reasons for both views, differs from the conflict between egoism and altruism, because in the latter case there is a way to compromise the issue between the two views that respects the most important elements of each: Favor high-ranking self-interested reasons over conflicting low-ranking altruistic reasons, other things being equal, and favor high-ranking altruistic reasons over conflicting low-ranking self-interested reasons, other things being equal.

This illustrates how the requirement of non-question-beggingness favors different solutions in different contexts. Thus, in contexts where action can be deferred, it favors deferring action until compelling reasons favoring one course of action can be found, for example, putting off your choice of a vacation spot until you have good reasons for going to one particular spot. However, in contexts where action cannot be deferred (and you do not have non-question-begging grounds favoring one alternative over the others), either it is or it is not possible to combine the best parts of the existing alternatives into a single course of action. If it is not possible to combine the best parts of the existing alternatives, as in the assumed case concerning naturalism and supernaturalism, the requirement of non-question-beggingness favors arbitrarily choosing between them, while periodically reexamining the situation to determine whether, at some time or other, compelling reasons can be found for favoring one alternative over the other. If it is possible to combine the best parts of existing alternatives, as in the case of egoism and altruism, the requirement of non-question-beggingness favors this course of action. It is on this account that I argue that morality as compromise is rationally preferable to both egoism and altruism.

In sum, I have argued that the compromise view does provide a non-question-begging resolution to the particular debate between the egoist and the altruist. This is because neither the egoist nor the altruist has any non-question-begging grounds for not allowing both sorts of reasons to have prima facie status. So the debate between these views is not about the existence of self-interested or altruistic reasons but about which reasons should have priority (egoists say self-interested reasons always have priority whereas altruists say that altruistic reasons always have priority). They are really not contesting the existence of the reasons they oppose. However, once both sorts of reasons are allowed prima facie status, we do have non-question-begging grounds for favoring high-ranking over low-ranking reasons, or so I argue. In that way, I claim, we get morality as compromise.

However, if the debate were construed differently, as one between the egoist and the moralist, then no such non-question-begging compromise position would emerge. But here, I maintain, there is a reason why a compromise would not, and should not, emerge. It is because morality is already the result of a compromise between egoism and altruism. To require further compromising here would involve an unreasonable double counting of egoistic reasons. In addition, the reason why, in particular, my morality as compromise would not emerge from a debate between the egoist and the moralist is because it is virtually equivalent to just one side of the debate.

It is also important to note that the idealization that was introduced to show the superiority of morality as compromise over egoism and altruism renders the view not as useful as it appears to be for determining particular practical moral requirements. This is because the relatively precise rankings of self-interested and altruistic reasons were simply hypothesized to better illustrate the choice over egoism, altruism, and morality. Unfortunately, such relatively precise rankings are not likely to be found in real life.

Another objection that has been raised to morality as compromise is that it violates the conservativeness of logic, according to which you cannot get out of a valid inference what you don't put in.[42] Stated formally, this thesis about logic maintains that "a predicate or propositional variable cannot occur non-vacuously in the conclusion of a valid inference unless it appears among the premises." David Hume's famous thesis that you cannot derive an "ought" from an "is" turns out to be just a special case of this general thesis about the conservativeness of logic. The particular form of the thesis that is relevant to morality as compromise simply claims that moral conclusions cannot be derived from nonmoral premises.

For some reason, this sort of challenge to a defense of morality has not been taken very seriously throughout the history of ethics. When Kant is taken to be arguing that morality is grounded in rationality, most attack the validity of his argument. To my knowledge, no one has argued that Kant was trying to do something impossible. Similarly, among contemporary philosophers, attempts by Alan Gewirth, Kurt Baier, Christine Korsgaard, myself, and others to ground morality in rationality have not been greeted with claims of impossibility but rather with specific objections to the derivations we provide. To my knowledge, no one has challenged Gewirth's claim to derive morality from logical consistency on the grounds that it just could not be done because the premises of Gewirth's argument are nonmoral. All the criticisms are directed at the particular steps of Gewirth's argument, which seem to imply that what he was trying to do is at least logically possible. Nor when Korsgaard argues that morality is the product of a certain type of constitutive unity of the self or self-reflectiveness have critics replied that you cannot derive the moral from the nonmoral, but rather they have tried to show that even immoral people have that same unity or self-reflectiveness, so it cannot be the grounds for our moral life.

Still, I do think that there is something to this thesis about logic. Consider how it applies to my argument for morality as compromise. The basic premise in my argument for morality as compromise is the principle of non-question-beggingness, which is a rational requirement for a good argument. Thus, my argument is an attempt to derive morality from this principle of rationality. Accordingly, it moves not from an "is" to an "ought," but from an "ought" to an "ought." In fact, I agree with Hume that you cannot derive an "ought" from an "is," unless the "is" already has an "ought" built into it. At the same time, I take the ought-ought gap to be bridgeable in the way that the is-ought gap is not.

Nevertheless, the conservativeness of logic thesis maintains that my argument from "ought" to "ought" can only succeed in defending morality if its premises are moral. The principle of non-question-beggingness, however, doesn't look like a moral premise. It looks like a rational principle for good arguments, which would make it a rational "ought," not a moral "ought." But there is a sense in which it can also be regarded as moral. What the principle of non-question-beggingness requires is that we be fair or unbiased in our use of premises in deriving conclusions. It is a requirement of fair argumentation. It proscribes arguments, irrespective of their validity, where the conclusion is explicitly or blatantly in the premises, but not arguments where the conclusion is implicitly or subtly contained in the premises. In my argument for morality as compromise, the requirement of fair argumentation leads to a fair standard for leading one's life, which is recognizably a moral standard. So there is a sense that in my argument, the morality of the conclusion is contained in its premises as well.

Even so, the argument for morality as compromise remains interesting and important, even with the admission that its moral conclusion is contained in its premises, because the sense that morality is in its premises is neither obvious nor well understood. It definitely takes some doing to show how the proto-morality of fair argumentation supports the morality of ordinary life. This explains why there are many people who accept the premise of my argument (the principle of non-question-beggingness) without thinking that they are thereby bound to accept its conclusion (the endorsement of morality in ordinary life). Hence, my argument does serve an important function of helping to bring people to endorse the requirements of morality, even if, as the thesis of the conservation of logic maintains, its moral conclusion is contained in its premises. Now I will argue that completing this conception of morality with respect to the enforcement question leads to substantial equality.

THE ENFORCEMENT-OF-MORALITY QUESTION

While morality as compromise can be seen as rationally preferable to both egoism and altruism, and thus helps to establish the justification of morality over those two perspectives, it is anything but a complete moral perspective.

Here is one way I like to think about the incompleteness or inadequacy of morality as compromise. Suppose that John Stuart Mill had given us a non-question-begging argument that utilitarianism is rationally preferable to egoism. I think that we would be happy to accept such an argument as useful in our defense of morality, but then we would still want to go on to indicate the ways in which utilitarianism is an inadequate morality that needs to be improved upon or reinterpreted in various ways. That is how I think about morality as compromise. It is a useful way to think about morality for the purpose of showing the rational superiority of morality over egoism, but it is not as useful for other purposes. In any case, in order to settle the question of which moral requirements should be enforced, I am now shifting the discussion to a comparative evaluation of the political-moral perspectives of libertarianism, welfare liberalism, and socialism.

This is because morality as compromise, so far defended, does not clearly specify when its requirements can be coercively enforced, so its requirements seem to be open to a libertarian, or a welfare liberal, or even a socialist interpretation. Agreeing with libertarians, it would appear that we could hold that high-ranking altruistic reasons have priority over conflicting low-ranking self-interested reasons, and that acting upon them would provide comparably greater benefit, and still hold that we should not enforce that priority by means of a welfare state. Alternatively, it seems, we could agree with welfare liberals that we should coercively establish a right to welfare, or agree with socialists that we should go further and require substantial equality. Morality as compromise appears open to all three interpretations.

Nevertheless, we now need to go further and address the enforcement-of-morality question. Here, it behooves us to start with the assumptions of the libertarian perspective, the view that appears to endorse the least enforcement of morality, given that I propose to show that this view, contrary to what its defenders usually maintain,[43] requires a right to welfare, and that further, this right to welfare, which is also endorsed by a welfare liberal perspective, leads to the substantial equality of a socialist perspective. So far, I have argued from a conception of rationality as non-question-beggingness to the incomplete moral perspective of morality as compromise. Now I will argue that completing this conception of morality with respect to the enforcement question leads to substantial equality.

THE IDEAL OF NEGATIVE LIBERTY

Let us begin by interpreting the ideal of liberty as a negative ideal in the manner favored by libertarians. Libertarians like to think of themselves as defenders of liberty. F. A. Hayek, for example, sees his work as restating an ideal of liberty for our times. "We are concerned," says Hayek, "with that condition of men in which coercion of some by others is reduced as much as possible in society."[44] Similarly, John Hospers believes that libertarianism is "a philosophy of personal liberty—the liberty of each person to live according to his own choices, provided that he does not attempt to coerce others and thus prevent them from living according to their choices."[45] And Robert Nozick claims that if a conception of justice goes beyond libertarian "side-constraints," it cannot avoid the prospect of continually interfering with people's lives.

Yet while libertarians endorse an ideal of liberty, they interpret it in different ways. For some, liberty is defined as follows:

The Want Conception of Liberty: Liberty is being unconstrained by other persons from doing what one wants.[46]

This conception limits the scope of liberty in two ways. First, not all constraints, whatever their source, count as a restriction of liberty; the constraints must come from other persons. For example, people who are constrained by natural forces from getting to the top of Mount Everest do not lack liberty in this regard. Second, constraints that have their source in other people, but that do not run counter to an individual's wants, constrain without restricting that individual's liberty. Thus, for people who do not want to hear Beethoven's Fifth Symphony, the fact that others have effectively proscribed its performance does not restrict their liberty, even though it does constrain what they are able to do.

Of course, some may wish to argue that even such constraints can be seen to restrict a person's liberty once we take into account the fact that people normally want, or have a general desire, to be unconstrained by others. But others have thought that the possibility of such constraints points to a serious defect in this conception of liberty,[47] which can only be remedied by adopting the following broader conception of liberty:

The Ability Conception of Liberty: Liberty is being unconstrained by other persons from doing what one is able to do.

Applying this conception to the above example, we find that people's liberty to hear Beethoven's Fifth Symphony would be restricted even if they did not want to hear it (and even if, perchance, they did not want to be unconstrained by others), because other people would still be constraining them from doing what they are able to do.

Moreover, it is important to note that being unconstrained from doing what one is unable to do does not constitute a liberty. Of course, some philosophers would object to this account, claiming, for example, that people might be free or have the liberty to run a four-minute mile even when they are unable to do so. However, if we allow that people can have the liberty to do what they are unable to do, then, presumably, they can also lack the liberty to do or be constrained from doing what they are unable to do, which seems absurd.

Of course, there will also be numerous liberties determined by the ability conception that are not liberties according to the want conception. For example, there will be highly talented students who surprisingly do not want to pursue careers in philosophy, even though no one constrains them from doing so. Accordingly, the ability conception but not the want conception would view them as possessing a liberty. And even though such liberties are generally not as valuable as those liberties that are common to both conceptions, they still are of some value, even when the manipulation of people's wants is not at issue. This seems, therefore, to be a good reason for favoring the ability over the want conception of liberty.

Yet even if we endorse the ability conception of liberty, problems of interpretation still remain. The major problem concerns what counts as a constraint. On the one hand, libertarians would like to limit constraints to positive acts (that is, acts of commission) that prevent people from doing what they are otherwise able to do. On the other hand, welfare liberals interpret constraints to include, in addition, negative acts (that is, acts of omission) that prevent people from doing what they are otherwise able to do. In fact, this is one way to understand the debate between defenders of "negative liberty" and defenders of "positive liberty." For defenders of negative liberty would seem to interpret constraints to include only positive acts of others that prevent people from doing what they otherwise are able to do, whereas defenders of positive liberty would seem to interpret constraints to include both positive and negative acts of others that prevent people from doing what they are otherwise able to do.[48]

Thus, in order not to beg the question against libertarians, suppose we interpret constraints in the manner favored by them to include only positive acts by others that prevent people from doing what they otherwise either want and are able to do, or are just able to do.[49]

Libertarians go on to characterize their political ideal as requiring that each person should have the greatest amount of liberty that is morally commensurate with the greatest amount of liberty for everyone else.[50] Interpreting their ideal in this way, libertarians claim to derive a number of more specific requirements, in particular, a right to life; a right to freedom of speech, press, and assembly; and a right to property.

Here, it is important to observe that the libertarian's right to life is not a right to receive from others the goods and resources necessary for preserving one's life; it is simply a right not to have one's life interfered with or ended unjustly. Correspondingly, the libertarian's right to property is not a right to receive from others the goods and resources necessary for one's welfare, but rather typically a right not to be interfered with in regard to any goods and resources that one has legitimately acquired either by initial acquisition or by voluntary agreement.[51]

A PARTIAL DEFENSE

In support of their view, libertarians have advanced examples of the following sort. The first two are adapted from Milton Friedman, the last from Robert Nozick.[52]

In the first example, you are to suppose that you and three friends are walking along the street and you happen to notice and retrieve a $100 bill lying on the pavement. Suppose a rich fellow had passed by earlier throwing away $100 bills, and you have been lucky enough to find one of them. Now, according to Friedman, it would be nice of you to share your good fortune with your friends. Nevertheless, they have no right to demand that you do so, and hence, they would not be justified in forcing you to share the $100 bill with them. Similarly, Friedman would have us believe that it would be nice of us to provide welfare to the less-fortunate members of our society. Nevertheless, the less-fortunate members have no right to welfare, and hence they would not be justified in forcing us to provide such.

The second example, which Friedman regards as analogous to the first, involves supposing that there are four Robinson Crusoes, each marooned on four uninhabited islands in the same neighborhood. One of these Crusoes happens to land on a large and fruitful island, which enables him to live easily and well. The others happen to land on tiny and rather barren islands from which they can barely scratch a living. Suppose one day they discover the existence of each other. Now, according to Friedman, it would be nice of the fortunate Robinson Crusoe to share the resources of his island with the other three Crusoes, but the other three Crusoes have no right to demand that he share those resources, and it would be wrong for them to force him to do so. Correspondingly, Friedman thinks it would be nice of us to provide the less fortunate in our society with welfare, but the less fortunate have no right to demand that we do so, and it would be wrong for them to force us to do so.

In the third example, Robert Nozick asks us to imagine that we are in a society that has just distributed income according to some ideal pattern, possibly a pattern of equality. We are further to imagine that in such a society someone with the talents of Wilt Chamberlain or Kobe Bryant offers to play basketball for us, provided that he receives, let us say, $1 from every home-game ticket that is sold. Suppose we agree to these terms, and 2 million people attend the home games to see this new Wilt Chamberlain or Bryant play, thereby securing for him an income of $2 million. Because such an income would surely upset the initial pattern of income distribution, whatever that happened to be, Nozick contends that this illustrates how an ideal of liberty upsets the patterns required by other conceptions of justice, and hence calls for their rejection.

Of course, libertarians allow that it would be nice of the rich to share their surplus goods and resources with the poor, just as Milton Friedman would allow that it would be nice of you to share the $100 you found with your friends, and nice of the rich-islanded Robinson Crusoe to share his resources with the poor-islanded Robinson Crusoes. Nevertheless, they deny that government has a duty to provide for such needs. Some good things, such as providing welfare to the poor, are requirements of charity rather than justice, libertarians claim. Accordingly, failure to make such provisions is neither blameworthy nor punishable. As a consequence, such acts of charity should not be coercively required. For this reason, libertarians are opposed to coercively supported welfare programs.

THE IDEAL OF LIBERTY AND
THE PROBLEM OF CONFLICT

Now, in order to see why libertarians are mistaken about what their ideal requires, consider a conflict situation between the rich and the poor. In this conflict situation, the rich, of course, have more than enough resources to satisfy their basic needs.[53] In contrast, imagine that the poor lack the resources to meet their basic needs to secure a decent life for themselves, even though they have tried all the means available to them that libertarians regard as legitimate for acquiring such resources. Under circumstances like these, libertarians maintain that the rich should have the liberty to use their resources to satisfy their luxury needs if they so wish. Libertarians recognize that this liberty might well be enjoyed with the consequence that the satisfaction of the basic needs of the poor will not be met; they just think that liberty always has priority over other political ideals, and since they assume that the liberty of the poor is not at stake in such conflict situations, it is easy for them to conclude that the rich should not be required to sacrifice their liberty so that the basic needs of the poor may be met.

Of course, libertarians allow that it would be nice of the rich to share their surplus resources with the poor. Nevertheless, according to libertarians, such acts of charity are not required because the liberty of the poor is not thought to be at stake in such conflict situations.

In fact, however, the liberty of the poor is indeed at stake in such conflict situations. What is at stake is the liberty of the poor not to be interfered with in taking from the surplus possessions of the rich what is necessary to satisfy their basic needs.

Needless to say, libertarians want to deny that the poor have this liberty. But how can they justify such a denial? As this liberty of the poor has been specified, it is not a positive liberty to receive something but a negative liberty of noninterference. Clearly, what libertarians must do is recognize the existence of such a liberty and then claim that it unjustifiably conflicts with other liberties of the rich. But when libertarians see that this is the case, they are often genuinely surprised, for they had not previously seen the conflict between the rich and the poor as a conflict of liberties. In responding to my work in recent years, libertarians Tibor Machan, Eric Mack, and Jan Narveson, among others, have come to grudgingly recognize that this liberty of the poor, as I have specified it, is indeed a negative liberty, but then they want to go on to argue that this liberty is illegitimate, or, at least, as Machan sees it, practically illegitimate.[54]

Now, when the conflict between the rich and the poor is viewed as a conflict of liberties, we can either say that the rich should have the liberty not to be interfered with in using their surplus resources for luxury purposes, or we can say that the poor should have the liberty not to be interfered with in taking from the rich what they require to meet their basic needs. If we choose one liberty, we must reject the other. What needs to be determined, therefore, is which liberty is morally enforceable: the liberty of the rich or the liberty of the poor.[55]

THE "OUGHT" IMPLIES "CAN" PRINCIPLE

I submit that the liberty of the poor, which is the liberty not to be interfered with in taking from the surplus resources of others what is required to meet one's basic needs, is morally enforceable over the liberty of the rich, which is the liberty not to be interfered with in using one's surplus resources for luxury purposes. To see that this is the case, we need only appeal to one of the most fundamental principles of morality, one that is common to all moral and political perspectives, namely, the "ought" implies "can" principle. According to this principle, people are not morally required to do what they lack the power to do or what would involve so great a sacrifice or restriction that it is unreasonable/contrary to reason to ask them, or in cases of severe conflict of interest, unreasonable/contrary to reason to require them to abide by.[56]

For example, suppose I promised to attend a departmental meeting on Friday, but on Thursday I am involved in a serious car accident that puts me into a coma. Surely it is no longer the case that I ought to attend the meeting, now that I lack the power to do so. Or suppose instead that on Thursday I develop a severe case of pneumonia for which I am hospitalized. Surely I can legitimately claim that I cannot attend the meeting on the grounds that the risk to my health involved in attending is a sacrifice it is unreasonable/contrary to reason to ask me to bear. Or suppose instead the risk to my health from having pneumonia is not so serious, and it is reasonable and not contrary to reason to ask me to attend the meeting (a supererogatory request). However, it might still be serious enough to be unreasonable/contrary to reason to require my attendance at the meeting (a demand that is backed up by blame and coercion).

This "ought" implies "can" principle claims that reason and morality must be linked in an appropriate way, especially if we are going to be able to justifiably use blame or coercion to get people to abide by the requirements of morality. It should be noted, however, that although major figures in the history of philosophy, and most philosophers today, including virtually all libertarian philosophers, accept this linkage between reason and morality, this linkage is not usually conceived to be part of the "ought" implies "can" principle.

This linkage between morality and reason is expressed in the belief that (true) morality and (right) reason cannot conflict. Some supporters of this linkage have developed separate theories of rationality and reasonableness, contending, for example, that while egoists are rational, those who are committed to morality are both rational and reasonable. In this interpretation, morality is rationally permissible but not rationally required, because egoism is also rationally permissible. Other supporters of the linkage between reason and morality reject the idea of separate theories of rationality and reasonableness, contending that morality, though reasonable, is not just rationally permissible and reasonable but also rationally required and that egoism is rationally impermissible. But despite their disagreement over whether there is a separate theory of rationality distinct from a theory of reasonableness, most in both groups usually link morality with a notion of reasonableness that incorporates a certain degree of altruism. However, for those who do not link morality with a notion of reasonableness that incorporates a certain degree of altruism but instead favor a self-interested-based Hobbesian perspective, the first part of my essay gives them a non-question-begging argument for now making that linkage.

Nevertheless, I claim that there are good reasons for associating this linkage with the principle, namely, our use of the word "can," as in the example just given, and the natural progression from logical, physical, and psychological possibility found in the traditional "ought" implies "can" principle to the notion of moral possibility found in my formulation of the principle. In any case, the acceptability of my formulation of the "ought" implies "can" principle is determined by the virtually universal, and arguably necessary, acceptance of its components and not by the manner in which I have proposed to join those components together.[57]

Now, applying the "ought" implies "can" principle to the case at hand, it seems clear that the poor have it within their power to relinquish such an important liberty as the liberty not to be interfered with in taking from the rich what they require to meet their basic needs. They could do this. Nevertheless, it is unreasonable/contrary to reason in this context to require them to accept so great a restriction. In the extreme case, it involves requiring the poor to sit back and starve to death. Of course, the poor may have no real alternative to relinquishing this liberty. To do anything else may involve worse consequences for themselves and their loved ones and may invite a painful death. Accordingly, we may expect that the poor would acquiesce, albeit unwillingly, to a political system that denied them the right to welfare supported by such a liberty, at the same time we recognize that such a system has imposed an unreasonable/contrary to reason restriction upon the poor—a restriction that we could not morally blame the poor for trying to evade. Analogously, we might expect that a woman whose life is threatened would submit to a rapist's demands, at the same time that we recognize the utter unreasonableness of those demands. By contrast, it is not unreasonable/contrary to reason to require the rich in this context to sacrifice the liberty to meet some of their luxury needs so that the poor can have the liberty to meet their basic needs. Naturally, we might expect that the rich, for reasons of self-interest or past contribution, might be disinclined to make such a sacrifice. We might even suppose that the past contribution of the rich provides a good reason for not sacrificing their liberty to use their surplus for luxury purposes. Yet the rich cannot claim that relinquishing such a liberty involves so great a sacrifice that it is unreasonable/contrary to reason to require them to make it; unlike the poor, the rich are morally blameworthy and subject to coercion for failing to make such a sacrifice.

Consequently, if we assume that however else we specify the requirements of morality, they cannot violate the "ought" implies "can" principle, it follows that despite what libertarians claim, the right to liberty endorsed by them actually favors the liberty of the poor over the liberty of the rich. Moreover, although application of the unreasonable/contrary to reason standard of the "ought" implies "can" principle can be disputable in some contexts, in the context where we have to coercively enforce either the liberty of the poor or the liberty of the rich, the standard does offer a clear resolution, one that favors the liberty of the poor over the liberty of the rich.

This means that within the bundle of liberties allotted to each person by the basic principle of libertarianism, there must be the liberty not to be interfered with (when one is poor) in taking from the surplus possessions of the rich what is necessary to satisfy one's basic needs. This must be part of the bundle that constitutes the greatest amount of liberty for each person because this liberty is morally superior to the liberty with which it directly conflicts, that is, the liberty not to be interfered with (when one is rich) in using one's surplus possessions to satisfy one's luxury needs. In this context, the "ought" implies "can" principle establishes the moral superiority and enforceability of the liberty of the poor over the liberty of the rich.[58]

Yet couldn't libertarians object to this conclusion, claiming that it would be unreasonable/contrary to reason to require the rich to sacrifice the liberty to meet some of their luxury needs so that the poor can have the liberty to meet their basic needs? As I have pointed out, libertarians don't usually see the situation as a conflict of liberties, but suppose they did. How plausible would such an objection be? Not very plausible at all, I think.

For consider: What are libertarians going to say about the poor? Isn't it clearly unreasonable/contrary to reason to require the poor to restrict their liberty to meet their basic needs so that the rich can have the liberty to meet their luxury needs? Isn't it clearly unreasonable/contrary to reason to coercively require the poor to sit back and starve to death? If it is, then there is no resolution of this conflict that is reasonable and not contrary to reason to coercively require both the rich and the poor to accept. But that would mean that libertarians could not be putting forth a moral resolution because a moral resolution, according to the "ought" implies "can" principle, resolves severe conflicts of interest in ways that it is reasonable and not contrary to reason to require everyone affected to accept,[59] where it is further understood that a moral resolution can sometimes require us to act in accord with altruistic reasons.[60] Therefore, as long as libertarians think of themselves as putting forth a moral resolution, they cannot allow that it is unreasonable/contrary to reason in cases of severe conflict of interest both to require the rich to restrict their liberty to meet some of their luxury needs in order to benefit the poor and to require the poor to restrict their liberty to meet their basic needs in order to benefit the rich. But I submit that if one of these requirements is to be judged reasonable and not contrary to reason, then, by any neutral assessment, it must be the requirement that the rich restrict their liberty to meet some of their luxury needs so that the poor can have the liberty to meet their basic needs; there is no other plausible resolution, if libertarians intend to put forth a moral resolution.[61]

It should also be noted that this case for restricting the liberty of the rich depends upon the willingness of the poor to take advantage of whatever opportunities are available to them to engage in mutually beneficial work, so that failure of the poor to take advantage of such opportunities would normally cancel the obligation of the rich to restrict their own liberty for the benefit of the poor.[62] In addition, the poor would be required to give back the equivalent of any surplus possessions they have taken from the rich, once they are able to do so and still satisfy their basic needs.[63] The case for favoring the liberty of the poor is also conditional on there being sufficient resources available to meet everyone's basic needs.

Of course, there will be cases where the poor fail to satisfy their basic needs, not because of any direct restriction of liberty on the part of the rich, but because the poor are in such dire need that they are unable even to attempt to take from the rich what they require to meet their basic nutritional needs. Accordingly, in such cases, the rich would not be performing any act of commission that prevents the poor from taking what they require. Yet even in such cases, the rich would normally be performing acts of commission that prevent other people from aiding the poor by taking from the surplus possessions of the rich. And when assessed from a moral point of view, restricting the liberty of these other people would not be morally justified for the very same reason that restricting the liberty of the poor to meet their own basic needs would not be morally justified: It would not be reasonable to ask all of those affected to accept such a restriction of liberty.

Notice, too, that it is not the mere size of the sacrifice required of the poor that is objectionable when considering the possibility of favoring the liberty of the rich over the liberty of the poor because sometimes morality does require great sacrifices from us. For example, it requires us to refrain from intentionally killing innocent people even to save our lives. Rather, what is objectionable about this possibility is the size of the sacrifice that the poor would be required to bear, compared to the size of the benefit that would otherwise be secured for the rich. In the case of the prohibition against intentionally killing innocent people, the sacrifice that violating this prohibition would impose on (innocent) people is normally greater than the benefit we ourselves and others would realize from violating that prohibition, hence the reasonableness of the prohibition. Correspondingly, in the conflict between the rich and the poor, the sacrifice that would be imposed on the poor by denying them the satisfaction of their basic needs is clearly greater than the benefit the rich would obtain from satisfying their nonbasic or luxury needs, hence the unreasonableness of imposing such a sacrifice on the poor. In this case, it is more reasonable to require a certain degree of altruism from the rich than to require an even greater degree of altruism from the poor. In all such cases, the goal is to avoid imposing an unreasonable sacrifice on anyone, where the reasonableness of the sacrifice is judged by comparing the alternative possibilities.

It is sometimes thought that there is a different interpretation of libertarianism in which rights, not liberties, are fundamental and for which another argument is needed to establish the conclusion I have just established here.[64] Under this presumptively different interpretation, the rights taken as fundamental are a strong right to property and a weak right to life. Yet, given that for libertarians such rights are also rights of noninterference, that is, (negative) liberty rights, the question arises of why we should accept these particular rights of noninterference (liberties) and not others—which is just the question that arises when we consider the conflicting liberties to which an ideal of liberty gives rise. What this shows is that the "rights" interpretation of libertarianism is not really distinct from the "liberty" interpretation we have just been discussing.

One might also think that once the rich realize that the poor should have the liberty not to be interfered with when taking from the surplus possessions of the rich what they require to satisfy their basic needs, it would be in the interest of the rich to stop producing any surplus whatsoever.

Suppose a producer who could produce a surplus didn't want to do so, even though she knew that others needed that surplus to meet their basic needs. Imagine that these others through no fault of their own could not produce enough to meet their own basic needs and that their basic needs would be met only if they took from the nonsurplus resources of the producer or threatened to do so in order to motivate her to produce more. In these circumstances, I think that the producer could be legitimately interfered with by those seeking in the only way possible to meet their basic needs by appropriating or threatening to appropriate her nonsurplus resources.

Of course, the producer in this case would probably respond to the appropriations or threat to appropriate by producing more.[65] Nevertheless, what the producer is morally required to do is not that, but rather not to interfere with the appropriation or the threat to appropriate her nonsurplus resources by others who are in need through no fault of their own and who cannot meet their own basic needs in any other way.

Of course, our producer could respond by doing nothing. The poor could then appropriate the nonsurplus resources of the producer, and then by not producing more, the producer would just waste away because she is unwilling to be more productive. If that happens, then both the poor and the producer would lose out, due to the inaction of the producer. Still, the producer is not obligated to respond to the negative welfare right of the poor by doing something productive, however self-destructive being unproductive would be for her. This is how the negative right to welfare differs from a positive right requiring the producer to do something. It falls short of what a positive right to welfare can do for the poor. Yet it falls short only when the producers of the world choose to act in a self-destructive way—a very unlikely possibility.

Nevertheless, libertarians might respond that even supposing welfare rights could be morally justified on the basis of the liberty of the poor not to be interfered with in taking from the rich in order to meet their basic nutritional needs and the liberty of third parties not to be interfered with in taking from the rich in order to provide for the basic nutritional rights of the poor, the poor still would be better off without the enforcement of such rights.[66] For example, it might be argued that when people are not forced through taxation to support a system of welfare rights, they are both more productive, since they are able to keep more of what they produce, and more charitable, since they tend to give more freely to those in need when they are not forced to do so. As a result, so the argument goes, the poor would benefit more from the increased charity of a libertarian society than they would from the guaranteed minimum of a welfare state. Yet surely it is difficult to comprehend how people who are so opposed to the enforcement of welfare rights would turn out to be so charitable to the poor in a libertarian society.

Moreover, in a libertarian society, the provision of welfare would involve an impossible coordination problem. For if the duty to provide welfare to the poor is at best supererogatory, as libertarians claim, then no one can legitimately force anyone who does not consent to provide such welfare. The will of the majority on this issue could not be legitimately imposed upon dissenters.[67] Assuming, then, that the provision of welfare requires coordinated action on a broad front, such coordination could not be achieved in a libertarian society because it would require a near unanimous agreement of all its members.[68]

There is also an interesting practical reason why coercive welfare systems are needed. For many people, coercive welfare systems provide them with the opportunity to be as morally good as they can be. This is because many people are willing to help the poor, but only when they can be assured that other people, similarly situated, are making comparable sacrifices, and a coercive welfare system does provide the assurance that comparable sacrifices will be made by all those with a surplus. Such people, and there appear to be many of them, would not give, or not give as much, to the poor without this coercive requirement.

Nevertheless, it might still be argued that the greater productivity of the more talented people in a libertarian society would increase employment opportunities and voluntary welfare assistance, which would benefit the poor more than a guaranteed minimum would in a welfare state. But this simply could not occur. For if the more talented members of a society were to provide sufficient employment opportunities and voluntary welfare assistance to enable the poor to meet their basic needs, then the conditions for invoking a right to a guaranteed minimum in a welfare state would not arise, since the poor are first required to take advantage of whatever employment opportunities and voluntary welfare assistance are available to them before they can legitimately invoke such a right. Consequently, when sufficient employment opportunities and voluntary welfare assistance obtain, there would be no practical difference in this regard between a libertarian society and a welfare state, since neither would justify invoking a right to a guaranteed minimum. Only when insufficient employment opportunities and voluntary welfare assistance obtain would there be a practical difference between a libertarian society and a welfare state, and then it would clearly benefit the poor to be able to invoke the right to a guaranteed minimum in a welfare state. Consequently, given the conditional nature of the right to welfare, and the practical possibility and, in most cases, the actuality of insufficient employment opportunities and voluntary welfare assistance obtaining, there is no reason to think that the poor would be better off without the enforcement of such a right.[69]

In brief, I have argued that a libertarian ideal of liberty can be seen to support a right to welfare by applying the "ought" implies "can" principle to conflicts between the rich and the poor. Here, the principle supports such rights by favoring the liberty of the poor over the liberty of the rich. Clearly, what is crucial to the derivation of these rights is the claim that it is unreasonable/contrary to reason to coercively require the poor to deny their basic needs and accept anything less than these rights as the condition for their willing cooperation.

Morality as compromise gave us the priority of high-ranking altruistic reasons over conflicting low-ranking self-interested reasons, but it left open the possibility that failing to act on the high-ranking altruistic reasons might involve simply not helping the poor meet their basic needs rather than interfering with the poor's meeting those needs. Thus, if we were only concerned with enforcing against such interference, there would be no need to do so in these cases. However, once we recognize that conflicts between the rich and the poor can be understood to involve either interfering with the poor meeting their basic needs or interfering with the rich meeting their nonbasic needs, the need for an enforceable resolution becomes apparent.[70] Applying the "ought" implies "can" principle to these cases, we were then led to favor the more important liberty (noninterference with the poor) over the less important liberty (noninterference with the rich), thereby justifying a right to welfare.[71]

Now, it might be objected that the right to welfare that this argument establishes from libertarian premises is not the same as the right to welfare endorsed by welfare liberals and socialists. This is correct. We could mark this difference by referring to the right that this argument establishes as "a negative welfare right" and by referring to the right endorsed by welfare liberals as "a positive welfare right." The significance of this difference is that a person's negative welfare right can be violated only when other people through acts of commission interfere with its exercise, whereas a person's positive welfare right can be violated not only by such acts of commission but by acts of omission as well. Nonetheless, this difference will have little practical import because in recognizing the legitimacy of negative welfare rights, libertarians will come to see that virtually any use of their surplus possessions is likely to violate the negative welfare rights of the poor by preventing the poor from rightfully appropriating (some part of) their surplus goods and resources. So, in order to ensure that they will not be engaging in such wrongful actions, it will be incumbent on them to set up institutions guaranteeing adequate positive welfare rights for the poor. Only then will they be able to use legitimately any remaining surplus possessions to meet their own nonbasic needs. Furthermore, in the absence of adequate positive welfare rights, the poor, acting either by themselves or through their allies or agents, would have some discretion in determining when and how to exercise their negative welfare rights.[72] In order not to be subject to that discretion, libertarians will tend to favor the only morally legitimate way of preventing the exercise of such rights:

They will set up institutions guaranteeing adequate positive welfare rights that will then take precedence over the exercise of negative welfare rights. For these reasons, recognizing the negative welfare rights of the poor will ultimately lead libertarians to endorse the same sort of welfare institutions favored by welfare liberals.

It is important to see how moral and pragmatic considerations are combined in this argument from negative welfare rights to positive welfare rights, as this will become particularly relevant when we turn to a consideration of distant peoples and future generations. What needs to be seen is that the moral consideration is primary and the pragmatic consideration secondary. The moral consideration is that until positive welfare rights for the poor are guaranteed, any use by the rich of their surplus possessions to meet their nonbasic needs is likely to violate the negative welfare rights of the poor by preventing them from appropriating (some part of) the surplus goods and resources of the rich. The pragmatic consideration is that in the absence of positive welfare rights, the rich would have to put up with the discretion of the poor, acting either by themselves or through their allies or agents, in choosing when and how to exercise their negative welfare rights.

Now, obviously, peoples who are separated from the rich by significant distances will be able to exercise their negative welfare rights only either by negotiating the distances involved or by having allies or agents in the right place, willing to act on their behalf. And with respect to future generations, their rights can be exercised only if they, too, have allies and agents in the right place and time, willing to act on their behalf. So unless distant peoples are good at negotiating distances or unless distant peoples and future generations have ample allies and agents in the right place and time, the pragmatic consideration leading the rich to endorse positive welfare rights will diminish in importance in their regard. Fortunately, the moral consideration alone is sufficient to carry the argument here and elsewhere: Libertarians should endorse positive welfare rights because it is the only way that they can be assured of not violating the negative welfare rights of the poor by preventing the poor from appropriating (some part of) the surplus goods and resources of the rich.

FROM WELFARE TO EQUALITY

Now, it is possible that libertarians, convinced to some extent by the above argument, might want to accept a right to welfare for members of their own society but deny that this right extends to distant peoples and future generations. Because it is only fairly recently that philosophers have begun to discuss the question of what rights distant peoples and future generations might legitimately claim against us, a generally acceptable way of discussing the question has yet to be developed. Some philosophers have even attempted to "answer" the question, or at least part of it, by arguing that talk about "the rights of future generations" is conceptually incoherent and is thus analogous to talk about "square circles." Accordingly, the key question that must be answered first is this: Can we meaningfully speak of distant peoples and future generations as having rights against us or of our having corresponding obligations to them?

DISTANT PEOPLES

Answering this question with respect to distant peoples is much easier than answering it with respect to future generations. Few philosophers have thought that the mere fact that people are at a distance from us precludes our having any obligations to them or their having any rights against us. Some philosophers, however, have argued that our ignorance of the specific membership of the class of distant peoples does rule out these moral relationships. Yet this cannot be right, given that in other contexts we recognize obligations to indeterminate classes of people, such as a police officer's obligation to help people in distress or the obligation of food producers not to harm those who consume their products.

Yet others have argued that while there may be valid moral claims respecting the welfare of distant peoples, such claims cannot be rights, because they fail to hold against determinate individuals and groups.[73] But in what sense do such claims fail to hold against determinate individuals and groups? Surely, all would agree that existing laws rarely specify the determinate individuals and groups against whom such claims hold. But morality is frequently determinate where existing laws are not. And at least there seems to be no conceptual impossibility to claiming that distant peoples have rights against us and that we have corresponding obligations to them.

Of course, before distant peoples can be said to have rights against us, we must be capable of acting across the distance that separates us. Yet as long as this condition is met—as it typically is for people living in most technologically advanced societies—it would certainly seem possible for distant peoples to have rights against us and for us to have corresponding obligations to them.

FUTURE GENERATIONS

In contrast, answering the above question with respect to future generations is much more difficult and has been the subject of considerable debate among contemporary philosophers. One issue concerns the referent of the term "future generations." Most philosophers seem to agree that the class of future generations is not "the class of all persons who simply could come into existence." But there is some disagreement about whether we should refer to the class of future generations as "the class of persons who will definitely come into existence, assuming that there are such" or as "the class of persons we can reasonably expect to come into existence." The first approach is more "existential," specifying the class of future generations in terms of what will exist; the second approach is more "epistemological," specifying the class of future generations in terms of our knowledge. Fortunately, there does not appear to be any practical moral significance to the choice of either approach.

Another issue relevant to whether we can meaningfully speak of future generations as having rights against us or our having obligations to them concerns whether it is logically coherent to speak of future generations as having rights now. Of course, no one who finds talk about rights to be generally meaningful should question whether we can coherently claim that future generations will have rights at some point in the future (specifically, when they come into existence and are no longer future generations). But what is questioned, since it is of considerable practical significance, is whether we can coherently claim that future generations have rights now, when they do not yet exist.

Let us suppose, for example, that we continue to use up the earth's resources at present or even greater rates, and, as a result, it turns out that the most pessimistic forecasts for the twenty-second century are realized.[74] This means that future generations will face widespread famine, depleted resources, insufficient new technology to handle the crisis, and a drastic decline in the quality of life for nearly everyone. If this were to happen, could people living in the twenty-second century legitimately claim that we in the twenty-first century violated their rights by not restraining our consumption of the world's resources? Surely, it would be odd to say that we violated their rights 100 years before they existed. But what exactly is the oddness?

Is it that future generations generally have no way of claiming their rights against existing generations? Although this does make the recognition and enforcement of rights much more difficult (future generations would need strong advocates in the existing generations), it does not make it impossible for there to be such rights. After all, it is quite obvious that the recognition and enforcement of the rights of distant peoples is also a difficult task.

Or is it that we don't believe rights can legitimately exercise their influence over long durations of time? But if we can foresee and control at least some of the effects our actions will have on the ability of future generations to satisfy their basic needs, why should we not be responsible for those same effects? And if we are responsible for them, why should not future generations have a right that we take them into account?

Perhaps what troubles us is that future generations are not yet in existence when their rights are said to demand action. But how else could people have a right not to be harmed by the effects our actions will have in the distant future if they did not exist at the time those effects would be felt? Our contemporaries cannot legitimately make the same demand, for they will not be around to experience those effects. Only future generations can have a right that the effects our actions will have in the distant future not harm them. Nor need we assume that in order for people to have rights, they must exist when their rights demand action. Thus, in saying that future generations have rights against existing generations, we can simply mean that there are enforceable requirements upon existing generations that will prevent harm to future generations.

A UNIVERSAL RIGHT TO WELFARE

Once it is recognized that we can meaningfully speak of distant peoples and future generations as having rights against us and that we have corresponding obligations to them, there is no reason not to extend the argument for a right to welfare grounded on libertarian premises that I have defended in this essay to distant peoples and future generations. This is because for libertarians, fundamental rights are universal rights, that is, rights possessed by all people, not just those who live in certain places or at certain times.

Of course, to claim that rights are universal does not mean that they are universally recognized. Rather, to claim that rights are universal, despite their spotty recognition, implies only that they ought to be recognized because people at all times and places have or could have had good reasons to recognize these rights, not that they actually did or do so.

Yet even though libertarians have claimed that the rights they defend are universal rights in the manner I have just explained, it may be that they are simply mistaken in this regard. Even when universal rights are stripped of any claim to being universally recognized or unconditional, still it might be argued that there are no such rights, that is, that there are no rights that all people ought to recognize. But how does one argue for such a view? One cannot argue from the failure of people to recognize such rights, because we have already said that such recognition is not necessary. Nor can one argue that not everyone ought to recognize such rights because some lack the capacity to do so. This is because "ought" does imply "can" here, so that the obligation to recognize certain rights applies only to those who actually have or have had at some point the capacity to do so. Thus, the existence of universal rights is not ruled out by the existence of individuals who have never had the capacity to recognize such rights. It is ruled out only by the existence of individuals who can recognize these rights but for whom it is correct to say that it is at least permissible, all things considered, not to do so. But we have just seen that even a minimal libertarian moral ideal supports a universal right to welfare. And I have argued earlier in this essay when "ought" is understood both morally and self-interestedly, a non-question-begging conception of rationality favors morality over self-interest when they conflict. So for those capable of recognizing universal rights, it simply is not possible to argue that they, all things considered, ought not to do so.

It is also worth noting that the question whether there are interpersonal conflicts of interest, and if so, how best to resolve them that seems to arise in pre-Enlightenment philosophy parallels the more modern question of whether there are interpersonal conflicts of liberty, and if so, how best to resolve them.

Nor need universal rights be unconditional. This is particularly true in the case of the right to welfare, which I have argued is conditional upon people doing all that they legitimately can to provide for themselves. In addition, this right is conditional upon there being sufficient resources available so that everyone's welfare needs can be met. So where people do not do all that they can to provide for themselves or where there are not sufficient resources available, people do not normally have a right to welfare.[75] Given the universal and conditional character of this libertarian right to welfare, what, then, are the implications of this right for distant peoples and future generations?

At present, worldwide food production is sufficient to provide everyone in the world with at least 2,720 kilocalories per person per day.[76] To meet the nutritional and other basic needs of each and every person living today, however, would require a significant redistribution of goods and resources. To finance such redistribution, Thomas Pogge has proposed a 1 percent tax on aggregate global income, which would net $312 billion annually.[77] Peter Singer, as an alternative, has proposed a graduated tax on the incomes of the top 10 percent of US families, netting $404 billion annually, with an equal sum coming from the family incomes of people living in other industrialized countries.[78] Both Pogge and Singer are confident that their proposals would go a long way toward meeting basic human needs worldwide. In fact, Singer remarks that before coming up with his recent proposal, he never "fully understood how easy it would be for the world's rich to eliminate, or virtually eliminate, global poverty."[79]

Although Pogge's and Singer's proposals would doubtless do much to secure a right to welfare for existing people, even in the current economic downturn, it is unfortunate that they do not speak very well to the needs of future generations. How, then, can we best insure that future generations are not deprived of the goods and resources that they will need to meet their basic needs? In the United States, currently more than 1 million acres of arable land are lost from cultivation each year as a result of urbanization, multiplying transport networks, and industrial expansion.[80] In addition, another 2 million acres of farmland are lost each year, on average, due to erosion, salinization, and waterlogging.[81] The state of Iowa alone has lost one-half of its fertile topsoil from farming in the last 100 years. That loss is about thirty times faster than what is sustainable.[82] According to one estimate, only 0.6 of an acre of arable land per person will be available in the United States in 2050, whereas more than 1.2 acres per person are needed to provide a diverse diet (currently 1.6 acres of arable land are available).[83] Similar, or even more threatening, estimates of the loss of arable land have been made for other regions of the world.[84] How, then, are we going to preserve farmland and other food-related natural resources so that future generations are not deprived of what they require to meet their basic needs?

And what about other resources? It has been estimated that currently a North American uses seventy-five times more resources than a resident of India. This means that in terms of resource consumption, the North American continent's population is the equivalent of 22.5 billion Indians.[85] So unless we assume that basic resources such as arable land, iron, coal, and oil are in unlimited supply, this unequal consumption will have to be radically altered if the basic needs of future generations are to be met.[86] I submit, therefore, that recognizing a universal right to welfare applicable both to existing and future people requires us to use up no more resources than are necessary for meeting our own basic needs, thus securing for ourselves a decent life but no more.[87] For us to use up more resources than this, we would be guilty of depriving at least some future generations of the resources they would require to meet their own basic needs, thereby violating their libertarian-based right to welfare.[88] Obviously, this would impose a significant sacrifice on existing generations, particularly those in the developed world, clearly a far greater sacrifice than Pogge and Singer maintain is required for meeting the basic needs of existing generations. Nevertheless, these demands do follow from a libertarian-based right to welfare. In effect, recognizing a right to welfare, applicable to all existing and future people, leads to an equal utilization of resources over place and time.

What makes this an equal utilization of resources over place and time is that the utilization is limited to fulfilling people's basic needs. Of course, once basic needs are met among existing generations, renewable resources may be used for meeting nonbasic needs in ways that do not jeopardize the meeting of the basic needs of future generations. In addition, existing generations can also justifiably meet their nonbasic needs if this is a by-product of efficiently meeting just their basic needs. Naturally, this holds equally for each subsequent generation as well.

Of course, it could be argued that even if we continue our extravagant consumption of nonrenewable resources, future generations will be able to make up for the loss with some kind of technological fix. We can even imagine that future generations will be able to make everything they need out of, say, sand and water. Although this might surely be possible, it would not be reasonable for us to risk the basic welfare of future generations on just such a possibility, any more than it would be reasonable for people starting out in the lowest-paying jobs in the business world to start wildly borrowing and spending on themselves and their families, relying just on the possibility that in fifteen to twenty years their incomes will rise astronomically so they then could easily pay off the large debts they are now amassing. There are also many examples of human civilizations that failed to find an appropriate technological fix.[89]

Now, it might be objected that if we fail to respect this welfare requirement for future generations, we would still not really be harming those future generations that we would deprive of the resources they require for meeting their basic needs. This is because if we acted so as to appropriately reduce our consumption, those same future generations that we would supposedly harm by our present course of action won't even exist.[90] This is because the changes we would make in our lives in order to live in a resource-conserving manner would so alter our social relations, now and in the future, that the membership of future generations would be radically altered as well. Yet to hold that we harm only those who would still exist if we acted appropriately is too strong a restriction on harming.

Consider an owner of an industrial plant arguing that she really did not harm your daughter who is suffering from leukemia due to the contaminants that leaked into the area surrounding the plant because only by operating the plant so that it leaked these contaminants was it economically feasible in this particular place and time. Hence, the plant would not have opened up, nor would you have moved nearby to work, nor would this daughter of yours even have been born, without its operating in this way.[91] In brief, the owner of the plant contends that your daughter was not really harmed at all because if there had been no contamination, she would not even have been born. Assuming, however, that we reject the plant owner's counterfactual requirement for harming in favor of a direct causal one (the operation of the plant caused your daughter's leukemia), as we should, then we have to recognize that we, too, can be held responsible for harming future generations if, by the way we live our lives, we cause the harm from which they will suffer.

Now, it might be further objected that if we did limit ourselves to simply meeting our basic needs—a decent life, but no more—we would still be harming future generations at some more distant point in time, leaving those generations without the resources required for meeting their basic needs. While our present nonconserving way of living would begin to harm future generations in, let's say, 200 years, our conserving way of living, should we adopt it, and should it be continued by subsequent generations, would, let's assume, lead to that same result in 2,000 years. So either way, we would be harming future generations.

There is a difference, however. Although both courses of action would ultimately harm future generations, if we do limit ourselves to simply meeting our basic needs, a decent life, but no more, and other generations do the same, then many generations of future people would benefit from this course of action who would not benefit from our alternative, nonconserving course of action. Even more important, for us to sacrifice further for the sake of future generations would require us to give up meeting our own basic needs, and normally we cannot be morally required to do this, as the "ought" implies "can" principle makes clear. We can be required to give up the satisfaction of our nonbasic needs so that others can meet their basic needs, but normally, without our consent, we cannot be required to sacrifice the satisfaction of our own basic needs so that others can meet their basic needs.[92] So although future generations may still be harmed in the distant future as a result of our behavior, no one can justifiably blame us, or take action against us, for using no more resources than we require for meeting our basic needs.

Of course, someone could ask: How do you distinguish basic from nonbasic needs? A person raising this question may not realize how widespread the use of this distinction is. While the distinction is surely important for global ethics, as my use of it attests, it is also used widely in moral, political, and environmental philosophy; it would really be impossible to do much philosophy in these areas, especially at the practical level, without a distinction between basic and nonbasic needs.

Another way that I would respond to the question is by pointing out that the fact that not every need can be clearly classified as either basic or nonbasic, as similarly holds for a whole range of dichotomous concepts like moral-immoral, legal-illegal, living-nonliving, human-nonhuman, should not immobilize us from acting at least with respect to clear cases. This puts our use of the distinction in a still broader context, suggesting that if we cannot use the basic-nonbasic distinction in moral, political, and environmental philosophy, the widespread use of other dichotomous concepts is likewise threatened. It also suggests how our inability to clearly classify every conceivable need as basic or nonbasic should not keep us from using such a distinction at least with respect to clear cases.

There is also a further point to be made here. If we begin to respond to clear cases, for example, stop aggressing against the clear basic needs of some humans for the sake of clear luxury needs of others, we will be in an even better position to know what to do in the less clear cases. This is because sincerely attempting to live out one's practical moral commitments helps one to interpret them better, just as failing to live them out makes interpreting them all the more difficult. Consequently, I think we have every reason to act on the moral requirements that I have defended here, at least with respect to clear cases.

CONCLUSION

Let me end by simply summarizing my argument, so far sketched. My argument has proceeded from a conception of rationality as non-question-beggingness to an endorsement of morality over egoism and altruism. I then further argued that even a libertarian version of the conception of morality that I defended leads to a right to welfare. Lastly, I argued that extending this right to welfare, particularly to future generations, as I claim we must, leads to the egalitarian requirement that as far as possible, we should use up no more resources than are necessary to meet our basic needs, securing for ourselves a decent life but no more. In addition, if the argument is successful, and it becomes widely accepted by moral and political philosophers so that they consistently make recommendations within its framework, then I think it would go some way toward improving the status of our profession by providing a promising account of morality, the why and the what of it.

PART II

Critiques of the Argument

CHAPTER 2

RATIONALITY AND MORALITY IN STERBA

Charles W. Mills

In "From Rationality to Equality," James Sterba—summarizing a body of work that now extends over many years—contends both that morality is "rationally required" of us and that morality demands a materially egalitarian social-democratic state. It need hardly be emphasized that these are both hugely controversial claims, the debate over which has exercised numerous ethicists and political theorists for generations. As someone on the political left myself, I am completely sympathetic to Sterba's second conclusion, if not entirely convinced by the route he takes to get there. But that is not going to be my focus in this essay. Instead, I will address his first argument. My claim will be that his argument fails. Morality cannot be derived from rationality, at least (more cautiously) not in this way.

STERBA'S METHOD

The attempt to derive morality from rationality is an ancient quest in the Western ethical tradition. Sterba cites Kant as his key reference point, but it goes back (in a different form, obviously) at least all the way to Plato. The general failure of these attempts has led most ethicists to conclude that the goal is unachievable. But Sterba is commendably undeterred. He offers what he sees as a new take on this question, one that does not fall prey to standard objections. Moreover, Sterba is not watering down the thesis to the claim that morality is merely rationally permissible, proof of which would be a less-demanding feat. Rather, he is putting forward the thesis in its strong and full-blooded form: the aim is to show "that morality is rationally required, thus excluding egoism and immorality as rationally permissible." He thinks the mistake other theorists have made is to appeal to consistency alone, whereas he is also going to appeal to "the principle of non-question-beggingness."

How does Sterba set about his task? His strategy is to distinguish between self-interested and altruistic/other-interested reasons, and then to argue that "morality" is a rationally required, "nonarbitrary" compromise between exclusivist motivation by either. For the purposes of the exercise, he is assuming that "an objective ranking" of these reasons for the person is possible and knowable, so that any epistemological problems of interpersonal comparisons are bracketed. An egoist will be someone who acts on the principle "Each person ought to do what best serves his or her overall self-interest." An altruist will be someone who acts on the principle "Each person ought to do what best serves the overall interest of others." In some cases, self-interested and altruistic motivation may both point in the same direction, so obviously here there is no problem about what to do. It is when there is conflict that the necessity for choice poses itself. Automatically giving priority to only one class of reasons, as both the egoist and altruist do, would beg the question. Instead, what is "rationally required" is a compromise: "In this compromise, sometimes self-interested reasons have priority over conflicting altruistic reasons, and sometimes altruistic reasons have priority over conflicting self-interested reasons." This nonarbitrary compromise is what morality is. And since such a compromise is rationally mandated, it means that morality has been derived from rationality.

MORALITY AND
NONARBITRARY COMPROMISE

Now, there are different possible ways to critique Sterba's argument. One would be to deny that his "nonarbitrary compromise" is in fact rationally mandated. But another way, which is the path I am going to take, would be to deny that his "nonarbitrary compromise," even if it is rationally mandated, corresponds to what we would normally call "morality." In other words, my claim is that Sterba's argument works only through a crucial weakening of what "morality" turns out to be.

Let me begin by rehearsing some familiar points. In the classic moral theories, it has always been taken for granted that one's own interests have a legitimate, demarcated role. This is most clearly the case—indeed, for later critics problematically, too saliently, the case—for some of the virtue theories, or character ethics, of the ancient world. Here, in what we would now categorize as agent-centered theories, the goal is to develop a certain kind of character, not primarily as an instrument to the performance of good deeds but as an end in itself. And classically, in the *Republic,* Plato sets out to refute the claims of Thrasymachus (with Glaucon and Adeimantus playing supporting devil's advocate roles) by showing that justice in the individual is good both in itself and for its consequences, that the just man experiences the most happiness and the most pleasure, in short, that being just pays. So one's own interests are in fact seen as crucial to the conception of justice itself, albeit with a partial moralization of what "interests" are. Thrasymachus is not refuted by a demonstration that we should be just even if it doesn't pay, but rather by a demonstration that because of psychological facts of which he is unaware, justice does pay, and pays better, than injustice. In a famous critique, H. A. Prichard points out "the identity of principle underlying the position of both [Plato and Thrasymachus]": "what in the end most strikes us is that at no stage in the *Republic* does Plato take the line . . . that the very presupposition of the Sophists' arguments is false. . . . He therefore, equally with the Sophists, is implying that it is impossible for any action to be really just, i.e., a duty, unless it is for the advantage of the agent."[1] So for at least one classic version of an agent-centered ethic, morality and self-interest do not really collide at all.

But in the act-centered theories of the modern period, the individual's interests are also included. If one distinguishes goal-based (consequentialist), rights-based, and duty-based theories, then in utilitarian consequentialism, each one is to count for one in the felicific calculus, where those ones include oneself; in natural rights theory, we too are assigned a schedule of rights that must not be encroached upon by others; and Kantian deontology includes not merely others' duties to respect us as equal persons, but our own duties to ourselves (for example, to cultivate our talents). So no plausible moral theory denies that the individual has legitimate self-regarding reasons to act, which morality must take into account.

In this respect Sterba is correct that morality reflects a compromise between altruism and egoism, at least if we take the terms in their "pure" senses. (I will soon raise questions as to whether we are really entitled to do this.) But the question is where this compromise is located. Sterba claims that rationality demands that we be moral, and obviously for his intervention in this classic debate to be a serious contender, it must presuppose the familiar sense of "moral." But I think that the content of "morality" has been crucially diluted, so that even if rationality does require us to be "moral" in Sterba's sense, it is not in a robust enough sense to give Sterba (and an anxiously awaiting world) what he wants.

To demonstrate this, let me introduce some terminology, appropriating the vocabulary conventionally used for different ways of balancing goods/values against one another. It is standard to distinguish a lexical (sometimes lexicographical) or serial ordering from a scalar ordering. A lexical/serial ordering (the logic of the term deriving from the way dictionary entries are arranged) has been made famous by John Rawls's use of it in *A Theory of Justice*.[2] Securing the basic liberties, at least under ideal circumstances, always trumps other values, so that the slightest decrease in liberty outweighs the greatest increase in other values. So trade-offs are precluded. The loss of one of Rawls's basic liberties cannot, in this framework, be exchanged for a guaranteed income of $10 million a year.

A scalar ordering, on the other hand, assigns different weights to different goods and values, so that trade-offs are possible. Even if we value V1 four times more than V2, so that given equal increments of both we would choose V1, a sufficiently large increase in V2 can change this outcome. So while one increment of ΔV2 will not outweigh one increment of ΔV1, five increments of ΔV2 will outweigh one increment of ΔV1.

Adapting this vocabulary, then, let us distinguish a "lexical" from a "scalar" egoist. But first, what is an egoist? Sterba's egoist, as we saw above, acts on the principle of doing "what best serves his or her overall self-interest." So an egoist is someone who systematically, as a point of principle, puts his interests before the interests of others. To make the two familiar points: This policy will be constrained by the desire not to be found out, and thus shunned by others; and this policy does not preclude taking an instrumental interest in the interests of others, since acting to benefit others may often be deemed to promote one's own long-term benefit.

Now, a lexical egoist as I am using the term always puts his own interests first, no matter how slight the increment to him, no matter how great the loss to others. So he assigns different finite weights to different components of his interests, but always assigns zero to the interests of others (at least intrinsically; as noted, their interests may under certain circumstances have instrumental value to him—what they will not have is intrinsic value). My lexical egoist is Sterba's pure egoist, someone for whom "the interests of others do not count for herself, except instrumentally."

Compare this familiar figure with the less familiar figure of the scalar, or impure, egoist. A scalar egoist also systematically puts her interests before the interests of others, but this is done according to a different, more moderate formula. There is a sense in which a consequentialist framework lends itself best to this project since by its nature, the theory is committed to calculations of various kinds. So consider what we could call, somewhat awkwardly, a scalar consequentialist egoist, an SCE (unfortunately, no more euphonious acronym leaps to mind, or at least to my mind; readers are invited to submit alternatives). An SCE will consistently assign a greater value, a greater weight, to her own interests, her own happiness, and her own welfare, in doing utility calculations. So each one will not count for one; the one that is, she will count for much more than one. But at the same time, it is not that others count for zero, as with the pure (or, in my framework, the lexical) egoist. Others' interests are taken into account; it is just that their interests are not given equal weight. We could think of this in terms of a coefficient, or operator, that differentiates the SCE from everybody else, and indicates how much more valuable the SCE is to herself than other people are. For the SCE, the operator is 1; for other people, it is some fractional figure, 0.8 or 0.5 or 0.2, depending on how egoistic the SCE is.

Refer now to Figure 2.1.[3] This represents a spectrum of possibilities, with pure/lexical egoism at the far right and pure/lexical altruism at the far left. At these ends, one has respectively zero (noninstrumental) concern for the interests of others and zero (noninstrumental) concern for one's own interests. Moving along the spectrum from right to left there is increasing concern for the interests of others and decreasing concern for one's own interests; we are moving through different scalar weightings.

FIGURE 2.1

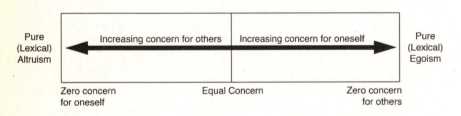

I hope the problem I have with Sterba's argument is now beginning to emerge. Apart from the two termini of the spectrum, all the positions along it are "impure" scalar positions, and as such all represent a compromise between "pure"/lexical egoism and "pure"/lexical altruism. Yet I think we would find it very strange to claim that every nonterminal position on this spectrum is a "morality." If we define "egoism" as pure/lexical egoism (the right-hand terminus), and exclude both it and pure/lexical altruism (the left-hand terminus) from morality, then everything in between counts as a morality. For everything in between assigns some non-zero weight both to self-interest and the interests of others. So as long as one does not actually give zero weight to the interests of others, then one is being moral. But this is obviously a very low benchmark indeed for the ethical. It would include extreme SCEs who are located just to the left of the right-hand terminus (by comparison with whom the moderate SCEs earlier discussed now emerge as paragons of morality), assigning the interests of others a co-efficient of 0.01, just one percent. So somebody who values her fellow humans' interests at one percent of her own, thus requiring the pain of one hundred of us lesser beings to equal the moral significance of her own pain, would count as a "moral" person!

Clearly, this is not how we would normally think of morality. For us, the ideally moral is not (as in Figure 2.2) anything in between the termini of the spectrum, but rather (as in Figure 2.3) a more restricted band, starting at the center and extending leftward. The middle point represents equal concern, equal weighting, for the interests of oneself and others, and as such represents what is the classic viewpoint of Western universalism, at least in its idealized (nonsexist, nonracist) form: each one's welfare to count equally; each individual to have the same natural rights; each person to be equally respected. Positions to the left of this represent increasing degrees of self-sacrifice, of assigning greater weight to the interests of others. The terminal point is sometimes represented as sainthood—the completely selfless person who has zero concern for himself, except in the instrumental sense of doing the minimum necessary to keep from starvation (a quick, tasteless meal before rushing back out to do more good deeds). But I think we would actually regard such behavior as pathological, deranged, rather than admirable. So perhaps at some point before this, we would cease to apply the judgment of "moral" and start to apply a different vocabulary. Correspondingly, I contend, we would apply the term "egoistic," and thus immoral, to a range of positions, not restricting ourselves to just the right-hand terminus ("lexical egoism") but to the band extending leftward from that terminus, even if the boundary is fuzzy and probably stops before the exact midpoint. In other words, we make allowances for our fellow humans and hope that they will likewise make allowances for us.

FIGURE 2.2

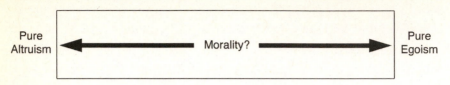

FIGURE 2.3

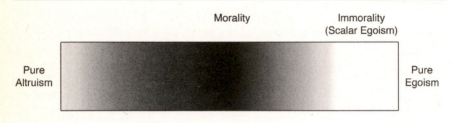

Now, before I turn to Sterba's possible replies, let me make some quick points about other objections.

First, it might be objected that operationalizing such a policy (the egoistic scalar coefficient) would not be easy. But this seems to me to be a pragmatic rather than a principled objection. And, in any case, to what extent are the difficulties any greater than those attending standard utilitarian calculations, which are notoriously problematic for a number of reasons (interpersonal comparisons, ordinal versus cardinal rankings, and so on)? So, to the extent that this objection goes through, it would tell against utilitarianism also. In any case, Sterba himself stipulates, for the purposes of his argument, that we should bracket such epistemological and operational concerns. He assumes "for the sake of argument—a relatively precise ranking of one's self-interested reasons from an egoistic perspective and a relatively precise ranking of one's altruistic reasons from an altruistic perspective, and the interpersonal comparability of these two rankings." The presumption, therefore, is that we already have such a ranking. My modification just requires that we now apply an egoistic operator to it, which adjusts the weights of the pertinent reasons appropriately, reducing the valence of others' interests by the particular fraction that indicates the SCE's degree of egoism.

Moreover, it needs to be emphasized that in certain respects this is not at all a hypothetical construct. Rather, in its structure (if not the population covered) it reflects the attitude that most people have historically had toward animals, and that most whites and men in the past few hundred years have had toward nonwhites and women. Most people think of animals neither as persons with rights nor as inanimate objects completely outside of the moral community, but as lesser beings with some claims on us. Most people are meat eaters and animal exploiters without being anti-animal sadists. Thus, we find the gratuitous torture of animals wrong (while not mentally dwelling on the practices of industrial agriculture), but in any serious conflict of interests, their welfare will in general go by the board. Similarly, there is, of course, ample precedent in the treatment of nonwhites and women as lesser beings, with fewer or diminished rights. So there is nothing at all psychologically impossible, or intrinsically structurally problematic, about this picture. On the contrary, it corresponds in its structure to the actual moral code by which many people have operated. All we need to do, then, is to imagine an individual who applies these tenets in a "principled" nondiscriminatory/nonsexist/nonracist way to humanity at large—that is, to everybody but himself.

Could Sterba reply, however, that this is not an egoism, since egoism is (definitionally) pure/lexical egoism, and insofar as scalar egoism does require us to take others' interests into account in a noninstrumental way, it is a contradiction in terms? Am I redefining terms in a tendentious way to advance my argument? Well, I earlier defined an egoist as somebody who systematically puts his interests before the interests of others. And the "before" here, of course, is not temporal but adjudicative. As such, it can be understood in more than one way. The scalar egoist is not putting her interests before others' in the sense of completely ignoring the interests of others. But she is putting her interests before others' in the sense of assigning them greater weight. And as we have seen, this can be vastly greater weight while still falling short of lexical egoism.

But finally, it doesn't really matter, for the simple reason that whether we make the semantic decision to call it "egoism" or not, it is clearly a position that is immoral, which is all I need to show the problematic nature of Sterba's argument. As he writes: "Generalizing, then, we can say that all immoralities involve an inappropriate (question-begging) favoring of the interests of self . . . over the interests of others, and in this way run afoul of the defense of morality I have just sketched." Under whatever designation, scalar egoism is obviously immoral.

Moreover, an interesting case can be made for the egoist's preferring scalar egoism to lexical egoism on various grounds, rational egoistic ones as well as others. It is a familiar point that, as earlier emphasized, the egoist needs to conceal his egoism from others so as to avoid ostracism, and also that even lexical egoism does not rule out acting in the interests of others, since they may be instrumentally of use to us. The additional point I am making here is that scalar egoism is likely to do a better job of self-concealment. Lexical egoism, even when cautiously operationalized, may simply be too dangerous because of the risk of being found out. Scalar egoism is less likely to be detectable, since the "shortfall" in the weights assigned to the interests of others (lesser weights, but non-zero) will, if noticed, be more likely to be attributed to human error, an occasional lapse into human selfishness, human weakness of the will, and so on, rather than to a systematic policy on the part of the agent.

Finally, it could well be that lexical egoism is not even psychologically possible except for sociopaths. Ironically, then, psychological egoism—that we all do put our interests first in decision making—far from being "obviously" true as some have thought (in part through failing to differentiate desires that are my own from desires aimed at serving my own interests), may actually be obviously false. Surely it is very unlikely for most of us, growing up and interacting with other human beings, not to spontaneously develop at least some feelings of empathy and self-identification with them. After all, the egoist does not spring from the earth as a fully formed adult, but as someone born, raised, and nurtured in a family and a larger community. Many ethicists have contended that the articulation of our moral ideals needs to pay attention to the facts of human psychology, and it could be that—in an ironic way—this principle could be applied to egoism also, in that lexical egoism as a prudential ideal is just not a psychologically viable candidate. "Ought" implies "can," though in a somewhat nonstandard sense of the phrase!

It seems to me that this modification does carve out a theoretical space for a policy recognizable as egoism. But since this space falls into the area Sterba has characterized as the realm of morality, we then see that many "compromises," though not all, will conform to what we think of as egoism, or at least immorality, rather than morality. Therefore, even if Sterba has shown us that rationality requires us to eschew the two termini of the spectrum, he has not shown us that what rationality requires is morality in the conventional sense that we would recognize. Insofar as the interests of others are taken into account, it is a "morality." Insofar as their interests are systematically assigned lesser weight, it is not.

POSSIBLE COUNTERARGUMENTS

Let me turn now to the reconstruction of some possible counterarguments by Sterba.

(i) Sterba emphasizes that the compromise in question must be a "nonarbitrary compromise." Couldn't he reply, right off the bat, that the compromise, or range of compromises, I have indicated above is "arbitrary" and is thus ruled out by his definition? Well, what do we normally mean by "arbitrary"? Isn't it something like: unmotivated, capricious, not rationally justified, inconsistent? I would deny that the compromise/range of compromises endorsed by the SCE is any of these things. It is motivated by the desire to privilege the SCE's interests at the expense of the interests of others—a motivation with a long history, if not an approved one, in ethics, political theory, economics, game theory, and so forth. As such, it is not at all random or capricious, but consciously and deliberately skewed toward the interests of the egoist, away from the midpoint of the spectrum. And this is "rational" in the sense of privileging and advancing our self-interest, as well as "rational" in the sense of better preserving the illusion that we are following the same rules as everybody else. Moreover, it will be internally consistent ("rational" in the minimal sense of noncontradictory) as long as the egoist is careful to adhere to the principle of systemic discounting, or undercounting, of the interests of others. So internal relations of transitivity and so forth will be preserved under this transformation of the weighting of interests by the scalar coefficient.

(ii) But couldn't Sterba argue that the size of the coefficient cannot be justified in a nonarbitrary way? In terms of size, for example, why should it be, say, 0.5 as against 0.3, or 0.7219, or whatever? Well, perhaps the SCE has a well-developed idiosyncratic ontology that explains this, in terms of her beliefs about her relative worth vis-à-vis the rest of the population. Do I myself have to try to give a plausible reconstruction of what such an ontology would be like? I don't believe that I do. Or perhaps the SCE has no elaborate rationale for a precise number but just fixes on some fraction for convenience in calculation. Say, 0.5, or 0.1, since it's easy to remember. The crucial parameters of choice for her are just that it should be significantly less than one, in keeping with the fact that other people really don't matter that much to her. She is emphatic about their lesser weight in her scheme of things. Does the fact that she can't quantify in a principled way how much lesser they are refute the reality of her conviction? Consider, then, how few things in this area are precisely quantifiable in the first place.

(iii) But can't Sterba licitly challenge the conviction itself? Never mind the question of mensuration—how can the conviction that there should be a nonequal weighting of others' interests be justified to begin with? But Sterba began by emphasizing the importance of not begging the question in favor of either the altruist or the egoist. This response would seem to me to come perilously close to begging the question in favor of (conventional) morality, for is it not just another way of asking egoism to defend itself?

(iv) However, it might seem that Sterba has an obvious fallback that I have not considered. Remember that he bracketed for the sake of argument standard epistemological difficulties in knowing others' interests well enough to provide an "objective ranking" of self-interested and altruistic reasons. Assume that he is correct, as he clearly is, to deny that epistemological problems in determining the interests of others are what the egoist uses as his justification, so the egoist must accept this "objective ranking" also. Couldn't he then say that the fact of this ranking itself precludes the kind of relative weighting I have proposed, since morality as a nonarbitrary compromise requires an ordering in which "high-ranking self-interested reasons have priority over conflicting low-ranking altruistic reasons, other things being equal, . . . [and] high-ranking altruistic reasons have priority over conflicting low-ranking self-interested reasons, other things being equal"?

The problem here, I would claim, is that once we take into account the distinction for the SCE between the internal ordering of the respective lists of reasons (self-interested, SR; altruistic, AR) and the external placement of these lists vis-à-vis one another, we will see that the same problem of differential weighting reappears and can be blocked only at the cost, once again, of begging the question against egoism (see Figure 2.4). The SCE will not be assigning equal significance to the items on the altruistic list but will be transforming them all by the scalar egoist operator/coefficient. Although their internal ordering (AR1, AR2, AR3 . . .) will be preserved under this transformation (that is, the sequence from more to less serious reasons and from high-ranking to low-ranking reasons will stay the same), their external relation to the self-interested list will shift. Items high up on the altruistic list will be placed above items low down on the altruistic list for both a normal moral agent and for the egoist (AR1 > AR4). But the lateral relation of the lists themselves will be different, because of the lesser significance the egoist assigns to such items (altruistic reasons) in general. So a high-priority altruistic reason (AR1) that would for a normal moral agent easily trump a particular self-interested reason (say, AR1 > SR2) will not necessarily do so for the SCE. What matters is not merely the rank ordering (the ordinal) but the particular value attached to each item (the cardinal).

Let me illustrate with a concrete example: different kinds of bad things happening to a human being's leg. Say the four possibilities are, in order of increasing seriousness: having someone step lightly on your foot; having

FIGURE 2.4

Moral agent's reasons				Egoist's reasons			
Self-interested	Altruistic			Self-interested	Altruistic		
SR1	AR1			SR1			
SR2	AR2			SR2		Downward	
SR3	AR3			SR3		displacement	
SR4	AR4			SR4			
					AR1		
					AR2		
					AR3		
					AR4		

somebody kick you forcibly in the shin; having your leg broken (but eventually healing); having your leg amputated. So for both kinds of reasons, whether this is happening to you or to somebody else (the self-interested list or the altruistic list), the ordering will be the same, in that the reasons to avoid amputation will be the highest ranking. But here's the problem. Sterba's pure egoist, my lexical egoist, who sets others' interests at naught, will not be willing to endure even a light step on his foot by a passerby if it would save someone else from leg amputation. The slightest egoistic reason for him will outweigh the largest altruistic reason. Because Sterba thinks it is question-begging not to admit such trumping factors, the pure/lexical egoist is, by Sterba's criterion, thereby ruled out. But what about the impure scalar egoist? For the SCE, other people's interests do have a non-zero weight. So it will be possible for there to be circumstances in which high-ranking altruistic reasons trump low-ranking self-interested reasons, and the SCE will choose so as to benefit others. But because it is not the same weight that a normal moral person would assign, this threshold will be to a greater or lesser degree quite distant from the point, or range of points, we would designate as deserving the judgment "moral." The reason is that though the ranking of altruistic reasons is the same for the SCE as for the normal person, they will all be shifted downward in significance. They undergo a scalar transformation, a fractional (<1) weighting that pulls them down the scale of importance.

Thus, what the scalar egoist sees as very serious in his own case (leg amputation), he sees as less serious (though not of zero seriousness) when it happens to somebody else. Whereas, for example, one kind of scalar egoist would be willing, if grumpily, to allow his foot to be trod on to save somebody else from having his leg amputated, he would not, let us say, be willing to be kicked in the shin to accomplish the same thing. He draws the line somewhere, as we all do, but he draws it in a much higher place than we do because of the diminished significance he attaches to others' well-being. And if he's the extreme scalar egoist, the 0.01 guy, he will, of course, draw it higher still, so that even the threat of several people having their legs amputated will not move him to submit to being kicked in the shin.

How can Sterba block this scenario? As before, note that the scalar egoist does allow some high-ranking reasons in the altruistic list to outweigh some low-ranking reasons in the self-interested list, so he cannot be accused of begging the question by always choosing self-interested reasons. But because of the scaling/weighting factor, the point at which this happens is not located where morality would demand it. The problem we saw earlier reappears here. What about arguing that the "objective ranking" he has stipulated rules out such a displacement? My claim would be that he cannot do this without presupposing the truth of conventional morality. The list is objectively ranked in terms of the ordering of reasons. But to demand that the reasons on the altruistic list have the same weight for the egoist as the reasons on the self-interested list is to smuggle in conventional, anti-egoistic morality under the guise of a neutral stipulation. An "objective" ranking that presupposes the equal valorization for the egoist of the egoist's interests and other people's interests is an anti-egoistic stipulation that begs the question from the start. To insist that the high-ranking altruistic reasons should be on the same plane of significance for the egoist as the high-ranking egoistic reasons is to incorporate conventional morality into the framework in terms of the lateral placement of the lists. For a scalar egoist, when comparing apples and apples, the terms in the altruistic column are all going to be displaced downward (though maintaining the same internal relation to one another) with respect to the terms in the egoistic column. It will just matter less morally to the egoist when bad thing X happens to someone else as against bad thing X's happening to her.

(v) Finally, consider this fallback option. Sterba could reason as follows. The problem with the nonhuman animal comparison is that rationality, autonomy, and so forth do constitute an independent rationale for not treating animals as moral equals, even if the work of animal rights advocates means that these considerations no longer carry the automatic conviction that they once did for us. But in the case of our fellow humans, there is no such rationale to be found for egoism, except, simply, that they are not we. Similarly, sexism and racism do have as their foundation particular false empirical claims about female and nonwhite (usually) inferiority. So as (reprehensible) normative theories, they do rest on a factual foundation, and as such should be abandoned by the rational cognizer if that foundation is shown to be nonexistent. But the egoist is not normally represented as saying that other humans are in fact inferior in these ways. Can't you then convict the egoist for inconsistency in conceding that others are equally human and that others' interests have some intrinsic weight, yet not going all the way to conventional morality? "If you've conceded this, then there is no principled stopping point. You have to go all the rest of the way with us, and it would be irrational not to do so!" But why can't the scalar egoist reply (anonymously, of course, behind one of those TV optical blurs): "No, I don't have to go all the rest of the way with you. I do far better staying here, and since looking out for number one is my primary concern, it would be irrational for me to follow you all the way to conventional morality. I am happy to remain right here, thank you very much, and my rational justification for not giving others' interests equal weight is quite simply that other people do not matter as much to me as I do to myself."

How do you answer that? In those terms—the egoist's terms (rationality)—I don't believe that you can.[4]

CHAPTER 3

REASONS TO BE MORAL

Candace A. Vogler

The question is: Why be moral? James Sterba has devoted considerable attention to this question and now gives a broadly Kantian response: Morality is grounded in rationality, where rationality rests in a refusal to beg the question when supplying justifications for action or policy. The account rests in a division of reasons for acting into self-interested, egoistic reasons and other-directed, altruistic reasons. Morality consists in a compromise between egoistic and altruistic reasons for action, such that strong self-interested reasons trump weak altruistic reasons, strong altruistic reasons trump weak egoistic reasons, and the relative strengths of reasons are not strictly a matter of how important a consideration happens to be for some agent, but rather how important the consideration is objectively. For example, my reasons to get food trump my reasons to spend a day at the spa, and, more to the point, my reasons to support your efforts to get food outweigh my reasons to purchase a timeshare in Bermuda. Now, whether an argument begs the question depends upon what question is being asked. Here, the "Why be moral?" question is equivalent to "Why act in accordance with a compromise between egoistic and altruistic reasons for acting?" Sterba rightly argues that answering this question by strict appeal to egoistic considerations begs the question against altruism, and vice versa. But the account relies, first, upon a division of practical considerations into the altruistic and the egoistic, and second, upon an understanding of morality as working a compromise between the competing claims of egoism and altruism on our practical orientations. I will complain about both moves and will try to do so in a way that does justice to the powerful intuitions in support of Sterba's picture of the two kinds of practical reasons.

WHAT ARE MORAL REASONS LIKE?

Suppose that I am at work on a new project. I describe it to you, "We should talk about it," you say, and I agree.

"When?" I ask.

We set a date for coffee and conversation. I send you some notes. You drop me a line. The day arrives. You sit down with my notes in the morning. "This is hopeless," you think. "What on earth am I going to say to her?"

You combat dread by attempting to find the strongest possible version of the sort of case I seem to want to make, so that your critical remarks will be organized in light of your highest hopes for a project of the kind I have sketched. But, in light of the notes, it is unlikely that I, in particular, will have the interest or the capacity to develop the kind of line that you can see as one possible way to grope toward the light from this sea of darkness. You fret, wishing that you hadn't offered conversation. You spend a moment lamenting the state of the discipline. You hope that I will break our date, but anyone dim enough to have sent you those notes is probably dim enough to show up to discuss them.

Meanwhile, across town, I am kicking myself for having sent you my notes. I know myself well enough to know that this is a good moment to receive heartfelt encouragement for my project, and a bad moment to be hit with criticism. You are not my mother. We are not close friends. I know your work well enough to know that you are unlikely to warm to my notes. It is hard to know how serious your criticisms will be. I fret, wishing that you hadn't suggested conversation, wishing that I hadn't sent you my notes, hoping that you will break our date.

At the appointed hour, we each arrive at the designated meeting place and have a long discussion of my project, based on the notes that I sent you. Each of us does this because we have agreed to meet.

I have no idea how many promises to meet and discuss work are kept by people who are quietly hoping that the other parties will fail to show up. A great deal of intellectual activity among academics is coordinated through agreements to discuss work-in-progress, and one excellent feature of coordinating discussion through giving and receiving promises to meet is that it does not much matter whether the parties would rather do something else when the day arrives.

Now, it is true that at the time that you promise to do something for me, we operate on the assumption that what you promise to do is something that we take to be in my interest. If we agree to meet and discuss a student's work, then the assumption has to be that what we undertake is in the student's interest. Perhaps I am not competent to advise my student on Aristotle's metaphysics and want to know whether what she has written is plausible, so I ask for your expert opinion. Perhaps we are both members of her dissertation committee, she has gotten stuck, and we want to figure out what to do. The assumption that what we promise is in the interest of the one on whose behalf the undertaking is given is part of what distinguishes promises from threats. So it's safe to assume that when you offered to discuss my project, both of us thought that I'd benefit from your help. I take it that each of us showing up for our date is a straightforward case of each of us acting from and for moral reasons. The moral reason in question looks like this: *pacta sund servanta;* promises are to be kept.

Sterba thinks that moral reasons may coincide with egoistic reasons, and may coincide with altruistic reasons, but often represent a reasonable compromise between self-interest and concern for others. It may look as though it is easy to see the egoism and the altruism at work in the example I've given. Your offer to look at my work was altruistic. My acceptance was egoistic. Where's the mystery?

But the question about being moral isn't a question about what might move me to accept an undertaking. Neither is it a question about what might move you to make one. In this example, the question about being moral is a question about why we do our word, given that each of us has undertaken to meet.

Are my reasons for keeping our appointment egoistic? Am I showing up because doing so is in my interest?

Not in any obvious sense. I hold out hope that you'll break our date all the way to our meeting place. And, notice, in this situation, it is more than likely that you are hoping that I will stand you up as well. It isn't at all clear, then, that egoistic reasons are moving either of us toward our meeting.

Frankly, even given a situation in which both of us are happy to keep the date, unless neither of us has enough imagination to think of anything that might serve her interests better than discussing my project, suggesting that considerations of self-interest get us to keep our date is implausible. It is implausible because, as Elizabeth Anscombe once put it, considering people whose purposes could be served by breaking promises, "one constantly has such purposes."[1]

I take it, then, that thought about self-interest is not what has each of us breaking off doing something interesting for the sake of the dreaded engagement.

Are our reasons altruistic, then? Am I concerned about the fact that you may have spent time thinking about my notes, that you are going out of your way to meet me, or that you might be disappointed if we don't have this chance to discuss my work?

Notice that any such thoughts that I might entertain presuppose that you have fidelity in you—that is, that you will do your word, barring a circumstance in which a more pressing obligation or some misfortune prevents you from being able to come. And, of course, there's no reason to be concerned about your work on my notes, your trip to the meeting place, or your disappointment unless I think that you will expect me to show up, prepared to have a conversation about my project. So my concern for you presupposes both that you will do your word, and also that you expect that I will do my word. If there is altruism here, it comes in after duty has already set the stage and informed the expectations of both parties.

As near as I can tell, then, both altruistic reasons and egoistic reasons that might move us to do our word come trailing after the department of morality that enjoins fidelity. I can see no way to analyze reasons of this kind as involving a compromise between altruism and egoism. The moral reasons already have to be in place, practicable, and active—in our understanding of our circumstances and in our deliberation about what to do—in order for altruistic concerns about you, or egoistic concern about me, to get a grip.

If I keep our date for your sake, my thought about what to do for you presupposes that you will keep your promise to me. If you keep our date for my sake, your thought about what to do for me presupposes that I will keep my promise to you. And if either of us acts from fear of disgrace, resentment, humiliation, or some such, or in hope of admiration, praise, building a good reputation, or some such, then our calculations about costs and benefits likewise make sense only in light of the assumption that each of us will do her word. Otherwise, neither of us can expect to gain or to lose, either by showing up or by failing to do so.

WHAT ARE MORAL REASONS FOR ACTING LIKE?

When they are reasons traditionally associated with justice—like considerations of fidelity—they are like the reasons for acting at issue between us when you have agreed to comment on my work. Far from being reasons that permit a clean and illuminating factoring into self-interested concern on the one side, concern for others on the other, they are reasons that have to be in place to inform any calculation of self-interest or concern over the welfare of others.

WHY THIS MATTERS

Why should that make any difference in our thoughts about how to move from rationality to equality?

Concern over equality surely belongs to concern over justice. But just because the concern belongs to justice does not mean that it belongs to concern over acting from and for the sake of considerations of justice. I can have all kinds of concern over justice that is not, in any interesting sense, practical. Justice can be one of my topics. I can think: "The government of Chile was right to impose strict building codes after a devastating earthquake some years back—they acted in the interest of their citizens on that point, at least." I can think, "It's wrong that debate over important policy measures should be held hostage by the neurotic terrors of a handful of vocal citizens." I can have all sorts of views about what justice requires in this or that situation. I might even be right about it, some of the time, at least. But unless I am in a position to do something in the service of my fine thoughts—something other than produce eloquent commentary on the state of the world in my blog, or over dinner, or on television—my thoughts about justice will be idle.

From this perspective, the fact that morality has to inform calculations of interest in order for us accurately to factor moral reasons into self-regarding and other-regarding components won't much matter. I am concerned with justice in the abstract, not with considerations of justice as these might inform concrete reasons for acting. My "Why be moral?" question is not the question that animated late-twentieth-century Anglophone philosophical concern. What the philosophers were after was an answer to a question about reasons for acting and motivation, not a general account of how things ought to be of the sort that might be produced over drinks in one's free time.

Sterba is not interested in idle chatter about how things ought to be. Sterba is interested in the nature of practical concern with human good—concern about actions, about practical deliberation, about reasons for acting, about motivation, and so on. He is, I think, dead right that we will get nowhere on those topics without supposing that people are capable of acting for the sake of private advantage and capable of doing things on behalf of others. However, I also think that he underestimates the difficulty of getting from these two capacities to a justification of that department of morality concerned with justice.

CONSIDERATION OF JUSTICE

The traditional stock of considerations of justice comes into play when different people going about their own business find themselves at cross-purposes. Justice inhibits our tendency to run roughshod over each other in such circumstances. To their credit, parties to just interaction do not wrong each other. That is, justice places constraints upon interpersonal interactions—action-guiding constraints recognized as such by each and every party to mutual, reciprocal just congress.[2] It is because they are of one mind about such things that it is to their credit when they act well. It belongs to modern moral philosophy to hold that two strangers meeting on a road who are as different as you please might show due restraint with respect to each other. That is, the possibility of just interaction exceeds the boundaries of customs and culture, as well as the limits of the parties' private concerns. This sketch of justice sets up at least these four requirements for philosophical work on the question about why one should act from and for the sake of justice:

1. There is the need to account for the identical practical precepts in the hearts and minds of the strangers.
2. There is the need to ensure that the strangers act from and for the sake of those very practical considerations.
3. There is the need to account for the normative authority of the moral precepts they share.
4. There is the need to say how and why a party to the exchange sides with justice, having crossed paths with a stranger who stands prepared to act well.

Providing an account of justice in these terms is not easy. I take it that we tend to assume that coming up with an account that meets the first three requirements will take us a long way toward meeting the fourth.

Sterba sides with Kant and with neo-Kantians on some of these matters. Like Kant, and like neo-Kantians, Sterba argues that rationality is on the side of justice. The normative authority of considerations of justice is no more or less mysterious than the normative authority of reason. That is how Sterba meets the third requirement. Presumably, he will rely upon this account of normative authority to explain why people side with justice, given that they see the sense in it.

Leave the second requirement to the side for a moment. In a sense, even Kant thought that we were in no position to meet the second requirement, since he argues that none of us can ever be sure, in her own case or anyone else's, that she has acted strictly from and for the sake of duty.

The real rub for foundational accounts of morality comes in meeting the first requirement.

To say why, I think it's useful to have a look at Anscombe's "Modern Moral Philosophy." She wrote:

> Now I am not able to do the philosophy involved—and I think that no one in the present situation of English philosophy can do the philosophy involved—but it is clear that a good man is a just man; and a just man is a man who habitually refuses to commit or participate in any unjust actions for fear of any consequences, or to obtain any advantage for himself or anyone else. Perhaps no one will disagree. But, it will be said, what is unjust is sometimes determined by expected consequences; and certainly that is true. But there are cases where it is not: now if someone says, "I agree, but all this wants a lot of explaining," then he is right, and, what is more, the situation at present is that we can't do the explaining: we lack the philosophic equipment.[3]

The expression of bafflement is uncharacteristic but warranted in light of what she thinks is needed in modern moral philosophy. She is asking how the capacity to do right by each other could belong to the mature human with her wits about her as such. For a Kantian, the question will be how reason alone could equip us for just interaction. Explaining the generality of the individual capacity for justice poses a problem because one cannot build up to just interaction, person by person.

THE PROBLEM

Although individual justice is a character trait, different people—parties to mutual, reciprocal just interaction—must, in acting from and for justice, act from the same source.[4] This is clearest in the case of conduct informed by full-blown social practices, such as those having to do with contract and promising. As John Rawls taught us,[5] a group of eighteen people who knew nothing of baseball could wander onto a baseball field. Their individual fascinations might lead four to arrange themselves around the diamond, one to kneel behind home plate, three to wander into the outfield, one to stand on the pitcher's mound and start tossing a baseball to the kneeling man, and the other nine to take turns attempting to spoil the game of catch by knocking the ball away with a baseball bat. It is not possible for these creatures to play baseball. In order to play baseball, each man needs to have baseball in him.[6] Even if each man has idiosyncratic ludic tendencies that lead him to formulate, endorse, and abide by a set of rules governing his movements that (as it happens) corresponds to the rules of baseball, such that each understands himself to be playing a position in the game that he has given to himself, it will be the merest accident that the aggregated individual actions look to add up to a game of baseball. We have eighteen individual amusements taking place simultaneously on the same field, not a game of baseball. And this will be so even if some players leave and others wander onto the field, each of whom sees a splendid opportunity to pretend to play the very game that he has given to himself (while those others go about doing whatever it is that they are doing, conveniently providing a perfect backdrop against which to live out the private fantasy).

Anscombe's essay on promising takes up a wider range of such cases.[7] There are two problems about "cases of this type," she explains. The first is to explain the content of the thought "I am playing baseball," or "I am making a promise," or "I have entered into a contract," or "This is my gift to you." This problem is solved for Rawls (in part) by introducing consideration of a social practice, for Anscombe by introducing and explaining some features of Wittgensteinian language-games.[8] The language-game, like the social practice, deposits the relevant identical source in the many participants (the fact that social contract theory tends to bypass this requirement is, for Anscombe, why contractualism is not philosophically promising as a starting place for work on moral philosophy).[9]

I mentioned earlier that the attempt to analyze considerations that favor promise keeping into egoistic and altruistic components looked to suffer from the fact that the morality of fidelity has to be in place to inform the calculation of individual interests. Talk about what I might do for you, what you might do for me, or how either of us might benefit or suffer individually from keeping our date can happen only on the assumption that each of us has promising in her already. Rawls's work on social practices, and Anscombe's invocation of language-games, helps to show how the relevant structure can be in each of the parties, and so can help us to understand what they are doing, and what they expect of each other.

This explains how entering into a game or an undertaking can restrict one's possibilities of acting without incurring reproach. People will criticize a player if she breaks the rules of play. People will complain about broken vows or promises, or attempts to reclaim a gift, as well.

The second problem about cases of this kind is to explain how they tend to restrict participants' possibilities of acting well. Here, mere invocation of language-games or social practices is not helpful. As Anscombe put it:

> It is at this point that I cease to use the notion of a language-game, since I should find further application of it useless and unintelligible. Unintelligible, because I can see no procedure to describe a language-game, other than that of using the language of "desert," of "keeping" and "breaking" your "word," of "justice" and "injustice" in the contexts where someone has, e.g., attached a certain sign to a statement that he will do so-and-so. Unless, indeed, all we mean by saying that a language-game is played is that the things we are discussing are said. But in that case the notion is useless; a mere superfluous bit of jargon.[10]

Although careful discussion of a practice or a language-game might explain how many different people can act from a single source, it cannot explain why any of them should act from that source. The mere exploration of the facts that people do such things, and of the stunning coincidence in their thoughts and actions when they do, is not enough to baptize such doings with justice. It is not enough to distinguish acts of, from, and for the sake of justice from beautifully played games of baseball. And pointing out that many (but not all) people tend to think matters of justice weightier or more important than baseball gets us no closer to an account of individual justice. It just adds to our discussion of the sort of talk and happenings routinely attracted by justice-associated language-games. In short, we require more in our discussion of the common source of the many actions than we can get from talk of practices and language-games.

A POSSIBLE RESPONSE AND A FINAL DOUBT

Why not take this route, then? Why not agree that a lot has to be in place (e.g., as much of whatever kind of institutional context is needed in order to locate altruistic and egoistic components in moral action) before we can turn to the question about justifying morality, and then give the justification in terms of the morally informed estimations of private interest? We could argue, for example, that having both internalized and endorsed the norms that enjoin fidelity and having learned to form my expectations of your conduct in light of these things that we must be presumed to share (otherwise, neither of us could have been on either side of giving and receiving an undertaking in the first place), I can easily see that reason sides with keeping our date.

There are a couple of problems here, I think. First, moral reasoning now both frames and permeates our story about what will count as egoistic concern, what will count as altruistic concern, and what will count as a reasonable expectation about what each of us might do, given that we have agreed to meet. Philosophers who hoped to provide an account of the rational foundation of morality were hoping for an extra-moral account.

Second, as Sterba knows, entire human societies have been oriented to systemic injustice and have instilled the norms and principles crucial to the orientation in the very young as part of customary education. One can at once have tremendous confidence in our moral knowledge that restricting a human being's access to political participation, education, food, clothing, shelter, and so forth on the grounds that it is female, or of sub-Saharan African descent, or Catholic, or Jewish, or Muslim is wrong, and that this very piece of moral knowledge is distinctively modern and liberal, hence not a thing that seems to have been timelessly promulgated in and to rational agents as such. The potential for justice deposited in us by reason has to reach all the way to our knowledge of the injustice in sexism, religious persecution, and racialism, as well as to the more traditional prohibitions on murder, torture, and procuring the judicial condemnation of the innocent. That this cannot be left to the vicissitudes of custom and conscience will be clear to anyone who thinks about the historic prevalence of systematic injustice.[11]

Faced with this difficulty, given an understanding that whole societies have misjudged good and evil, Anscombe imagines one of us deciding to do the best he can with what he's got through acculturation and habituation, realizing that he will be lucky if this does the trick. She remarks: "Such an attitude would be hopeful in this at any rate: it seems to have in it some Socratic doubt where, from having to fall back on such expedients, it should be clear that Socratic doubt is good; in fact rather generally it must be good for anyone to think 'Perhaps in some way I can't see, I may be on a bad path, perhaps I am hopelessly wrong in some essential way.'"[12]

I am inclined to sympathy with the modesty of the remark. To argue that reason alone grounds morality in the sense in which many of us were hoping to find a rational ground for morality is to make a very bold claim. It is to argue that the capacity for reason that we share with sane adults now, and with many of our ancestors, all by itself, favors justice over injustice, and so on. It is to argue that not only does every just agent act from the same source as I do, insofar as we do what justice requires, but also that acts of justice in ancient societies and in societies yet to come are acts grounded in precisely the kind of rational capacity that guides us now. I confess that I still think that we lack the philosophical equipment needed to make that case. But I could be mistaken.

CHAPTER 4

FURTHER THOUGHTS ON THE MORAL SKEPTIC

Anita M. Superson

In "From Rationality to Equality," James Sterba takes on the onerous task of defeating the skeptic about morally required action. Such a skeptic, traditionally construed, denies that rationality requires acting in morally required ways and accepts that reason requires that one act in ways that best promote one's own interest. Sterba's project, praiseworthy at least for taking on one of the most challenging issues in contemporary philosophy, is to show which reasons—moral or self-interested, or in his terms, altruistic or egoistic—win out. His arguments raise the deep and interesting issue of how best to set up the skeptic's position in order to mount a successful and complete defeat of skepticism.

STERBA'S STRATEGY

The general strategy of Sterba's paper is as follows. First, Sterba aims to reject two standard arguments for defeating the egoist (his version of the skeptic) by invoking the principle of consistency. Next, he argues for supplementing the principle of consistency with the principle of non-question-beggingness and sets up a different dichotomy from the one standardly used in attempts to address the skeptic about acting morally. Then he argues that we should reject the traditional model of the skeptic in favor of his own. He argues finally that sometimes altruistic reasons outweigh self-interested reasons, although sometimes the reverse is true, by using the principle of non-question-beggingness. My objections concern (1) the ranking Sterba assigns to altruistic and self-interested reasons, (2) the difference between the skeptic's and the egoist's position, and (3) the reason Sterba believes the traditional account that pits morality against self-interest does not work, having to do with moral reasons already being the result of a nonarbitrary compromise between self-interested and altruistic reasons. I challenge the principle of non-question-beggingness, promising though it is as a factor in our argument against skepticism. This leaves us with the principle of consistency to defeat skepticism. I believe there is a kind of consistency to which we can appeal, one that is at base similar to what I believe Sterba appeals to in his answer to the racist or sexist. Finally, I will raise some concerns about whether this argument from consistency goes far enough to provide a robust defeat of skepticism.

I will begin with an account of the traditional view of the skeptic, since one of Sterba's main concerns is to recast it, which he takes as essential to defeating skepticism in the way he believes he has shown. In general, the skeptic's position is meant to capture the kind of actions that are rationally required in opposition to morally required acts as defined by the moral theory at issue. Philosophers going back to Plato,[1] through Hobbes,[2] Hume,[3] Kant,[4] Sidgwick,[5] and others, until most recently, David Gauthier,[6] take the skeptic about moral action to deny that there is reason to act morally and to endorse only reasons of self-interest. More specifically, in Gauthier's words, the skeptic endorses the expected utility theory of practical reason, according to which rationality dictates that the agent act in ways that maximize her expected utility, which is commonly identified with promoting one's own interest, benefit, or advantage, or satisfying one's desires or preferences.[7] The skeptic is taken to believe that it is rational to have desires whose satisfaction promotes one's self-interest. In the strongest accounts, including those offered by Hobbes and Gauthier, self-interest is understood subjectively, as defined by the individual herself. Even though the expected utility theory does not rationally assess desires themselves, and according to it rationality requires acting in ways that maximize the satisfaction of whatever desires the agent happens to have, for purposes of defeating skepticism, philosophers assume that a rational person can have any desires but moral ones, which involve taking an intrinsic interest in the interests of others.[8] The skeptic's position is one of rationality: It takes a certain set of reasons to be the ones we ought, rationally speaking, to follow. Philosophers have defined the skeptic this way for at least these reasons: The expected utility theory is, despite objections, the best defended theory of rational choice and action; self-interested action is assumed by many philosophers to be the farthest removed from or the most in opposition to moral action; and the position of the rationality of self-interested action avoids begging the question in favor of morality by assuming that anyone has moral desires or that it is rational to have or act on moral desires.

Rather than dichotomize moral reasons with self-interested reasons, Sterba pits altruistic reasons against egoistic or self-interested reasons. Since he uses some terms differently from the way I understand them, and since, I believe, his setup of the skeptic's position ultimately poses problems for his account, it is best to begin with the terminology he employs. Sterba takes egoism to be the view that each person ought to do what best serves her or his overall self-interest.[9] He takes egoism to be synonymous with immorality.[10] And egoism is at odds with morality, he says, because it never requires a person to sacrifice her overall interest for the sake of others.[11] Altruism is the view that each person ought to do what best serves the overall interest of others. Altruism differs from morality in that morality, or, I assume, moral reasons, represent(s) a nonarbitrary compromise between self-interested reasons and altruistic reasons by virtue of the fact that morality includes requirements for both self-regard and a constraint on the pursuit of one's self-interest. Thus, altruism might require sacrifices to the promotion of one's self-interest when morality would not. Sterba takes the moral skeptic to represent the view that we do not know that morality is justified over egoism and altruism. The skeptic, I understand him to be saying, is agnostic between egoistic and altruistic reasons. The traditional view, in contrast, has it that the skeptic is not at all agnostic between moral reasons and self-interested reasons—the skeptic favors the latter and denies the existence of the former. To understand Sterba's view of the skeptic, we need to examine why he sets up the dichotomy between self-interested and other-interested reasons.

STERBA'S PREMISES

Sterba begins by asking which of self-interested and altruistic reasons we should take to be supreme. Here is one place he invokes the principle of non-question-beggingness, which "requires that we not argue in such a way that only someone who already knew or believed the conclusion of our argument would accept its premises, or, . . . that we not assume what we are trying to prove or justify." Sterba believes that by assuming either that egoistic reasons override altruistic reasons or that altruistic reasons override egoistic reasons, we beg the question against either altruism or egoism. So the first step in his argument is to grant the prima facie relevance of both self-interested and altruistic reasons to rational choice, because otherwise we would beg the question in favor of either the egoist or the altruist (Premise 1). Sterba believes that the egoist, unlike the traditional skeptic, would not reasonably object to a ranking of one's altruistic reasons from an altruistic perspective. The pertinent issue is what rationality dictates when these two kinds of reasons conflict. The egoist believes that self-interested reasons, even low-ranking ones, always override altruistic reasons, even high-ranking ones. To defeat the egoist, Sterba needs to show that this position is wrong. The next step in his argument is that the principle of non-question-beggingness—the second place it enters his argument—requires that priority not be given always to either self-interested reasons or to altruistic reasons (Premise 2). Therefore, there must be a (nonarbitrary) ranking of self-interested reasons and altruistic reasons, one that gives priority to those reasons that rank highest in each category (Premise 3). We should think it would be another set of reasons, and indeed this is what Sterba says: morality (or, moral reasons) serves as this nonarbitrary compromise that serves to rank self-interested and altruistic reasons (Premise 4). This is because morality requires some self-regard, while it limits the extent to which one should pursue one's self-interest. Morality thus gives us a nonarbitrary ranking of self-interested and altruistic reasons: High-ranking altruistic reasons override low-ranking self-interested reasons, and high-ranking self-interested reasons override low-ranking altruistic reasons (Premise 5). Thus, moral reasons override self-interested reasons (and altruistic reasons) (Premise 6), and the egoist is defeated (Conclusion).

In essence, Sterba is suggesting that there are three sets of reasons: self-interested, altruistic, and moral. To take either self-interested or altruistic reasons always to be overriding is to beg the question against the alternative perspective. Invoking moral reasons as a nonarbitrary compromise between self-interested and altruistic reasons is a non-question-begging way to defeat the egoist, since moral reasons will allow altruistic reasons to override self-interested reasons, at least when the former are high-ranking and the latter low-ranking.

Does Sterba's argument succeed in defeating the egoist and the skeptic?

I phrase this critical question this way because Sterba believes that his defeat of the egoist will serve as a defeat of the skeptic. He states: "As far as the moral skeptic is concerned, she cannot be denying what the egoist grants for the sake of argument [i.e., that there are altruistic reasons that from an altruistic perspective override self-interested reasons]. Rather, what the moral skeptic must be claiming is that we do not know . . . that morality is justified over egoism and altruism. So to defeat the egoist, here, really is to defeat the moral skeptic as well."

FLAWS IN THE ARGUMENT

The argument seems quite compelling, but on closer inspection I find some flaws with it. The first point I want to challenge is the passage I have just quoted. I do not think that a defeat of egoism serves as a defeat of the traditional skeptic, precisely because the skeptic does not accept the legitimacy of altruistic or moral reasons, as Sterba has defined these terms. The skeptic does not accept the first premise of the argument, nor does he accept the last premise, which invokes moral reasons as a compromise. The traditional skeptic endorses only self-interested reasons and denies the existence of moral reasons, though he is open to a better theory of practical reason that includes moral reasons, should one be defended.[12] The task of the moral philosopher is to defend such a theory. Sterba will likely object that the traditional skeptic's position begs the question in favor of self-interested reasons, or, egoism, because it accepts only self-interested reasons. But, traditionally, the skeptic is set up this way precisely because the position does not beg the question in favor of morality because self-interested action is taken to be in direct opposition to morally required action. To strengthen the case against morality, assume in addition that persons can have any desires but moral ones that involve taking an intrinsic interest in the interests of others (Gauthier), and that one's own good is defined subjectively, in terms of the maximization of the satisfaction of one's desires or preferences (Hobbes and Gauthier). The moral philosopher's goal is to establish, in the face of these strong assumptions against morality, that rationality requires acting in morally required ways, even in cases of conflict with self-interested reasons.

Now, this has been a difficult thing to establish. Hobbes famously, but unsuccessfully, tried to show it by arguing that every instance of acting morally was an instance of acting rationally just because it was an instance of acting in one's self-interest. This was so, he believed, because if one acted immorally by reneging on the hypothetical contract one made with others, one would risk detection and being placed back in the State of Nature, where others were free to treat one immorally. Gauthier tried to show that adopting a moral disposition was rationally required in the sense that doing so best promoted the maximization of the satisfaction of one's interests. Being morally disposed means that one can expect to benefit from a system of morality in place, even though one expects to have to make moral sacrifices from time to time. But Gauthier's view faces problems with demonstrating that the rationality of the moral disposition carries over to the actions expressing this disposition.[13]

Sterba alludes to two further reasons he is opposed to the traditional view of the skeptic. First is that even if we could defeat the traditional skeptic, the defeat would not yield the kind of answer we are looking for.

Sterba notes that an account such as Gauthier's that attempts to derive morality from purely egoistic premises will justify "at best a truncated morality." I am not sure what he means here, but maybe he is agreeing with Gauthier that were we to show that every morally required action was rationally required because it was in one's self-interest, we would make morality otiose, which is to say that all talk of moral reasons could be replaced with talk of self-interested reasons.[14] This is a damning criticism for this strategy, but it does not require relinquishing the traditional strategy of defeating the skeptic, because we could employ Gauthier's dispositional move or something like it. Alternatively, Sterba might mean that any morality that would emerge from the traditional skeptical starting point would be minimalist. Sterba adds that altruists would have little or no reason to accept what results from the Gauthier-type strategy that attempts to derive morality from the starting point of the traditional skeptic. Jean Hampton criticizes the traditional view of the skeptic and its grounding in expected utility theory for the reason that it will inevitably yield a morality that allows us to treat people instrumentally.[15]

I agree with Sterba and Hampton and others that there are significant problems with expected utility theory.[16] Nevertheless, I think the solution is not to soften the skeptic's stance against morality, which is what I believe Sterba's own dichotomy between egoistic and altruistic reasons does in assuming that the egoist can accept altruistic reasons from an altruistic perspective. To emphasize this point, consider that the strategy of defining the skeptic in the traditional way, as endorsing the view that rationality always requires self-interested action, covers all the cases where anyone from the worst immoralist to the morally disposed person who could on occasion cheat on her taxes, tell a white lie, or inflate her cab receipts to get a higher travel reimbursement, does not accept the overridingness of moral reasons. Perhaps defining the skeptic in this way will yield reasons that would not appeal to the altruist, but this might be the price we have to pay to avoid importing morality into the skeptic's position, because we cannot assume that anyone has any disposition toward morality on any occasion without begging the question in favor of morality. Thus, I think that regardless of past failures to defeat the traditional skeptic, the difficult nature of defeating this skeptic, and the problems with expected utility theory, philosophers must set up the skeptic in a way that is as far removed from morality as possible to avoid a question-begging defeat.

The second reason Sterba might be opposed to the traditional account of the skeptic is his denial that we act self-interestedly most of the time. Sterba believes that the behavior of women exhibits considerably more altruism than egoism, whereas the behavior of men, under patriarchy, exhibits more egoism than altruism, but that this difference is more a matter of nurture than nature. He believes that "it is beyond dispute" that humans are capable of both self-interested and altruistic behavior, and that we move along a spectrum from egoism to pure altruism. This is in contrast to those who endorse expected utility theory for the reason that it best explains and predicts behavior.[17] Sterba is in good company here, as many others have thoroughly criticized expected utility theory for falling short on these aims.[18] However, regardless of how persons in fact act, it is a strategic move to set up the skeptic to incorporate the view that persons act only in self-interested ways. Indeed, regardless of his description of persons in the State of Nature, Hobbes did not have to endorse psychological egoism, according to which we always act in ways that best promote our own self-interest, but merely assume it as a strategic move to set up what he took to be the worst-case scenario against morality. I disagree with Hobbes that self-interest represents the worst-case scenario against morality; other immoralities, such as negligence, indifference, or even doing evil for its own sake, are just as bad, in intention and outcome. My view is to define the skeptic's position such that it captures all immoralities by what they have in common, namely, privileging of oneself and one's reasons over others and their reasons. But I agree with Hobbes that our strategy should put the moralist in the strongest position, should her argument against skepticism succeed. Although my view increases the difficulty of defeating skepticism, if we do defeat it, we will have shown that most if not all immoral action is irrational.

Finally, the two reasons I have just examined why Sterba rejects the traditional account of the skeptic go beyond his principle of non-question-beggingness. It is this principle that is supposed to ground the defeat of skepticism, not the fact that the traditional view will not yield the kind of answer we are looking for, or that it does not speak to our actual behavior. Invoking this principle is the main purpose that is served by talking in terms of the egoist rather than the skeptic in the way Sterba favors. Suppose Sterba is correct that the egoist begs the question in favor of self-interested reasons by not admitting the existence of altruistic reasons. I do not think this is problematic because the reasons for setting up the skeptic in the traditional way, especially that we avoid begging the question in favor of morality, outweigh his worries about begging the question in favor of self-interested reasons.

FURTHER PROBLEMS WITH THE ARGUMENT

Let's put aside these worries about the traditional skeptic and return to the argument, the conclusion of which is that the egoist is defeated because moral reasons serve as a nonarbitrary compromise between self-interested and altruistic reasons. Moral reasons are a nonarbitrary compromise because, according to Sterba, they include both self-regard and a constraint on the pursuit of one's self-interest. But not all moral theories have a requirement of self-regard built into them. Act utilitarianism, for instance, requires the agent always to aim to promote the good for all, even if this means sacrificing one's own welfare or even one's own life.[19] And most moral theories do not build in a requirement that the agent aim to promote self-regard in a desire-satisfaction sense that the traditional skeptic deems to be rationally required. Instead, they enjoin us to promote the good life for ourselves, which they take to mean something like Aristotle's version of eudaimonia.[20] Maybe Sterba means that ideally, morality would include self-regard, and that this, if not identified with desire-satisfaction, at least includes it. I think this is right: I agree with philosophers such as Judith Thomson and Jean Hampton, who argue for the importance of interest-satisfaction to morality for understanding what it is to make a moral sacrifice and for avoiding subservience. I think the issue of whether morality includes a requirement for self-regard, and in what sense, is an important one that ultimately has bearing on the defeat of skepticism. For if we can justify a legitimate shift in what self-interest entails, we would change the skeptic's position in a way that might make it easier to defend morality against it. But I would like to hear more from Sterba in the way of a defense of the claim that morality involves a requirement for self-regard.

Let's consider further Sterba's solution to the egoistical problem, that moral reasons serve as a nonarbitrary compromise between self-interested and altruistic reasons. I understand this to mean that moral reasons are always overriding, from the standpoint of rationality, when we are faced with a choice with respect to moral, self-interested, and altruistic reasons. This is because moral reasons themselves supply us with the ranking between self-interested and altruistic reasons in cases of conflict and so "contain" or reflect these other reasons in them. This has bearing on why Sterba forgoes the traditional dichotomy between self-interested and moral reasons in favor of the dichotomy between egoistic/self-interested and altruistic reasons. He remarks: "To ask [as the traditional view of the skeptic does] that moral reasons be weighed against self-interested reasons is, in effect, to count self-interested reasons twice—once in the compromise between egoism and altruism that constitutes a conception of morality, and then again, assuming moral reasons are weighed against self-interested reasons—and this double counting of self-interested reasons would be clearly objectionable from a non-question-begging standpoint."

Since the traditional view of the skeptic pits moral reasons against self-interested reasons, it allows self-interested reasons to count twice. Thus, we should reject it in favor of the dichotomy Sterba proposes.

But I wonder whether Sterba's view allows a double counting of moral reasons, and so is question-begging in the opposite direction? Suppose that moral reasons already "contain" a weighting of self-interested and altruistic reasons. We then must choose between self-interested/egoistic and moral reasons. If we choose moral reasons, we have allowed moral reasons to count twice. Alternatively (for those who reject the traditional skeptical dichotomy), moral reasons are typically thought of as altruistic, or, other-directed, rather than self-directed. If we must choose between egoistic/self-interested reasons and altruistic reasons, and we choose moral reasons because they reflect both of these kinds of reasons, then our choosing moral reasons double counts altruistic reasons. The deeper, larger problem is the authority of moral reasons. Sterba seems to grant moral reasons authority just by virtue of their compromising nature—moral reasons serve as the arbiter between self-interested and altruistic reasons just because they "contain" both of these kinds of reasons. But to avoid double counting, it seems that the way out of the dichotomy Sterba proposes in lieu of the traditional one is to appeal to a set of reasons having nothing to do with either altruistic or self-interested reasons. But then this set of reasons would stand in need of defense: How do we defend their authority? My general worry about Sterba's solution of morality as nonarbitrary compromise is my skepticism about what, for him, justifies the authority of moral reasons. Their compromising nature does not seem to be the proper grounding of their authority to adjudicate between self-interested and altruistic reasons. Rather, I think it is something prior to and independent of their compromising nature that grounds their authority. Of course, much more needs to be said to defend this force—but this is just what needs to be decided to defeat skepticism.

A third problem I have with the solution involving the overridingness of moral reasons is about what in the end grounds the ranking of self-interested and altruistic concerns. How do we know when altruistic concerns are higher-ranking than self-interested concerns such that moral reasons reflect this ranking rather than the opposite one? Because all the work gets done by the ranking, it seems that we have pushed back the problem of how to adjudicate between the requirements of self-interest and morality to the very ranking that takes place with moral reasons. But this is just the issue: How do we know which concerns—self-directed or other-directed—outweigh the others, from the standpoint of rationality? It is not enough to assert that altruistic reasons sometimes outrank self-interested reasons, because the issue for anyone who is skeptical about moral reasons is whether and when they do.

In the end, I do not believe that this ambitious attempt to defeat the egoist succeeds because of worries about double counting and authority. Nor do I believe that this attempt to defeat the egoist will also defeat the skeptic as traditionally defined, because this skeptic will not take the first step and admit the existence of altruistic reasons, nor take the latter step and admit the existence of moral reasons. Concerns about the dichotomy Sterba proposes, as well as about the principle of non-question-beggingness, lead me to reject this novel attempt, grounded in the principle of non-question-beggingness, to defeat the skeptic and egoist.

ARGUMENTS FROM CONSISTENCY

This leaves us with the principle of consistency. Sterba offers two reasons he believes we should not attempt to defeat the skeptic with this principle, at least not without supplementing it with the principle of non-question-beggingness, which he takes to do most of the work in his argument against the egoist. But maybe he was too quick to reject it. Let's turn to why he does, and see whether it can be salvaged in some form. I will argue that there is room for him to appeal to it, and say a bit more about how such an appeal might work as a way of defeating skepticism.

Sterba rejects the principle of consistency as a defense against skepticism first because of the universalization argument, which is that consistency requires that one be able to universalize one's claims. The egoist or immoralist (whom he identifies with the skeptic) must, on pain of inconsistency, universalize his position that one has reason to pursue one's own freedom and well-being so that others who are similarly situated also have reason to pursue their own freedom and well-being, even if this is not what the egoist wants because it might hamper his pursuit of his own freedom and well-being. Sterba's complaint is that if the egoist universalizes his prudential claim, we get only another prudential claim—that everyone ought to pursue their own freedom and well-being. He objects that this is not a claim about morality, which would require that one should help or not interfere with others' pursuit of freedom and well-being. The idea, I believe, is that we end up with a kind of Hobbesian state of morality, where each person pursues her own self-interest, leading to, as it were, a "sum of self-interests," rather than a real change in the object of what is to be pursued, which is the interest of others. This may have been Gauthier's point when he argued that a real defeat of skepticism requires showing that rationality requires us to become "truly moral persons," ones who are disposed to morality and follow it even when the system of morality collapses, rather than "moral persons" who did the right thing but only when they stood to benefit from a moral system in place, even if they did not benefit from the occasion of acting morally.[21] It is what we end up with if we limit our defeat of skepticism to self-interested reasons. I think Sterba and Gauthier are right about this, and it shows that there might be a better way to describe the skeptic's position than as the view that rationality requires merely a pursuit of one's self-interest. I will explore this alternative shortly.

The second argument from consistency that Sterba rejects is grounded in public reasons: Egoists cannot make public their reason for action, that everyone ought to do what best serves her overall interest, when their reasons conflict with the reasons of others. So egoism is a myth. Sterba rejects this argument for the reason that the egoist's reasons are public in that they are communicable to others, even if the egoist does not want others to know his reasons when this might make the egoist lose out. I think he is correct about this, too. Sterba concludes that consistency is not a sufficient reason for defeating the skeptic, and goes on, as we have seen, to supplement it with the principle of non-question-beggingness.

Despite his rejection of these arguments from consistency, and his claim that he is appealing to the principle of non-question-beggingness in his argument against the racist and the sexist, I think Sterba appeals to the principle of consistency in this argument. He claims that in group-based immoralities such as racism and sexism, "there are no non-question-begging grounds for the way those who are dominant favor their interests over the interests of those they dominate . . . those who dominate use biased, that is, question-begging, information, to conceive of their interests as superior to the interests of those they dominate, which they then think entitles them to their privileged status." They appeal to a shared feature of the group to justify their group-based preference, and this appeal begs the question in favor of their interests.

Now, I think this argument at base appeals to consistency. To see this, let's begin with the assumption that all persons are equal in a Kantian sense—they have dignity by virtue of having the capacity for rationality, as evidenced by their having interests, desires, plans, and goals. This assumption does not import morality into the skeptic's position, should the skeptic accept it; rather, it provides the grounds for the very possibility of morality. At base it says that persons are allowed into "the moral game" by virtue of the fact that they are interest-bearers. Hobbes argued similarly that being an interest-bearer allows one to enter rational bargaining schemes from which moral agreement arises, and positions one to consider whether a system of morality or the occasion of acting morally will bring one greater expected benefit than the benefit one could otherwise expect.[22]

I have argued elsewhere for redefining the skeptic's position from that of self-interest to privilege: Rationality requires acting in ways that privilege oneself by disrespecting the humanity or dignity of others.[23] Privileging oneself displays an inconsistency in treating the humanity of self and others. It involves: caring negatively about others' humanity by rendering it void or discounting it; not caring about others' humanity; not being aware of others' humanity by failing to focus on it and succumbing to emotion instead; or even enjoying undeserved benefits from an unjust system. Racism and sexism take the form of one or more of these immoralities. Thus, the racist and the sexist privilege themselves and their own reasons over others and their reasons; they fail appropriately to respect the humanity of others outside their group. The principle of consistency requires that we not disrespect others' humanity; it is inconsistent, we might say to the skeptic, and so irrational, not to respect others fully, but to respect one's own humanity and to expect that others do so as well.

A defeat of skepticism grounded on the principle of consistency faces a similar charge about universalizability as does egoism. Individual egoism is the view that one's own desires or good gives one reasons, but denies that the desires or good of others gives one reasons. An inconsistency remains unless the egoist explains what is so special about one that only one's own desires give one reasons. Universal egoism tries to diffuse this inconsistency, because according to it, each person's desires give that person a reason—the principle of egoism is universalized to everyone, even if no one person wants the others to follow it, lest her good be jeopardized.

One might object to my argument about consistency by giving the skeptic a similar way out of the inconsistency involved in respecting one's own worth but not the worth of others. That is, the skeptic can claim that there is no inconsistency in privileging oneself, so it is not irrational to do so. The skeptic, in diffusing the inconsistency, can follow the universal egoist in saying that taking oneself to have a reason to privilege oneself means that it is rational for each person to privilege herself, which gives each person the same status. Each person is rationally allowed to favor her reasons having to do with her own worth, and because each gets to do so, there is no inconsistency in treatment of self and others.

But I think that the inconsistency charge still holds in my account of the privileged person like the racist or sexist. The reason is that there are two different senses of consistency at issue. My objector construes inconsistency as a violation of universalizability, of favoring one's own reasons and not taking others' reasons to factor into one's own. But in my account of privilege, the privileged person aims to make another person inferior in worth by not appropriately respecting her intrinsic worth. But morality requires impartiality: Each counts for one, without favoritism of one or one's group. The inconsistency that best explains privileging oneself is a violation of impartiality. So although we can universalize the principle that one's own desires or good gives one a reason, this goes no way toward diffusing the violation of impartiality, which requires that we treat everyone's worth equally. The racist and sexist endorse partiality, and treat others as inferior in worth to them and to their group. Acknowledging consistency as impartiality rather than universalizability avoids the problems Sterba discusses that face traditional inconsistency arguments.[24]

This is just the start of an attempt to defeat skepticism, a suggestion that we should go the way of appealing to reasons of consistency, rather than meeting the skeptic on his own terms by invoking reasons of self-interest (or appealing to non-question-beggingness). Still, rationality as consistency, though it packs a lot of punch by granting persons intrinsic worth, is a rather minimalist conception of rationality.[25] It may not go far enough for a robust defeat of skepticism, which, I believe, would not leave any further skeptical challenge remaining. It should show that rationality requires being morally disposed, acting morally on the occasion, having the right reasons for one's disposition and actions, and having the appropriate motives. I believe that reasons of consistency are likely the most plausible to invoke against the skeptic. Elsewhere I argue for invoking consistency as coherence among one's reasons, dispositions, actions, and motives.[26] Setting up the skeptic's position in a way that captures privilege, and then attempting to debunk the rationality of acting in ways that privilege oneself and one's reasons by appealing to reasons of consistency, avoids the problems inherent in the self-interested account of the skeptic and captures many more immoralities than mere self-interested action. Nor does it beg the question in favor of morality, so it addresses Sterba's main concern about the traditional account of the skeptic. Nor does it invoke double counting of self-interested reasons. Sterba's insightful essay is important for at least the reason that it has gotten us thinking once again about the best way to characterize the skeptic's position so as to enact a successful defeat of the skeptic. Successfully defeating the skeptic is, after all, a goal on which we can all agree.

CHAPTER 5

THE JUSTIFICATION OF MORALITY

Russ Shafer-Landau

There are at least two things that we might be talking about when talking of "the justification of morality."

We might be speaking, first, of the rational authority of morality. Here, we are asking whether it is rational to be a moral person or to behave morally on a given occasion. We are also discussing what reasons there are for people to cultivate moral dispositions or to act in a way that morality demands.

Or, second, we might be asking about how the content of morality is fixed. To justify morality, in this sense, is to explain how moral requirements are generated. It is to provide a general method, or some sort of foundational account, that explains why the basic moral norms are what they are. In other words, we might be trying to offer a plausible account of the source of various moral requirements.

Very ambitiously, Sterba has set out to offer both kinds of justification. He wants to show how it is rational to be moral, and also show how the content of our moral requirements is fixed. And he seeks to do this in a way that is unified by a single sort of consideration—the importance of avoiding question-begging arguments.

Before commenting on the central strategy of Sterba's new view, I want to comment on the goal that he has set himself. He writes that "what needs to be shown is that morality is rationally required." I take it that this means that success in the project of justification can be had only if we can show that morality is always rationally required, since everyone thinks that reason demands that we at least sometimes do what is moral—if only because that tallies with self-interest, or with what we most want.

I don't think that we can achieve this goal, for there are times when moral demands are slight and conflicting concerns of self-interest very great. In such cases we are, it seems, at least rationally permitted to take a pass on morality. Of course, in saying such a thing I am making assumptions about what morality requires, and as we'll shortly see, Sterba rejects these assumptions. And so my pessimism about morality's supreme rational authority at this point begs the question—a cardinal sin in this context. I will try to make good on my doubts by presenting what I take to be Sterba's master argument, critically examining it, and then drawing some lessons from the exercise.

THE MASTER ARGUMENT

Here, as I understand it, is the master argument of Sterba's justification of morality:

1. We are rationally required to avoid begging questions.
2. When contemplating amoralism or immoralism, we avoid begging questions only if we:
   (a) assign relevance to all and only applicable egoistic and altruistic reasons, and then
   (b) strike a certain kind of compromise between them.
3. Therefore, when contemplating amoralism or immoralism, we are rationally required to assign relevance to all and only applicable egoistic and altruistic reasons, and to strike a certain kind of compromise between them.

4. Assigning such relevance and striking such a compromise is being moral.
5. Therefore, when contemplating amoralism or immoralism, we are rationally required to be moral.

I have tried to be faithful in my reconstruction, and I have no qualms about the logic of the argument as set out here. Now I'd like to raise some questions about each of the three premises, in order.

Premise 1

If one is rationally required to do something, then failing to do it entails irrationality. But I don't think that those who beg questions are necessarily being irrational. There are contexts in which one may beg a question without either defeating one's own goals or acting contrary to the best applicable reasons.

In my understanding of the matter, begging a question means advancing an argument that includes a premise that is acceptable only to those who already accept the conclusion. If my goal is to convince an interlocutor of something, then begging a question is indeed irrational. But I may have other, perfectly legitimate goals when advancing an argument that seeks to vindicate morality. I may be trying to rally the faithful, to shore up their confidence against skeptical doubts, to reveal to them why morality isn't just a sucker's game, to get them to see that their irrevocable commitments entail a renunciation of amoralism or immoralism. There are all sorts of good reasons for adopting such goals. Moreover, it may be that an effective way to secure them is to offer arguments that include premises that dedicated amoralists or immoralists would reject.

But what if my goal is to convince the amoralist or immoralist? In that case, a question-begging argument won't do. It would be irrational of me to offer it. But that does not show that the argument is unsound. It may be the case that we cannot avoid begging a question at some philosophical junctures. And the likeliest such places are those in which we are seeking to defend our fundamental normative commitments. There may really be nothing to say to the immoralist who places no value on kindness and feels no repugnance at the thought of torturing another human being. If that were so, then when confronted with such a person, it would be irrational to try to argue him out of his position. But that doesn't show that our views are false. Nor does it show that we are irrational or epistemically unjustified in retaining the moral beliefs that we are unable to convince the skeptic to embrace.

To see this last point, consider my belief in my embodied existence. Any argument I offer on behalf of this claim is bound to beg the question against an idealist or a skeptic about the external world. The evidence and argument I offer to support my belief that the earth is roughly round are going to beg a question against a member of the Flat Earth Society. The student who is convinced that I hate him and have graded him poorly on that basis may take any explanation I offer of his grade as further confirming his suspicions about my unfairness. In each of these cases, all arguments I offer to my interlocutor are bound to beg the question. I am nevertheless justified and rational in continuing to hold such contested beliefs.

What this means for the present endeavor is that our worst-case scenario may not be crippling. That scenario is one in which we are unable to provide a non-question-begging argument for the rational authority of morality. We may be justified and avoid irrationality in believing that there is excellent reason to do as morality says—even when it calls for the most serious self-sacrifice or the gravest suppression of what we want from life. I applaud Sterba's efforts, and those of other philosophers, to find a neutral starting point from which we might convince open-minded immoralists and amoralists of the errors of their ways. But I am not optimistic about the success of such efforts. My point here is simply that reliance on question-begging assumptions would not consign moralists to irrationality or a lack of epistemic justification for our allegiances.

Premise 2

The need to assign prima facie relevance to altruistic and egoistic reasons is supported by an assumption that Sterba has not argued for, but one that I agree with. The assumption is that the only arguments there are for rational egoism are either unsound, because of a reliance on psychological egoism, or question-begging.

Although I agree with Sterba's rejection of rational egoism, I do not think that this rejection fully supports Premise 2. And the reasoning he does give for this premise strikes me as problematic. Let me briefly reconstruct that reasoning, and then explain my worries.

As I understand the argument, there are two basic steps that constitute the support for Premise 2:

(A) If we assume, as Sterba does, that arguments for and against the existence of altruistic reasons will be question-begging, then we have no choice, he says, but to assign both kinds of reasons prima facie relevance in determining what we have most reason to do.

(B) Once we assign such relevance to both altruistic and egoistic reasons, the only fair way to determine which is to have priority is to give the nod to the reason that ranks higher on its own scale of importance.

I have two concerns about Step A. I'll postpone discussion of Step B for now, and will return to it when considering Premise 4.

About Step A: First, I am not sure how this manages to avoid begging a question against the rational egoist. And that is because the importance that Sterba is asking us to assign to altruistic reasons is not really prima facie, but pro tanto. Prima facie importance denotes the appearance of importance, but is compatible with the appearances being mistaken. Pro tanto relevance signifies a consideration that is always relevant, but whose relative importance can vary with context.

It seems innocent to assign prima facie relevance to egoistic and altruistic reasons only because this looks like it allows for the possibility that such reasons might have no importance at all. But that is not Sterba's view. His position is committed to moving from the absence of a question-begging argument for rational egoism to the claim that we must assign altruistic reasons pro tanto importance. It is, in effect, asking rational egoists to abandon their position, by admitting the permanent normative relevance of altruistic reasons. Such reasons won't always win the day, of course. But in deciding what we have most reason to do, we are always required to assign weight to any existing altruistic reasons.

FURTHER PROBLEMS WITH THE ARGUMENT

In effect, Sterba's reasoning looks like this:

1. Every argument for rational egoism is question-begging.
2. If every argument for rational egoism is question-begging, then we must assign pro tanto normative importance to altruistic reasons.
3. Therefore we must assign pro tanto normative importance to altruistic reasons.

I have already invited Sterba to say more in defense of Premise 1. But even if we grant it, what is the defense of Premise 2? In the absence of a non-question-begging argument for the moral and rational relevance of altruistic reasons, Sterba urges us to assign them pro tanto relevance. But why shouldn't the default view be that these reasons have no such relevance—they get it only when they earn it, and not before? I remain unclear about how Premise 2 avoids begging the question against rational egoists.[1]

I have a second concern about Step A: Why are the sources of our reasons restricted to just altruistic and egoistic ones? Even if we were to agree that both kinds of reasons have pro tanto relevance to normative inquiry, why do only these two kinds enter the equation? I was particularly struck by the absence of any discussion of practical instrumentalism. Indeed, in ordinary thought, as well as in much philosophical writing, there are standardly three sources of reasons that we must consider—self-interest, morality, and personal commitments (desires, wants, goals, cares, concerns, and so on).

In my reading, Sterba offers no argument for excluding considerations of personal commitment from constituting one of the elements out of which the rational or moral balance is struck. The closest he comes to defending this restriction is when he writes that "all immoralities involve an inappropriate (question-begging) favoring of the interests of self (or a particular group of selves) over the interests of others." This makes immorality essentially a matter of poorly balancing egoistic and altruistic reasons. If that were so, then we would have a plausible basis for restricting the relevant moral inputs to egoistic and altruistic considerations.

But that isn't so. Some immoral acts involve self-sacrifice. Others involve disinterested malice. Yet others represent paternalistic efforts designed precisely to enhance the interests of others. Not every immorality involves wrongly elevating self or group interests over those of others.

Indeed, we might ask how altruistic and egoistic reasons get into the balance in the first place, and then see whether the same considerations apply to desires. As far as I can tell, Sterba cites two supporting reasons for thinking that we must take both altruistic and egoistic reasons into account when determining what is rationally and morally required.

First, denying the relevance of either type of reason will beg a question, and that we must not do. At best, however, this gives us cause to treat both kinds of reasons as equivalent. It doesn't yet argue for giving them any weight, rather than no weight. Further, denying the relevance of desires or commitments generally will just as surely beg the question at this stage against the instrumentalist.

Second, we must take both egoistic and altruistic reasons into account because we are capable of being motivated by both sorts of consideration. Yet this justification, like the preceding one, obviously applies to our desires as well. So, by parity of reasoning, we must also consult our desires and enter them into the mix when striking the compromise that represents our normative requirements.

But this is very troubling. There are at least two problems that arise once we allow that desires can be a nonderivative source of reasons.

(1) There is the difficulty of trying to strike a balance among items on three distinct ordinal scales, without a common measure to do the work. This is a familiar problem, not unique to Sterba's theory, but it is no less worrying for that. The problem is there in any event for

Sterba's original proposal, in which we must strike a balance between egoistic and altruistic reasons, without the aid of some common measure.

(2) Many desires seem to be completely irrelevant to fixing our moral duty, even if they are relevant to determining what is rationally required of us. Malevolent desires need not be rooted in egoistic concerns or a concern to further the interest of some third party (contrary to Sterba's assumption early in his essay). So they cannot be subsumed under the other two classes when striking the appropriate balance. Such desires may be very powerful—indeed, sometimes all-consuming—and yet we should be loath to give them pride of place in fixing our moral duties, even if in such a situation these desires rank higher on their scale than competing egoistic or altruistic desires do on theirs.

In short, it isn't clear how the mandate to assign prima facie (really—pro tanto) relevance to both altruistic and egoistic reasons avoids begging the question against the rational egoist. Further, we need more argument to show why the demands of rationality and morality stem from a balance struck between only egoistic and altruistic reasons, rather than, in addition, reasons that stem from commitments that serve neither self-interest nor the interests of others.

Premise 4

I now want to set aside these last complications and return to the thought that morality and rationality are a matter of balancing only egoistic and altruistic reasons. Let's just assume for now that desires do not provide an independent source of reasons.

Still, there is trouble for the claim that what is morally and rationally required is a matter of compromise between egoistic and altruistic reasons. We must strike the relevant balance in a nonarbitrary way. Sterba believes that the only nonarbitrary way is to assign priority to the reasons that rank higher on their respective scale. The action supported by the strongest such reason is the one that is both rationally and morally required. For instance, if an egoistic reason is, relative to other egoistic reasons, very weighty, and an altruistic reason is, relative to other altruistic reasons, not very weighty, then the action supported by the egoistic reason is in that particular case rationally and morally required. This vision of compromise gives rise to two specific concerns that I'd like briefly to discuss.

The first has to do with the way in which it makes the content of morality deeply contingent. Those who believe in the existence of absolute moral requirements—those that may never be permissibly broken—should be especially worried here, because Sterba's view offers no guarantee that the highest-ranking reasons in every situation will always tally with the recommendations set forth by those absolute rules.

But even for those of us who are agnostic about the existence of absolute moral rules, it does seem that Sterba's view makes paradigmatically moral requirements too vulnerable to being overridden. One way to put this is to say that there seems to be no place in Sterba's account for peremptory reasons—those that silence any competing considerations in a given kind of context. Considerations of a rapist's self-interest are entirely irrelevant to determining whether he is morally bound to refrain from what he would most like to do. And we don't need to see how the altruistic and egoistic reasons line up before knowing that sadistic torture is wrong—even if, very unusually, the victim is easily able to get over it, and nothing else would serve the torturer's interests as well. It seems that there are contexts in which egoistic reasons have no weight at all in determining our moral duty, no matter how high on the self-interest scale such reasons rank.

The natural way to try to assuage such worries is to invoke a moralized conception of self-interest. This would make moral virtue an essential element of well-being, so that the hypothesized scenarios I've just drawn are impossible—one couldn't really best advance self-interest by doing things that are paradigmatically immoral. But aside from the optimism that underlies such a view, it is in any event not open to Sterba to rely on it. That's because this view presupposes a conception of morality that exists independently of self-interest and serves to constrain it, rather than one that sees morality as emerging from a compromise between self-interest and altruistic reasons.

The second concern I have with the compromise procedure at the heart of Premise 4 is that it yields deeply counterintuitive results. It does this in at least two ways. It morally licenses (indeed, requires) us to commit actions that appear to be paradigmatically immoral. And it forbids actions that to all appearances are morally admirable.

As I understand Sterba's view, it implies that in any case in which one stands to gain a great deal through very harmful and unfair behavior, and the victim's stakes are just a bit lower, then we are morally and rationally required to give the nod to self-interest. But this paints a false picture of our moral duty, as actions that we intuitively regard as gross immoralities will in this view sometimes qualify as our moral duty. For it's possible that an intuitively evil action does more than any alternative to promote self-interest, whereas the reasons that oppose such actions do not rank at the very top of the list of applicable altruistic reasons.

Now, Sterba does say that morality and rationality require us to assign priority to the higher-ranking reason, other things being equal. But I have no idea what other sorts of considerations could come into play here to alter the balance. We can't, of course, say that the higher-ranked reason takes precedence except when it would require some serious immorality, because that assumes that there are moral duties whose content is fixed independently of the relevant compromises. I'd like to hear more about the cetera in this ceteris paribus clause.

A less worrying implication, but still counterintuitive enough to warrant mention, occurs when there is little at stake, for either oneself or others. Suppose in a given context that a self-interested reason is the strongest applicable reason. In such a case, acting altruistically will be immoral, because such action is counter to the highest-ranking applicable reason. That is hard to swallow.

Now, Sterba, in both conversation and in written correspondence, denies that this balancing strategy is designed to serve as a perfectly general method for assigning moral requirements. Its scope is said to be limited, so that in only certain contexts are compromises struck in this way determinative of our moral duty. I have two problems with this reply.

First, it isn't clear how, in a principled way, Sterba is going to be able to restrict the application of the compromise mechanism. If it works in some cases to fix the content of our moral duty, why doesn't it work in all cases? I don't offer this as a knockdown criticism, but as an invitation for him to do more positive work that lays out the scope and limits of morality as compromise.

Second, if there are sources of moral duty other than the one given by the balance struck between egoistic and altruistic reasons, then we have as yet no guarantee that we will be rationally required to adhere to the moral duties derived from such a source. One of the beautiful aspects of Sterba's vision of morality as compromise is the way in which it purports to show how every moral requirement is also a rational requirement. It does that by offering a theory of rational requirements that makes such requirements identical with those of moral requirements. But if that theory—morality as compromise—has only a limited scope, then there is simply no reason to think that the supplemental theory of moral requirements, whatever it is, will provide all rational agents with an overriding reason to obey its edicts. The main goal that Sterba has set himself—to show that we always have best reason to comply with moral requirements—would remain elusive. For even if all of my earlier concerns about this project could be answered, the claim that morality as compromise yields only a portion of our moral duties still leaves us wondering what the other source of our moral duties is, and whether that source can invariably supply us with decisive reasons to act as it recommends.

FINAL THOUGHTS

For the reasons I've just given, I remain unconvinced by Sterba's efforts to justify the content and rational authority of morality. And I am pessimistic about other efforts to offer such unified justifications. So where does that leave us?

There is much to say at this point and very little time to say it in. In short, I want to be clear that I am not offering a counsel of despair. I haven't provided a case to show that all neutral arguments for moral rationalism or proceduralism must fail. So my doubts about such efforts may be misplaced. But suppose they are not. Still, an inability to convince open-minded immoralists of the content of morality, and amoralists of its reason-giving power, does not by itself yield the verdict that we moralists are unjustified in our beliefs about the content and normative status of moral requirements.

I liken the moralist's position here to that of a believer in a 3-D external world, when pitted against a very smart skeptic. There is no neutral argument that I know of that will convince a skeptic of the material existence of this world. It would be ideal if we could devise such an argument. But philosophically, as well as in all other respects, we live in a non-ideal world. Yet just as the absence of an ideal anti-skeptical argument is compatible with our justified belief in an external world, so too, I think, the absence of an ideal (i.e., neutral and sound) argument for the content and intrinsic normativity of moral requirements is compatible with our beliefs about where our duty fundamentally lies and about the power of our duty to supply us with reasons for action. It would be lovely to have our convictions on this score ratified by means of an argument powerful enough to convince anyone, no matter her moral and metaethical starting points. The effort to construct such an argument is a noble one. But its failure—if, at the end of the day, failure is what results—would not undercut whatever justification we already enjoy for our moral beliefs, or for our beliefs in the intrinsic reason-giving power of our moral duties.

CHAPTER 6

STERBA'S VINDICATION OF MORALITY

Allan F. Gibbard

In his essay "From Rationality to Equality," James Sterba offers a vindication of morality that is quite different from other vindications in the philosophical literature. His central arguments have considerable attraction for me. I'll begin by examining the vindication, asking some questions about how it is meant to work, and pursuing some worries I have with it. Later, I'll look at Sterba's treatment of libertarian bases for requirements that resources go toward meeting peoples' basic needs. For the most part, I am fully on board with this argument, but I think it leads further than Sterba may think it does.

Sterba and I agree that we can't get morality out of sheer requirements of consistency.[1] A vindication of morality could succeed only by relying on judgments that we find plausible, even though we could invent less plausible alternatives that aren't self-defeating in their own terms. I am far from hostile, then, to trying to vindicate morality by appeals that fall short of ironclad conceptual necessity; I think that this is the only way to proceed. Sterba appeals to judgments that, I take it, normal human beings will share, at least in a prima facie way: that one's own good provides reasons to do things, and that the good of another provides reasons to do things. Sterba, then, addresses his vindication to those capable of acting both for prudential and for other-regarding reasons. He takes the prima facie relevance of each kind of reason as basic. I find this an entirely reasonable way to proceed.

The way he goes on from here is familiar in the present context, and I won't try to summarize it exactly. Any way of arguing that at base we have only egoistic reasons to act, Sterba says, begs the question against our prima facie judgment that the good of others can provide a reason independent of further grounds. Correspondingly, any way of arguing that we have basic reasons only to act for the good of others must beg the question against our prima facie conviction that a person has basic reason to act for her own good. (Indeed, I take it, this position would strike us in Sterba's actual audience as utterly implausible. If I am to act for the good of others, why not for my own? But Sterba's argument addresses as well a hypothetical audience that, unlike any of us humans, accords far more prima facie plausibility to the claim that one must act for the good of others than to the claim that one must act for one's own good.) The only way not to beg the question against either of these prima facie convictions of ours, Sterba concludes, is to regard both kinds of purported reasons as genuine. This doesn't tell us which such compromise to adopt, and as I read Sterba, he thinks that a number of competing accounts of the nature of morality will remain in contention, for all his argument in this essay establishes. It doesn't confine us to a morality that consists in such a compromise, confining the reasons it recognizes to egoistic and altruistic ones. What the argument does is eliminate pure egoism and pure altruism from contention as accounts of how to live, by showing that they beg a question that a compromise between them doesn't beg.

I should pause here for two preliminaries. First, the term "reason": I'll take it to mean what T. M. Scanlon calls a "reason in the standard normative sense." Sterba, as I understand him, is likewise using the term in this way. Reasons in this sense contrast with what is sometimes called a person's "operative reasons," what she took to be a reason and acted on. Robert Audi points out the distinction we make in language between "her reason for doing" such-and-such and "a reason to do" it; the latter, to my ear and his, suggests reasons in the standard normative sense.[2] How to make sense of claims about reasons is of course highly controversial, but I have my own views of the meaning of such claims.[3] I'll assume that assertions about reasons in the standard normative sense can be intelligible, and I'll join Sterba, as I read him, in using the term "reason" in that sense.

My second preliminary is a matter of reading. Sterba speaks of "altruistic" reasons. Strictly speaking, altruism is concern for the good of others, and Sterba clearly adopts this reading.[4] In a looser sense, though, we might hear altruism as something more like Sidgwickian universalism: taking a person's good as grounding basic reasons regardless of whether that person is oneself or another. (Altruism in this sense wouldn't require full Sidgwickian universalism, weighing the good of a person equally no matter who the person is or what relation the person bears to oneself. One might be somewhat altruistic, but still, at root, somewhat favor oneself, or somewhat favor oneself and one's friends or compatriots.) Sterba makes clear in a note that he is using the term "altruistic" in the strict sense. By "morality as compromise," he tells us, he means a compromise between egoism and altruism, a compromise that weighs in both kinds of reasons. Sidgwickian universalism would qualify as one such compromise, weighing into one's decisions, at base, each other person's good equally with one's own. The other reading, though, wouldn't have been entirely implausible, apart from the note. In a version of the argument that Sterba is not running, morality weighs in both egoistic reasons and universal reasons. Universal reasons heed the good of each person equally, and so this kind of compromise— the one Sterba isn't speaking of—will accord one's own good more weight than the good of another. This would fit the widespread conviction that although we morally owe others consideration, it is morally all right to favor oneself over others to some degree. Sterba's argument doesn't eliminate such a view, but also doesn't require it.[5]

Sterba's rationale might work better for this false reading than for the correct one. Sidgwick thought that the intuitions between which we are pulled are egoistic on the one hand and universal on the other hand. On the one hand, clearly we find reasons of our own good especially clear and salient. On the other hand, clearly we sometimes find the good of another person to ground nonderivative reasons. Is that, however, because the person is not me, or just because she is a being with a good that can be affected? I don't think I ever help anyone on the grounds that it isn't my own good that is at stake—unless out of pride in my selflessness.[6] If I'm not helping the person because of some special relation she has to me—she's my sister, say, or my friend—I help because she is a person who could use the help. That reason applies just as well to my helping myself. If this is right, a Sterba-like argument might more plausibly end up favoring a compromise between egoism and universality.

Such a compromise would have to weigh one's own good more heavily than the good of another, since one's own good gets counted both universalistically, as an instance of the good of some person or other, and egoistically. Such an argument, then, purports to rule out a pure Sidgwickian universalism, just as it rules out pure egoism. Some will find this upshot plausible, but some will think that it shows that this form of argument proves too much. Now, I agree—as Sidgwick himself in effect did—that we have a prima facie conviction that we each have reason to act for our own good, as our own and not just as an instance of someone's good in general. The universalist, though, is convinced that this is an illusion. Any bald claim that it is begs a question, to be sure—but doesn't, too, the claim that the special urgency of the self is no illusion?

Begging the question against a strong prima facie conviction does, though, seem worse than begging it in favor. Shouldn't we let a prima facie conviction stand unless it bumps against one that is stronger? I'm not sure. I worry about other kinds of reasons that may strike us as prima facie plausible; we can ask about these other reasons as well. It may seem prima facie plausible that we have reason to return good for good and evil for evil, and that reasons for revenge don't entirely depend on its advantages for oneself or others. Could I nevertheless reasonably conclude that seeming reasons of retaliation for wrongs aren't genuinely basic, that I don't really have fundamental reason to mete out pain to those who pain me or pain those who are dear to me? I don't know what non-question-begging argument I could give that these seeming reasons are illusory. I don't think that an eye for an eye and a tooth for a tooth is a good fundamental moral principle, but I can't find any inconsistency in supposing that it is. And if it is question-begging to dismiss reasons of retaliation as nonfundamental, I don't find that this precludes me from judging, on due consideration, that reasons of retaliation are indeed illusory, so long as they are not rooted in some good, apart from the sheer putative advantage of getting back at those who harm one. This isn't because I'm not capable of acting to get back at people for no further reason. Maybe I shouldn't confess that I am, but I suspect that if shoved enough, I am entirely capable of acting for such reasons and finding them compelling and basic—even though in a cool hour, I might conclude that such reasons had no fundamental validity.

Sterba does consider purported malevolent reasons.[7] Such reasons, he says, "are ultimately rooted in some conception of what is good for oneself or others," and so "would already have been taken into account" as egoistic or altruistic. Such an answer would presumably apply to revenging wrongs inflicted on oneself or others. My worry here, though, isn't that Sterba's argument eliminates reasons of revenge, but that his argument from question-beggingness might preclude us from rejecting putative reasons of revenge as fundamental.

I would dearly love the question-beggingness argument to work to refute egoism. I don't find pure egoism a plausible stance to take to the world, though I share the pull that I suppose we all feel toward such a view. I also find sheer egoism repugnant—again, I think, a reaction I share with most other people. It even arouses in me quasi-retaliatory feelings: "If you are going to be indifferent to everybody else's good except when it's to your advantage to be nice, t' hell with you! We'll do with you whatever suits us, and if you protest, we'll say it serves you right!" I am disquieted, though, by the worry that if Sterba's argument refutes sheer egoism, it might also refute giving zero fundamental weight to purported reasons of retaliation and revenge.

I myself think that there are many seeming reasons for various aspects of morality, all with prima facie fundamental weight. W. D. Ross lists reasons of gratitude, fidelity to promises, and various others. Rawls in *A Theory of*

Justice claimed positive reciprocity to be a strong grounding reason for justice, and he dismissed general altruism as a ground that not only doesn't strongly motivate us, but, as he concluded, might reasonably not do so.[8] Sidgwick examined grounds for morality not fully grounded in people's good, with astounding thoroughness, and concluded that none stood up to examination. He didn't, though, consider the framework of prima facie duties that Ross proposed, and I don't find it clear that Sidgwick's methods of evaluation vitiate Ross's position. My hunch is that establishing which of the putative reasons we are capable of responding to have fundamental weight in reasonable action will require the kind of long and searching examination that Sidgwick gave to the moral theories of his day.[9] I will, of course, celebrate any quicker way to unravel the Gordian knot of these many kinds of putative reasons, so long as it works. Arguments from non-question-beggingness might accomplish such a thing, if we can figure out when question-beggingness disqualifies a view and when it doesn't. I'm not convinced, though, that we understand when a question-beggingness argument should convince us and when it shouldn't.

In summary, suppose a non-question-beggingness requirement works to refute sheer egoism, compelling us to retain our prima facie judgment that seeming altruistic reasons can be genuine and fundamental. Then, I worry, the same kind of argument will compel us to retain the prima facie judgment we have from time to time that seeming reasons of retaliation can be genuine and fundamental. This might beg the question against a position that I find to have some plausibility: that reasons of revenge, compelling though they will seem when one has been wronged, are not genuinely reasons to do things, reasons with fundamental weight. I don't present this worry as an airtight refutation of an argument from question-beggingness of the kind Sterba gives. There may be something further to be said about why such an argument works to vindicate altruistic fundamental reasons but not to vindicate retaliatory fundamental reasons. I haven't, though, seen my way to discerning how to discriminate the cogency of these two applications of the style of argument that Sterba presents—except that the conclusion is welcome in one case and not in the other.

THE COMPROMISE

Let me pursue the hope, though, that Sterba's kind of argument can be rescued, by telling us how to discriminate among the variety of kinds of seeming reasons that we, his audience, can be drawn to. Perhaps we can be led to understand that some such seeming reasons don't require a non-question-begging argument to be rejected as illusory. Or perhaps we can be shown that suspect fundamental reasons like those of revenge can indeed be refuted by a non-question-begging kind of argument. (As I say, whether they can, and whether fundamental reasons of revenge are illusory, Sterba doesn't purport to establish in this essay.) I'll now explore what kind of conclusion is meant to follow.

Sterba speaks of one form of morality as a compromise between egoism and altruism. Having recognized as fundamental both egoistic and altruistic reasons, we should act, in a given instance, on the one that ranks highest. This requires comparing the rankings of reasons of different kinds. This is meant to leave various possibilities open. We begin, it seems, with two separate rankings, one of egoistic reasons and one of altruistic reasons. We then, if I follow, somehow combine these rankings to give us a ranking that is to guide us in our actions.

I'm not entirely clear how such rankings work. In a way, it might not much matter exactly how a compromise between egoism and strict altruism is supposed to work. For such a compromise, in Sterba's view, need not be the right answer to how to live; his claim for the compromise in this essay is just that it beats out egoism and strict altruism. Still, the way reasons are treated in the compromise may indicate how competing reasons are to weigh more generally, and I'll say a little about Sterba's talk of "ranking" reasons.

It seems natural to conceive of many kinds of reasons as weighing one way or another. If I'm weighing reasons to get sleep against reasons to finish a paper that's overdue, some of my reasons might weigh toward going to bed right away and others toward staying up and working longer. When I conceive of reasons this way, I don't know how to interpret talk of ranking.

The ranking can't be by weight, since I don't always have reason all told to act on my weightiest reason. My weightiest reason to do a thing might be outweighed in toto by a combination of reasons against, each individually less weighty but having greater weight all told.

Perhaps, then, the reasons with rank are combined reasons. I might compare everything to be said for going to bed now with everything to be said for working longer. The rank might then be the total strength of these favoring reasons. Or perhaps the total reason for going to bed now combines considerations pro and con. "Although if I go to bed now, I'll be even later with my paper, but I'll feel miserable if I don't and be less effective with my class tomorrow." Maybe we can understand the rank of such a total reason as how all this balances out. Where there are only two alternatives, the strength of the total reason to do A rather than B will be the negative of the total reason to do B rather than A. I won't, though, scrutinize further whether sense could be made of such a way of treating the reasons, self-interested and other-interested, that weigh for and against one act as opposed to another. The natural way to give heed to both kinds of reasons, I would think, is somehow to weigh reasons of each kind into the decision. If with an act I'd suffer today but benefit tomorrow, and Adam would suffer but Eve would benefit, won't these considerations all weigh into a proper decision of whether to do it?

Perhaps the idea is that reasons of some kinds outrank reasons of other kinds, in that if a higher-ranking kind of reason favors an action, then that's the thing to do, lower-ranking reasons against notwithstanding. Reasons of health perhaps outrank reasons of amusement, in that no amount of amusement justifies going against health. The reply from orthodox decision theory, controversial though it is, strikes me as convincing, at least for reasons like these. A tiny risk to health may be worth taking for enough amusement. Going to the movies carries a small risk of a car accident on the way, but the risk is not always decisive against going out for the evening. Health gets great weight compared to amusement, but not a weight that is incomparable.

The question of how kinds of reasons rank against each other is beyond the scope of this essay. My puzzlement is just how to interpret this talk of ranking so that the highest-ranking reason settles what to do. I have broached the orthodox decision theorist's argument from small risks, which concludes, in the application I am giving it, that differences among reasons are differences of weight, so that putative cases of lexical priority of a consideration are really cases of overwhelming weight. Such arguments are controversial, though, and their legitimate scope isn't something that we could settle quickly, even in light of the state of the debates. Some moral systems do things like prohibit suicide under all circumstances but permit acts that are sure or almost sure to result in one's death. These systems, I agree, may not fit into the rubric of weighing that I am advocating. Still, where reasons that do weigh against each other come in, like the goods that would stem from finishing a paper and from getting enough sleep, I don't see that talk of rank could provide systematic guidance that we would find reasonable.

Sterba tells us that many systematizations of morality might, for all his arguments establish, be supportable by arguments that aren't question-begging. One kind of compromise between egoism and altruism, I would think, weighs in reasons of equal strength equally, whether they are egoistic or altruistic. Doing this requires that the strengths of egoistic and altruistic reasons be comparable. The comparison must be of their strength as reasons for the agent to do one thing or another: How am I to weigh the strength of an intrinsic reason for me to promote your good for its own sake to that of an intrinsic reason for me to promote my own? One solution would be universalistic: Given a choice between a gain to your good and a gain to mine, choose the greater gain. Promote the good of all people without regard for whose good is in question. (Rawls seemed to think that such universalism fails to recognize the separateness of persons. But we can fully recognize the separateness and still think that when circumstances force a choice between the good of two people, we should prefer the good that is the greater of the two. Such a preference will be equivalent to maximizing the total good of all affected, but can fully recognize that they are separate persons.) Perhaps also I could compromise by counting my good as of equal import as the good of ten others—so long as I recognize that others are justified in similarly discounting my good in favor of theirs. I voiced the opinion at the outset that the chief prima facie grounds we respond to aren't egoistic and altruistic, in the strict sense of "altruistic," but egoistic and universalistic. Seeing it this way may force us to conclude that I should favor myself over others to a degree. Otherwise, egoistic reasons are ignored except as a special case of universalistic reasons, no more special than the reasons to promote the good of anyone other than me.

Such an upshot is in some respects utilitarian. Altruistic reasons are reasons to promote the good of others, we might think, and egoistic reasons are reasons to promote one's own good. A compromise is to promote the good of all, though perhaps with some favoritism toward oneself. Sterba seems to reject this, but not on the basis of arguments that go beyond what is in this essay. He labels his project as Kantian, and many Kantians abhor utilitarianism—as Kant himself did, if he understood it. I have never myself understood how Kant could be seen as consistently deriving a systematic position distinct from utilitarianism in this broad sense, and Kant's system (as opposed to his other dicta) can be read as utilitarian. R. M. Hare gives a powerful argument to this effect.[10] Most philosophers other than Hare who call their views Kantian, though, oppose utilitarianism, and Sterba, as I read him, envisages further arguments that will refute utilitarianism.

Back, though, to the possibility of weighing my own good more heavily than the equal good of others. Once we do this, we get the kinds of Prisoner's Dilemmas that may seem to support some kind of contractarianism. It's true that Prisoner's Dilemmas are mitigated if each prisoner gives some weight to the good of the other, but so long as there is any divergence of interest, Prisoner's Dilemmas can arise. In those instances, each, by favoring her own good to a certain degree, acts in a way that jointly produces less good for either than what they could achieve by pursuing the totality of their joint good—or indeed, by pursuing in common any weighted sum of their goods. What follows for rational action is controversial, as we all know. Egoists say that the moral is to pursue enforceable agreements if one can gain by doing so, but to accept that sometimes no such agreement can be obtained. In that case, they lament, one rationally pursues one's own good while suffering grievously from the other's like pursuit of her own good. A like conclusion could be argued by the compromise egoist-universalist. These are the sorts of situations, though, that bring to the fore another class of reasons we are capable of acting on, a kind of seeming reason apart from egoism, altruism, and revenge. I have in mind the sorts of reasons that Rawls stressed in *A Theory of Justice,* reasons of positive reciprocity, returning good for good. Prisoners who can trust each other may indeed be trustworthy, returning cooperation for expected cooperation. The same lesson applies to partial altruists. Whether Sterba wants to bring such reasons into his system remains to be seen when his essay finishes.

Another kind of seeming reason Sterba does discuss in the essay: group favoritism, stemming from loyalty, group pride, and a special fellow feeling. He places this under the heading "Other Immoral Views." He dismisses group favoritism, though, as question-begging in claiming a privileged status for the group. I would agree that most forms of group favoritism that we see in the world do this. Or if they don't quite do this, they attribute special virtues to the group beyond what the evidence supports, drawing moral conclusions favoring a particular group that proponents would find ludicrous were the group not their own. More insidiously, where there is room for doubt as to what the considerations support morally on balance, people embrace the resolution that favors their own group, changing sides when it's their own group's ox that's gored. The logical status of group favoritism, though, I would have thought, is just the same as with egoism. Preference for one's own group can be universalized: It is consistent to maintain that everyone should favor her own group. As with egoism, this has a drawback from the point of view of someone loyal to her own group but concerned with consistency: If I universalize my claim that I should favor my group, then I can't in consistency object if members of other groups do so, too. This is an important consideration, since we want to claim the protections of morality as legitimate demands to make, and in consistency we must regard such demands on the part of others as legitimate if our own are. We aren't taking our own protests seriously, either, if we don't accord what we claim for hypothetical cases. If I license my own group to ride roughshod over other groups when we have the power, I can't in consistency complain when other groups with the power ride roughshod over us, in actuality or in hypothetical cases. Familiarly, group favoritism gives rise to Prisoner's Dilemmas and even wars of attrition. Still, if it is honestly universalized, I don't see that it begs a question. And there indeed is some tendency to universalize it: We are told that it is glorious for a man to die for his country, usually at great cost to another country.

I should stress that in all this, I am asking about considerations that might arguably lie at the root of morality. The considerations that should guide us in daily life will have rationales in terms of such basic reasons, but perhaps indirectly. Group and personal loyalty can be immensely valuable motives when kept in proper bounds. They elicit energy and a passion for goals other than one's personal advantage. The question Sterba is discussing, I take it, is not whether we should be loyal in various ways to our families, towns, or countries, or whether professors should be loyal to their departments, colleagues, students, and universities. We have special responsibilities and reason to act on specific attachments. The question is what the rationale for these loyalties comes down to at root. Is it a universal, basic requirement to favor groups and people one has some kind of particular relationship to, such as marriage and other family relationships, collegiality, responsibility, friendship, and the like? Or do these requirements have a deeper rationale, in a balance of egoism and altruism, say, or in some basis like reciprocity? We are familiar with various forms of indirect utilitarianism such as rule utilitarianism or intuitive morality supported by an indirect application of utilitarian standards. How to specify the relation of deep rationale and the standards that it supports is a vexed and much-debated question, but I don't see how we could reasonably think that such indirect support of mores isn't central to why various strictures of morality, loyalty, integrity, and the like matter. Even those drawn to the thought that rather than betray a friend it would be better to betray humanity defend this preference by picturing how bleak it would be if everyone guided himself fully by the common good. I take it that on this score, Sterba and I are in agreement. A view like this, I take it, lies behind the more specific things that Sterba says in this essay.

NEGATIVE LIBERTY FOR THE POOR

I have been worrying that seeming reasons other than egoistic or altruistic ones might have the same kind of prima facie plausibility as the altruistic reasons that Sterba is concerned to vindicate. To one such other kind of reason Sterba gives ample heed: reasons of negative liberty. On this point, I fully agree with Sterba, except that I think that the arguments he gives should take us further than he appears to go himself.

I argued long ago that an extreme libertarian true to his convictions that liberty triumphs over all other considerations would have to accord anyone a liberty to use anything he wanted as he saw fit. Even being precluded from using the product of the sweat of another's brow without his consent is a restriction on liberty. Rights to liberty justify a special relation of a person to what is her own only once moral property rights have been established by argument, and the arguments that libertarians like Nozick give for property appeal not to liberty but to how miserable things would be without some system of property.[11] I agree that things would be miserable without some system of property rights, but as I once heard a libertarian say, "A moral world is not a pretty world." I myself favor the pretty world, with morality grounded in the good that it can work, but if one scorns such a rationale, one can't defend property as preventing ugly outcomes. A system of property rights can mimic some aspects of negative liberty, giving an individual a range of choices that don't depend on anyone else's judgment of what they need, but at base, a rationale for property rights will be rooted in considerations of positive liberty, not negative. Property can expand one's range of choice. And so we need a system of property that expands choice even for those who wouldn't thrive in a system of pure laissez faire.

Or that's so, given usual justifications of property from John Locke, Robert Nozick, and beyond. Still, I argued, there's another way to defend some sort of a welfare state, with rights of ownership taxed in a scheme of social insurance. Even if liberty does triumph above everything that gives it value, morality will still demand a fair degree of equality among people. If a strong right to use anything one wanted were established, people would rationally bargain for a system of property rights that saw to everyone's needs. I didn't stress, as Sterba does, that the liberties I was arguing from are purely negative liberties, but I did stress that any right of ownership restricts the liberty of others to use the thing owned. In thinking about the kind of system of property rights that best avoids misery and fosters commodious living, we aren't confined to systems of full ownership and untaxed voluntary transfers and exchanges, and I see no reason that a person with a right to use anything would accept such a system in preference to some sort of welfare state. A system of free, untaxed exchange of ownership rights wouldn't hold out best prospects of catering to a person's needs and preferences. Sterba puts forth an argument along these lines with great clarity, and I can only applaud.

Still, Sterba endorses requirements on the poor that, it seems to me, his argument doesn't support. He requires a willingness of the poor to engage in mutually beneficial work if they can. I think that such a requirement can be defended, but it requires an argument of a different kind. He requires of the poor that they repay the aid they have received to meet their basic needs once they can do so consistently with satisfying their basic needs. In effect, the otherwise destitute are to get loans, not the kind of entitlement to income that comes from US Social Security or would come from a negative income tax. I accept—indeed, I insist—that everyone has responsibilities when they are in a position to meet them, but I don't think that considerations of negative liberty, once granted primacy, would by themselves lead to these conclusions. And the responsibilities, I would think, fall irrespective of whether one has at some point been saved by a safety net. That's a matter of whether one's entitlements under a just system have at times exceeded what they would be under pure laissez faire, and I don't see why a baseline of pure laissez faire has any moral significance.

Negative liberty alone, I think we can see from Sterba's arguments, doesn't offer the rich any rights at all to property, let alone rights to property surplus to their basic needs. Indeed, it doesn't offer any rights to property at all, except as common property. To establish such rights, we need to add some other kind of basis for our moral conclusions. I suggested in my paper of long ago how we could get property rights, and do so in a way more or less congenial to considerations that a libertarian might recognize. We can go by way of contractarian thinking. Libertarians will allow contracts that are actual, such as "I'll leave 80 percent of the things you produce alone so long as you leave 80 percent of the things I produce alone. (This might sound like an illegitimate shakedown, but it is illegitimate only if there's a threat of illicit coercion or if it's illicit to try to bargain away someone's property rights in this way. But I am talking here of a stage in the justification of claims where no property rights have yet been established.) The bargaining that might lead noncoercively to an actual social contract, though, would be intractable, and I agree with Rawls and others that we must move to a hypothetical contract, one that would be arrived at under ideal, fair conditions. An argument from negative liberty and the right of contract won't get far toward any sorts of property rights, I am claiming, unless it makes some such move as this.

We still have to account, though, for the seeming plausibility of arguments like Nozick's, in spite of the defect in cogency that Sterba identifies. I am convinced by Sterba and by my own thinking and that of many others that the appeal of Nozick-like arguments can't be explained by their overall cogency. I consequently think that we need to look for a psychological explanation. Alan Fiske, an anthropologist, argues that universally, social cooperation is based on four general schemas: equality, hierarchy, communality, and property exchange.[12] Whether or not this listing is entirely accurate and complete, I think it may well be that all human beings are genetically equipped with powerful wired-in moral schemas for assessing social goings-on. Much moral argument is over which schema to invoke for a particular question concerning terms of social cooperation. Libertarians give primacy to the property-exchange schema, while acknowledging something that Fiske classifies under communality, namely, gift giving. Utilitarians give primacy to communality, fostering the total good of members of the community— though I have been arguing that the property-exchange schema can be pressed in this direction, once we recognize that the schema doesn't tell us who has what property at the outset, so that a justification of a system of property rights must come from outside the property-exchange schema. Still, our tendency is to see de facto property rights as moral property rights and then force them into a schema of full rights to untaxed exchange. As Hillary Rodham told me when she was new to college, "It's my money, and they have no right to tax it away to help poor people."[13] Our problem as philosophers is to know, as we work toward a coherent and plausible view, which of our moral promptings to take as having independent validity, which ones to treat as having derivative validity, and which ones to reject. I have been arguing that no coherent view that anyone would find plausible stems purely from the property-exchange schema, unless from a contractarian argument that proceeds from a default moral state of everything's being commonly at our disposal. On due examination, then, we must conclude that whatever moral validity property has stems from schemas other than one of full, unfettered ownership: a communal schema, or such a schema along with a hypothetical contract schema. But the property-exchange schema is bound to have a powerful grip on us, a grip that resists the mitigation needed to render the schema cogent.

THE IDEAL SOCIAL CONTRACT

What, then, would be in an ideal social contract? Parties will grant particular urgency to meeting their basic needs, I agree. And for people's basic needs to be met, we may well need some sort of system of property—though not the kind that "libertarians" stress, with untaxed exchange of property rights or at least exchange of rights not subject to taxation to maintain the economic level of others. What, though, of the surplus over what is needed to meet basic needs? A lot of this surplus, I agree, will be needed to provide incentives for the production needed to meet basic needs and beyond. Social experiments, grand and small, to do without such incentives have regularly been disastrous. It isn't immediately clear, though, who is entitled to consume what is surplus to basic needs and the wherewithal of economic incentives. We can get an answer, though, by thinking about what bargainers to a social contract would agree on. If the bargaining isn't wasteful, then roughly, ideal bargainers will maximize the expectation of some weighted sum of their utilities—where by a person's "utility," we mean a gauge of what goals the person is pursuing in the bargaining. That is the upshot of standard theories of bargaining. If a person's utility in this sense is her good and the outcome gives equal weight to each individual's utility, then this amounts to utilitarianism. Bargainers choose to maximize their expectation of good, and they do that by maximizing average prospective individual good. John Harsanyi has a theorem that bears heavily on all this, and parts of the argument stem from a theorem that is ubiquitous in the mathematical theory of maximization. John Broome laid out these considerations in his magnificent book *Weighing Goods*, and my Berkeley Tanner Lectures volume *Reconciling Our Aims* tries to take the subject further—with the aid, among other things, of a commentary by Broome.[14]

What, then, of the economic surplus above that is needed to satisfy basic needs? To establish the claim of the rich on the lion's share of the surplus, I have been saying, we would need to establish a moral basis for property rights. And every basis that doesn't collapse appeals to welfare, the range of choices a person has, or something of the sort.[15] The basis for social cooperation and self-restraint that can be morally supported is a moral requirement to play one's part in a fair, mutually beneficial scheme of cooperation. The scheme will assign rights, but for the sake of things worth wanting that the scheme will yield.[16] Almost equivalently, we can base the requirements of social justice on utilitarianism as a compromise between egoism and altruism of the kind that Sterba's argument supports over egoism and altruism. Negative liberty taken as far as anyone would want to go with it converges with utilitarianism in its upshot.[17]

Welfare economists have long studied how this can work, and an illuminating treatment in our own time stems from Hal Varian.[18] Our question is how basic needs should be protected and what the rules should be that eventuate in a distribution of the economic surplus. We can put this as a problem of social insurance. What kind of income insurance is it rational to want universalized, given the constraints of what's possible? A problem with insurance is moral hazard: that the security of being insured reduces the incentives to take care. In the case of income, this moral hazard takes the form of altering incentives to take pains to be productive. With guesses about what form preferences and economic feasibility will take, Varian comes to the conclusion that the system of social insurance it is rational for us to want will give scope for fairly pronounced inequalities of economic outcomes. In light of the special urgency, for each person, of meeting her basic economic needs, I take it that such a scheme of social insurance will guarantee basic needs in any economy sufficiently productive to do this and leave ample surplus. (Extremely expensive medical procedures might be an exception to this, and we have to think whether they should be guaranteed if, prospectively, it would be a rational piece of risk taking for the recipients to pocket the cost of the guarantees and forgo the guarantees. But for anything like ordinary medical expenses, insurance is something it is rational to want if you can't easily pay the expenses out of pocket.) As for the rest of the economic surplus, I don't think there is anything simple to say about what it's prospectively rational to want from an impartial point of view. If Varian is right, it may not be tremendously egalitarian in the outcomes the economic system leads to. Or at least it won't be if, apart from morality, economic level is all it is rational for an individual to be concerned with for herself. Problems of the tendency of economic inequalities to bias politics toward the rich and the rewards of equality in our social dealings with others are considerations that need to be brought into the discussion—but I won't do so in the analysis I give here. Even with these other considerations set aside, a basis that stresses negative liberty won't yield a moral requirement like this: that the rich can keep what they get by minimally taxed exchanges of the economic rewards they can bargain for individually within a framework of property rights, limited only by what is needed to meet everyone's basic needs. I'm not sure whether this gives me a different take from Sterba on the obligation to engage in mutually beneficial work and repay, once one can, aid one has received to cover one's basic needs. Both rich and poor have responsibilities in a just society, and they include responsibilities to work and support the just scheme. What these are, though, I think, depends on characteristics of how a person's good depends on income and what social arrangements are economically feasible.

With any contractarian thinking along such lines, there remain all sorts of problems about how far off the scheme can be from what is ideally fair and still produce moral requirements of voluntary cooperation. (This is Rawls's problem of "partial compliance.") A utilitarian rationale for the same ideals may produce a more straightforward answer to questions of when the poor should refrain from what counts as stealing by the rules of the system. But the literature on indirect forms of utilitarianism shows that rule utilitarianism and the like give rise to similar puzzles. How far off from ideal moral rules can accepted social practices and moral judgments be before one is no longer morally required to abide by the accepted rules of the society? Slavery is a clear case: It is hard to see that there could be a moral duty on the part of slaves to respect the property rights accorded to owners, except for reasons of self-protection. Other cases may not be so easy.

INTERNATIONAL JUSTICE

For the international case, I applaud the 1 percent tax idea, or the idea of a larger surtax on the wealthy. True enough, there are many complexities in establishing justice for the poor in poor countries, where donors don't control the government and probably shouldn't. There may be another severe problem, too: that aid that is large scale in proportion to the recipient economy may distort exchange rates and so reduce opportunities to achieve economic development by selling to the rest of the world. Some economies have an impressive record of going from poverty to moderate plenty without substantial external aid, and the results of external aid programs have often been disappointing. Growth sustained by trade is more reliable than the political kindness of strangers, and a chief goal should be to foster such growth. Still, there are areas where aid clearly can do good, in improving health, ameliorating extreme want, and promoting infrastructure. Education may be particularly important, especially for girls, in leading to the demographic transition that allows society to escape the Malthusian trap. We currently face the dilemma that population growth rates are high where there isn't such a demographic transition but where the dire Malthusian equilibrium of birth and starvation no longer holds. Population growth has stopped in many parts of the world, but it's a mathematical fact that fast-growing populations, if they keep growing at the same rate, soon come to dominate in numbers. Fostering development and a demographic transition requires both commitment and clear analysis. Promoting education isn't just a matter of will, because we don't understand what determines children's and parents' drive for education. We also need to understand what makes for economies that can take advantage of education. A letter to the *Economist* the week I first drafted this paper quotes from Thomas Malthus himself: "The first grand requisite to the growth of prudential habits is the perfect security of property and the next perhaps is the respectability and importance which are given to the lower classes by equal laws and the possession of some influence in framing them. We have been miserably deficient in the instruction of the poor, perhaps the only means of really raising their condition."[19]

As for the worry about farmland, the worry shouldn't be that most farmland will disappear. Scarcity will lead to higher prices for food, and hence higher rent for farmland. The horror is that the higher prices can starve people. Amartya Sen has long argued that the key to famine is lack of economic entitlements.[20] Often, too, there may be perverse incentives concerning farmland, as those who farm it may lack clear enough title to it and protection of that title. An honest capitalism with strong property rights won't by itself accomplish everything that is needed for the poor, but the poor should enjoy the benefits of capitalist entitlements, and not just reap the horrors.

As for providing for future generations, I'm not sure that this requirement can be derived from considerations of negative liberty and reciprocity alone. One way it might is to appeal to the fact that generations overlap; I'll come to that shortly. Absent such overlap, however, the kind of bargaining theory I sketched earlier won't ground a moral requirement to heed the needs of later generations. Take a world where generations don't overlap. Later generations can't do anything about it if previous generations leave them bereft of resources. Whatever negative liberty they might otherwise have to the resources we totally consume, they can't get to the resources before we consume them. Whatever they do, there is not backward causation in time, so there's no way they could exercise such a negative liberty to those resources. They have no threats to use in the bargaining. Could we establish in some other way that the negative liberty of future people is violated if they are left destitute or worse through our consumption? If we could establish from considerations of negative liberty that future people have property rights in the resources of the planet, all might be well for libertarian arguments establishing obligations to them. I have argued, though, that hypothetical contracts aside, considerations of negative liberty by themselves don't yield moral claims to anything beyond a tragic commons. If—as I would insist—we have obligations to future generations and these aren't only a matter of how generations overlap, then the moral bases of these obligations don't lie purely in negative liberty.

With overlapping generations, there may be scope for an argument from negative liberty and hypothetical contract to obligations to distant generations, through a series of overlaps. We depend on the next, overlapping generation to let us benefit from their productive efforts. We may count as entitled to buy these benefits with wealth accumulated over much of adult life, but the requirement that these entitlements be respected is a moral one, and the terms of morality are what we are inquiring into; it is not something we can take as given in our inquiry. If when we are old and unproductive, we claim "our" savings, retirement benefits, and the like, the young could reject our pleas that we benefited them and need their help in turn. "What have you done for us lately?" they can demand. "What will you be doing for us next? Why shouldn't I treat your past benefits to me as water under the bridge?" That wouldn't be fair, but to claim fairness when we are old from younger adults, we need to practice it with respect to the young when we ourselves are middle-aged and productive. They in turn will have like obligations to their children's generation, and we need to deal fairly with the next generation in light of their own obligations to deal fairly with the generation after. Our underinvestment is ground for complaint and perhaps nonreciprocity—though the stability of the political system means that the young aren't good at collectively pursuing their interests. These considerations might allow us a vindication of our obligations to posterity along roughly libertarian lines. However, I have never been able to work out any more specifically how such a vindication might go. I don't, by the way, mean that the younger should give the older, in the course of their overlapping lifetimes, as much as the older should give the younger. Net investment should presumably flow in the direction of the young, as with schooling and the burdens of child raising. (Note that depletion of nonrenewable resources is not the only way we can shortchange the young and later generations. Underinvestment matters, too—a great deal.)

All this exploring is not a basis for morality that Sterba advocates, but the basis that he can force a libertarian to accept on pain of incoherence. As for Sterba's own argument, he regards it as leaving open the question of what a defensible compromise between egoism and altruism would look like, and what other moral considerations need to be brought into the story. If morality requires some degree of altruism toward all whom we can affect, then moral requirements of some degree of altruism toward later generations would emerge obviously enough.

LOOKING BACK

This response to James Sterba's rich, cogent, and innovative essay is mostly a somewhat quick and breezy survey of thinking that others have conducted and that I myself have pursued in my previous work. The work I have touched on spans a number of fields: philosophical theories of morality and justice, including utilitarianism and contract theory, bargaining theory within game theory, welfare economics and development economics, and evolutionarily and anthropologically informed theory of human nature. Touching on so much, I could develop very little of what I said—but for the most part I didn't need to, because many of the points I touched upon have been well developed elsewhere. I am intrigued and somewhat drawn to the innovative basic line of argument that Sterba develops, though I voiced a number of worries. I accepted almost everything in his treatment of where bases of negative liberty would lead in moral theory. And I applaud the things Sterba has to say about the implications of a morally cogent view for public policy and personal morality, though I added some quick commentary of my own.

I'm not sure that all moral philosophers should enter seriously into public policy debates as experts and not just as educated citizens. The skills needed for policy assessment go beyond the skills we cultivate in analytical philosophy. I do think that our special skills are needed in such debates, but they won't be enough. Breaking new ground in public policy requires, along with clear philosophical reasoning, abilities to assimilate and keep track of vast amounts of information about the world. I consider myself an informed reader on problems in the world and in evolutionarily informed psychology, and to have expertise, somewhat dabbling though it is, in aspects of philosophy and economics. My judgment on these bases is that James Sterba has excellent judgment about how his philosophical arguments apply to the problems of the world, and my chief response is agreement.

CHAPTER 7

EGOISM, ALTRUISM, AND OUR COOPERATIVE SOCIAL ORDER

Gerald F. Gaus

"MORALITY AS COMPROMISE"

As James Sterba recognizes in "From Rationality to Equality," humans in society are often confronted by a conflict between self-regarding and other-regarding reasons. We are creatures devoted to our ends and concerns that give us self-regarding reasons, yet we are inherently social creatures and as such recognize other-regarding reasons. Morality, he claims, is a way of commensurating these reasons. In particular, he argues for an "incomplete" conception of morality—"morality as compromise"—according to which (1) both altruistic and egoistic reasons are relevant to choice, and (2) although reason cannot necessarily provide the complete ranking of these two reasons, it can be rationally demonstrated that higher-ranked altruistic reasons outweigh lower-ranked egoistic reasons. Many readers, no doubt, will be most interested in Sterba's striking claim that this "incomplete" conception of morality can be derived from very basic canons of good reasoning. Although I shall briefly address this ambitious thesis, my focus will be on where, if we accept it, it will take us. I wish to ask: If we accept Sterba's conception of morality as an incomplete compromise between egoism and altruism, how might we think about "completing" it—developing a more specific view of how a plausible human morality might "balance" egoism and altruism?

TWO ORDERINGS OF REASONS

Basic to Sterba's argument is that both altruistic and self-interested reasons "are relevant to rational choice." Our question when deciding what to do in some context is which of these two types of reasons should have "priority." Sterba introduces the idea of two orderings or rankings of reasons: an altruistic ordering $\{a_1 \ldots a_n\}$ and a self-interested or egoistic ordering $\{e_1 \ldots e_n\}$ of reasons.[1] Let us suppose that each of these orderings satisfies the standard conditions of being (within each) complete and transitive. The question for a practically rational agent is how one is to combine these two partial orderings into an overall ordering of reasons to act.

The key move in Sterba's analysis is the contrast among three different ways of transforming these two partial (or sub-) orderings ($\{a_1 \ldots a_n\}$, $\{e_1 \ldots e_n\}$) into an overall ordering. Sterba compares three possibilities. First, $\{a_1 \ldots a_n\}$ may strictly dominate $\{e_1 \ldots e_n\}$ such that for any member a_i of $\{a_1 \ldots a_n\}$ and any member e_j of $\{e_1 \ldots e_n\}$, $a_i \succ e_j$ (i.e., a_i is preferred to e_j). Second, the egoistic ordering $\{e_1 \ldots e_n\}$ might strictly dominate $\{a_1 \ldots a_n\}$, such that $e_j \succ a_i$. The third possibility is that in the overall ordering, neither sub-ordering strictly dominates the other, but in the overall ordering, there are some altruistic reasons that are ranked higher than some self-interested, and some self-interested that are ranked higher than some altruistic. Sterba holds that the third option is "rationally required":

> Once the conflict is described in this manner, the third solution can be seen to be the one that is rationally required. This is because the first and second solutions give exclusive priority to one class of relevant reasons over the other, and only a question-begging justification can be given for such an exclusive priority. Only by employing the third solution, and sometimes giving priority to self-interested reasons, and sometimes giving pri-

ority to altruistic reasons, can we avoid a question-begging resolution. . . . Such a compromise would have to respect the rankings of self-interested and altruistic reasons imposed by the egoistic and altruistic perspectives, respectively.

Accordingly, any nonarbitrary compromise among such reasons in seeking not to beg the question against either egoism or altruism would have to give priority to those reasons that rank highest in each category. Failure to give priority to the highest-ranking altruistic or self-interested reasons would, other things being equal, be contrary to reason.

I cannot see any reason to think dominance solutions necessarily, as a matter of logic or basic principles of good reasoning, beg any questions. That we can order the set of considerations $\{a_1 . . . a_n\}$, and that we can order the set $\{e_1 . . . e_n\}$, and that both are relevant to choice in context C does not tell us anything whatsoever about the combined ordering of C-relevant reasons (beyond that it should be consistent).

To be able to show that the canons of reasoning themselves, apart from any substantive considerations, allow us to say something substantive about the features of the combined ordering would certainly be remarkable. Suppose one introduces a principle of set union of the following sort: When combining two complete orderings it must be the case that one ordering cannot dominate the other in the complete ordering. This would yield Sterba's result, but surely it "begs the question" by eliminating all possibility of dominance solutions without considering the substantive case.

However, at least in one interpretation Sterba's core claim is so modest and reasonable that even if we are suspicious of the strong claims about its rational necessity, we should still accept it. When he says that according to an acceptable ordering, "high-ranking self-interested reasons have priority over conflicting low-ranking altruistic reasons, other things being equal, . . . and high-ranking altruistic reasons have priority over conflicting low-ranking self-interested reasons, other things being equal," we might take him as simply saying that in the comprehensive ordering of reasons, at least the very highest-ranked reasons of one ordering must be ranked above the very lowest of the other. Although that does not seem mandated by reason, if one admits that there are both egoistic and altruistic reasons, only an extraordinarily self-indulgent or self-sacrificial view would hold that in absolutely every case one type must trump the other. Instead of a simple ordering, think of the issue in terms of continuous values: Surely, in any plausible system of trade-off rates, there must be some case in which the marginal importance of the self-interested (or altruistic) reason is so low that the value of acting on the other type is greater. I am not entirely confident that Sterba has only this minimalistic interpretation in mind; at some points there is the suggestion of prima facie equal importance.[2] That certainly would be a strong claim. In any event, this raises the core question posed by morality as compromise: In the overall ordering, how important are altruistic reasons, and how important are self-regarding ones?

SELF-INTEREST AND ALTRUISM IN HUMAN SOCIETY

Decision Functions

If principles of reason and rational argumentation do not tell us much about how we must compare self-interested reasons and reasons of altruism, how do human communities come to resolve these issues in their conceptions of morality? Let us continue with Sterba's supposition that we are confronted by two rankings of reasons, altruistic and self-interested. As he points out, the important cases for morality concern conflicts—when altruistic reasons point us one way, and self-interested ones another. What to do? Consider Figure 7.1, which depicts three decision rules as to how to resolve the conflict.

We can map any conflict situation between reasons of self-interest and altruism in this space; thus, in case α, the chooser is faced between acting on strong reasons of altruism and strong reasons of self-interest. Each curve (*e, h, a*) divides the decision space into essentially two parts: Above and to the left of a curve, a person will choose in the case of a conflict to act altruistically; below and to the right, a person will act on self-interested reasons. (If a case falls exactly on a curve, the person will be indifferent.)

FIGURE 7.1

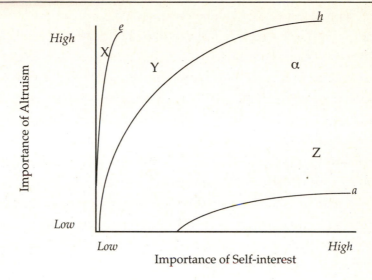

Curve *e* depicts a pretty thoroughgoing egoist; she will act on altruistic reasons only in cases in area X. Only when reasons of self-interest are very low, and altruistic concerns are very high, will she act on altruistic reasons. Curve *h* has a somewhat more altruistically inclined trade-off rate, with altruistic reasons chosen over self-interested ones in all cases in areas X and Y. Finally, curve *a* depicts the trade-off rate of a highly altruistic person, acting on altruistic reasons in areas X, Y, and Z. Consider again case α: Here, a person is faced with a choice between strong reasons of self-interest and strong altruistic reasons; persons *e* and *h* will act on self-interest, whereas agent *a* will act on altruistic reasons. Notice that all three decision rules satisfy Sterba's requirement for a reasonable commensuration: The highest reasons on one dimension are chosen over the lowest on the other.

Following Sterba, we might think of a morality as specifying a decision or commensuration function as in Figure 7.1, demanding when we must act altruistically. Thus, understood moral philosophy is, ultimately, interested in seeking to justify some decision function, or at least some family of functions. But before analyzing the commensuration that is demanded of us, I propose to first consider what functions seem plausible for communities of humans. As Sterba rightly indicates, like most other traits, a tendency to act altruistically varies among us. With no pun intended, let us suppose it to be distributed on a Gaussian curve: There will always be those on the tails who are much more altruistic, or much more egoistic, than morality assumes. Human morality, though, is something directed at the typical or normal moral person. To slightly alter Kant's insight, our morality is directed neither to the saints nor the villains among us, but to a normally good person going about her life. Given this, a morality cannot demand much more altruism than, given her nature and character, our normal moral agent can deliver. As Rawls would say, the "strains of commitment" cannot be overwhelming.[3] A free and equal person cannot endorse a morality that she cannot live up to, or one that she could honor only with great difficulty. So, before we know where we should draw the line, as it were, we must have some idea of the types of lines most humans can live with.

Hamilton's Rule

The most elegant, and in many ways accurate, analysis of the strength of our tendency to act altruistically was advanced by W. D. Hamilton.[4] What is now known as "Hamilton's rule" (Equation 1) essentially specifies a function for the strength of altruism, where r is the coefficient of relatedness between the helper and helped (essentially the probability that the helper shares the helped's genes), b is the benefit to the helped, and c is the cost to the helper. Altruism is favored by evolution when the weighted benefits exceed the costs, as specified in:

$$\text{Equation 1: } rb > c$$

In humans, the value of r is 1 for identical twins, .5 for parent-siblings and between siblings, and (without inbreeding) .25 between grandparents and grandchildren, and between half siblings. It is .125 between first cousins. Hamilton's rule quantifies the extent to which altruism—one organism sacrificing its fitness for another—can determine the behavior of an organism without endangering its genotype.

Hamilton's rule is a powerful (though, as we shall see, not the only or even the most adequate) explanation of a fundamental yet in many ways puzzling aspect of the development of an altruistic species: At least on the face of it, an organism that sacrifices its own fitness for the sake of others should go to extinction. The Social Darwinists were wrong about much, but they appreciated the problem that natural selection poses for altruism (though they were deeply wrong about the solution): That humans are altruistic at all is a puzzle that requires explanation. Take any group divided between altruists and selfish agents, where the altruists have a generalized tendency to help their fellow group members at some fitness cost to themselves, while the selfish individuals do not. Under such conditions the altruists will be good for the group, but in every generation they will constitute a diminishing percentage of the population. Unless we tell a more complicated story, they go extinct.[5]

To see this better, consider the problem posed for even modestly cooperative behavior in Figure 7.2:

FIGURE 7.2

		Column: Cooperate	Column: Defect
Row	Cooperate	3, 3	1, 4
	Defect	4, 1	2, 2

This, of course, is a Prisoner's Dilemma (4 = best, 1 = worst for each). Assume that these payoffs correspond to the fitness of individuals in an evolutionary setting. We can readily see that a society of mildly altruistic people, who cooperate with others, will receive an average payoff of 3. (I call this "mildly" altruistic because both do better at the cooperate-cooperate payoff than the defect-defect outcome.) The problem is that our society of cooperators can always be invaded by a mutant defector: The average payoff will be 3 for the general population, but 4 for the mutant, allowing it to grow. Thus, pure co-operation is not an evolutionarily stable strategy.[6] On the other hand, pure defection is a stable equilibrium: A society of pure defectors has an average fitness of 2; an invading cooperator would have a fitness of 1, and so could not get a foothold in the population.

Hamilton's rule explains one (let us say, a special) case under which altruistic behavior will not go extinct in a species: when it is directed at close kin. And Hamilton's rule explains a good bit of human altruism. There is a very strong tendency of parents to sacrifice for their children, and siblings to sacrifice for each other (in the United States, 86 percent of kidney transplants go to close kin, whereas less than .5 percent come from anonymous strangers).[7] Hamilton's rule also explains large-scale social cooperation among the eusocial insects, such as ants, bees, and wasps, which are haplodiploid.[8] In such insect groups, sisters have an r of .75, thus making altruism, as it were, the normal course of things. But the core problem for the study of humans is that we are an ultra-social species that often relies on each other, but in which genetic relatedness does not account for altruism between strangers. In my view—and I think this would be the view of almost every scholar who has studied the evolution of altruism—Sterba is altogether too sanguine in his assumption that we are a highly altruistic species. He asks: "But is there really this difference in motivational capacity? Do human beings really have a greater capacity for self-interested behavior than for altruistic behavior?" The answer, I believe, is a clear and resounding "yes" ("no" for the eusocial insects). Humans are ultra-social creatures who do indeed help those who are not closely genetically related, but this helping is limited. In the evolution of human beings, there were always two opposed forces: a selection toward self-interested behavior and one toward cooperative, altruistic behavior.

Direct Reciprocity

The development of human ultra-sociality has depended on getting the most, and most socially effective, altruism at the least cost to altruistic individuals. We are typically interacting with those whose *r* approaches 0, not .75. Given this, the study of the development of human altruism is complex and controversial. There is, I think, consensus that no single mechanism explains human altruism toward strangers, though there is great debate about the operative mechanisms (genetic group selection, cultural group selection, direct reciprocity, indirect reciprocity) and their relative importance.[9]

For the last thirty years, those working on the evolution of cooperation, inspired by the pathbreaking work of Robert Axelrod, have put a great deal of weight on the idea of direct reciprocity. As is well known, Axelrod demonstrated that in repeated Prisoner's Dilemmas, the strategy of tit-for-tat (cooperate when you first meet another, and then do to her on the ith play whatever she did to you on the $i-1$ play) allows cooperation to evolve in a large variety of settings.[10] More generally, assortative interactions, in which cooperators tend to cooperate only with other cooperators, is effective in allowing cooperation to evolve.[11] Indeed, this idea of "direct reciprocity"—helping a person if she helps you—is actually a version of Hamilton's rule, as expressed in Equation 2:[12]

Equation 2 (Modified Hamilton Rule for Reciprocity): $eb > c$

In equation 2, *e* is the expectation that the helped will return the favor, which replaces Hamilton's *r*, the degree of genetic relatedness (*b* continues to be benefits to the person helped, while *c* designates the costs to the helper). According to equation 2, Alf will engage in altruistic action φ toward Betty if the benefits of the act to Betty, weighed by *e*, exceed the costs to him. On the face of it, this seems a promising general analysis of how altruistic behavior can evolve in groups that are not closely genetically related.

It seems doubtful, however, that direct reciprocity can be the prime basis for the evolution of cooperation in medium to large groups.[13] And in any event, although much of human altruism has strong features of reciprocity, morality in particular appears to require unrequited altruism.[14] But unrequited altruism is the most perplexing of all forms of altruistic action.

The Evolution of Unrequited Altruism

The core question for the evolution of human pro-social tendencies is: How are we to explain unrequited altruism? As we saw in Figure 7.2, our unconditional cooperators are always at a fitness disadvantage, and can thus always be successfully invaded by defectors. Unrequited altruists (unconditional cooperators) are always at a fitness disadvantage of 1. But now suppose another sort of cooperator enters into the population: a punishing cooperator.[15] A punishing cooperator cooperates, but also punishes defectors. Let us suppose that the punishers inflict a punishment that is sufficient to more than remove the benefits of defection. In this case, the cooperators can drive the defectors from the population, and cooperation can stabilize and resist invasion by defectors. The problem, though, is that a society of our punishing cooperators can be invaded by "easygoing" cooperators who cooperate (and so get all the gains from cooperation) but never inflict punishment. So it now looks as if the cooperating punishers will simply be driven from the population by the easygoing cooperators—and should the easygoing cooperators take over, they can be successfully invaded by the defectors! However, as Figure 7.3 shows, the gap in fitness between the cooperating punishers and the easygoing cooperators is not constant: As the number of defectors in the population decreases because of the altruistic work of the punishers, the cooperating punishers punish less often. But the less they punish, the more their fitness converges with the easygoing cooperators (they suffered a fitness differential only because of the costs of punishment). Indeed, the gap in the fitness between easygoing cooperators and cooperating punishers reduces to zero if defectors are eliminated from the population. Of course, we would not expect this to actually reach zero—mutations, errors in determining defection, and immigration from other groups will result in greater than zero rates of punishing. Nevertheless, under a large range of values of the relevant variables, the discrepancy in relative fitness may be small enough so that punishers remain a high proportion of the population and defection thus declines.[16] However, it is certainly possible that a group may evolve to a "mixed" or polymorphic equilibrium, composed of punishers, easygoing cooperators, and perhaps defectors as well.[17]

FIGURE 7.3

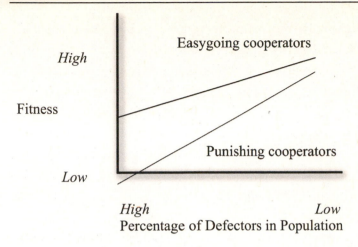

Percentage of Defectors in Population

Punishers are genuinely altruistic in the sense that they engage in activities that do not best maximize their own goals, but are advantageous for the group. Punishing a violator of cooperative norms is a public good; as the easygoing cooperators share in the good, they do better by cooperating but never punishing. And of course an agent solely devoted to her own interest will defect if she is not punished; cooperators will not. Empirical investigation provides support for the importance of altruistic punishment in cooperative interactions. A study conducted by Armin Falk, Ernst Fehr, and Urs Fischbacher shows the importance of punishment for norm violation.[18] In this study, in the first round the subjects played a Prisoner's Dilemma, which was depicted as contributions to a cooperative enterprise with the possibility of free riding. In the second round, subjects were informed of others' choices (identities of participants remained anonymous) and were given the opportunity of punishing others for their play on the previous round. In the low-punishment treatments, subjects could spend up to y units of money to punish the defectors up to a y amount (a payment of y yielded a punishment of y); in the high-punishment treatments, y units spent in punishment could reduce another's gains by up to $2.5y$ and $3y$. Here, one can expend money to reduce others' gains by a multiplier. Falk, Fehr, and Fischbacher found:

- When cooperators punished, they punished only defectors. In both treatments, 60–70 percent of the cooperators punish.
- In the high-punishment treatment, defectors also chose to punish. When they did so, they punished other defectors and cooperators randomly. We might call this "spiteful punishment." Such defectors thus will punish if doing so betters their relative position vis-à-vis the punished.
- Cooperators imposed higher punishments by far.
- In low-punishment treatments (where a unit spent punishing could not reduce the relative payoffs of the punishers and the punished), only cooperators punished.

After reviewing their data, Falk, Fehr, and Fischbacher conclude that "theories of inequality aversion cannot explain why cooperators punish in the low sanction condition. Despite this, 59.6 percent of the cooperators punished the defectors. . . . This suggests that the desire to retaliate, instead of the motive of reducing unfair payoff inequalities, seems to be the driving force of these sanctions."[19]

From First- to Second-Level Altruism

It is natural to think that human altruism must basically consist in the tendency to be altruistic in one's relations with others: For example, playing cooperatively in Prisoner's Dilemmas (Figure 7.2), even when one could get away with defecting. But we have seen that a society of easygoing cooperators would be vulnerable to invasion by ruthless defectors. Students of the evolution of altruism increasingly have come to understand altruism not as a first-order tendency to cooperate, but as a tendency to enforce cooperative social norms. Indeed, what is really crucial is that punishment renders first-order cooperation no longer necessarily an altruistic act; the altruistic component of human society is thus focused on the punishing of those who break the cooperative norms. Note that in this case, unrequited altruism—altruistic punishment—is the core of the account.

Of course, we do not go so far as to say that first-level altruism—the tendency to cooperate rather than defect on cooperative arrangements—is unimportant to human social cooperation. Surely, our altruism is not expressed just in our tendency to punish those who violate social rules, but in our tendency to voluntarily follow these rules ourselves, even when we could escape punishment. There is good reason to think that the basis of human sociality is the altruism of rule-following punishers: those who follow the rules and punish those who do not.[20] The power of such altruism is that it allows us to avoid the cooperative dilemmas expressed in Figure 7.2, while minimizing the costs of altruistic action—the decrease in the fitness of altruists as compared to non-altruistic members of the group.

ALTRUISM AND THE MORAL ORDER

The Asymmetry of Morality

I have been concerned with how we might explain and understand a unique feature of human life: ultra-sociality and altruism under conditions of low genetic relatedness. Now, I still have not said how much altruism morality should require of us. But I believe there is an important, if very general, implication of the analysis. We are right to think of altruism toward strangers as the basis of human ultra-sociality, especially in our complex modern world,[21] but there are compelling reasons to think that such altruism is a precious resource that must be efficiently and effectively employed. It is because altruism is such a precious and relatively scarce resource for humans that morality demands of us a minimum of altruism, and almost always leaves the pursuit of self-interest up to the actor. Elliot Sober and David Sloan Wilson, who conceive of morality in this way, point out, "Commonsense morality seems to set minimum standards concerning how much self-sacrifice is required, but it allows individuals to sacrifice *more* if they wish."[22] If we adopt Sterba's point of view and conceive of morality as simply demanding a nonarbitrary balancing of both reasons, we are left with the puzzle: "Why doesn't morality place a lower bound on how much selfishness we are required to exhibit, but allow people to be more selfish if they wish?"[23] Once one adopts the view of morality as reconciling egoism and altruism, we are immediately confronted with the puzzle of morality's asymmetric attitude: It characteristically demands minimum altruism but allows more but very seldom (in some views, never) demands minimum egoism.

At least in my reading of his essay, Sterba does not fully appreciate this asymmetry. He holds that "a certain amount of self-regard is morally required, and sometimes, if not morally required, at least morally acceptable. Where this is the case, high-ranking self-interested reasons have priority over conflicting low-ranking altruistic reasons, other things being equal." Some moral theories accord an important place for duties to self; many others deny that there are any such duties. In general, they are not the core of moral systems. Apparently Sterba does not think that it is important whether morality requires or merely permits one to act on self-interest, but surely it matters a great deal that it does not merely permit us to act altruistically: It demands. And it is an unusual moral complaint to insist that another just needs to be more egoistic (though it is common enough in self-help books). Indeed, Sterba, too, recognizes that first and foremost morality demands minimum altruism; still, he is so insistent that the crux of morality is to dictate the correct commensuration function that he loses sight that its main concern is to require a minimum of altruism in all acceptable commensurations. The important question is how much altruism we can demand of others; we can leave it to each to look out for her self-interest. Perhaps curve *h* in Figure 7.1 is the most we can hope for in a humanly realistic morality (a eusocial morality would no doubt be in the vicinity of *a*). Perhaps even *h* is too altruistic.

Cooperative Norms and Human Altruism

We cannot commence a realistic social and political philosophy with the supposition that unrequited altruism to strangers comes easily to us, or that we easily see reason to override our self-interest for the good of the anonymous other. Our altruism is expressed in the fact that we are rule-following punishers: We generally comply with cooperative norms, though almost all cooperative norms require punishment to stabilize them. Moral rules that overstrain our altruistic resources will be unstable. Of course, philosophers and priests can preach that much greater altruism is required, but there is good evidence that mere exhortation makes little difference: People act as they think others act.[24] If this is right, the main ways that political orders build on altruism is to ensure that fair and socially beneficial rules are followed by all with a genuinely altruistic concern that everyone plays according to the fair rules.

Do modern welfare states overstretch these resources? Perhaps some do, but it is clearly wrong to say that unrequited altruism is alien to humans: We are most definitely creatures of limited altruism. But we should not forget Rawls's lesson that the core idea of a just society is that it is a truly cooperative social and economic order characterized by reciprocity. Rawls was entirely right that social orders thus understood—as opposed to social orders in which many conceive of a large class of others as mere recipients of unrequited altruism—can be both free and stable. The debate within political philosophy—or, rather, that aspect of it focusing on distributive justice—properly concerns the conditions under which all participants can conceive of their order in this way. The crucial issue is under what conditions all reasonably benefit from the norms and institutions to which they are subject. No doubt, in our very wealthy societies this will involve some sort of social minimum to help ensure (it can never be fully ensured) that no one subjected to the norms and institutions ends up in truly dire straits. Friends of the market believe, overall, that a market order with a modest state framework performs this task the best; those who favor a more robust state take a different view.[25]

I have no intention of joining this debate here. But I must confess that I do not think we make much progress in resolving our deep perplexities by focusing on the sort of problem Sterba presents: a broadly specified case of a rich person with luxuries confronting a poor person with unmet needs. Sterba describes the case in the broadest of brushstrokes: "The poor lack the resources to meet their basic needs to secure a decent life for themselves, even though they have tried all the means available to them that libertarians regard as legitimate for acquiring such resources." I worry about focusing on this sort of case. We need to know a lot more about the background institutions and norms, and the facts of the situation that has given rise to this unacceptable state of affairs. Are the property rules unfair, discriminatory, or exploitative? Is the problem that the poor are not benefiting from an otherwise fair system of cooperation in which they participate? Why—is the educational system a culprit? Is the problem that there is deep lack of trust, and is norm violation so widespread that it greatly retards cooperative projects? Is the problem (perhaps with recent immigrants) that they have yet to be integrated into the cooperative enterprise, say, because of residency restrictions, language barriers, or restraints on entering professions and trades? Is part of the problem that draconian and oppressive drug laws have decimated the employment prospects of much of the male population and neighborhoods of a large group of citizens, as in the United States today? At the outset of his essay, Sterba aspires to philosophers being taken more seriously in political decision making. Until they are willing and competent to deal with this broad range of normative, political, sociological, and economic questions, it may be better for them to entertain more modest aspirations.

The Limits of Morality as Compromise

This brings me to a worry about Sterba's notion of "morality as compromise." To be sure, as I have argued, it points to a deep insight. Humans are ultra-social creatures who cooperate in large groups not characterized by genetic relatedness. Given this most fundamental of facts, it is enlightening indeed to see morality as a way in which the self-regard of such agents is channeled into cooperative action with an efficient use of altruism. However, we should not really think that morality is quite so simple as simply balancing egoism and altruism. Many of the deepest conflicts are within altruism. Consider Sterba's case of some who have as yet unmet basic needs advancing claims on those who are in the position to pursue luxuries, such as an excellent education for their children and an attractive home for their family. It is not just "selfishness" but human altruism that leads us to work for, and claim our right to keep, luxuries for our family and friends even in the face of the unmet needs of strangers. One spends sleepless nights worrying about one's children's welfare, and one undertakes a variety of onerous tasks with the aim of providing the resources that will allow them to achieve a good and interesting life. We must resist the temptation to think that all altruism is toward strangers, and all preference for our family is simply a form of selfishness. As Hamilton showed us, our altruistic tendencies vary with respect to those with whom we are interacting. We have some capacity for unrequited altruism toward strangers; more capacity for altruism toward those who have engaged in reciprocal relations with us; and much greater altruism toward close kin. We must be careful not to overtax the first of these by deeming it alone to be "truly altruistic." The main function of demanding unrequited altruism toward strangers is to ensure that all conform to the basic moral rules of cooperative social life. A social and political morality that too readily demands that we act altruistically toward strangers rather than act altruistically toward those whom we love is not, in my view, genuinely human.

CHAPTER 8

WHY LIBERTARIANISM DOES NOT LEAD TO WELFARE AND EQUALITY

Tibor R. Machan

James Sterba and other champions of Franklin D. Roosevelt's so-called "Second Bill of Rights" would maintain that the United States, and indeed any constitutional government, should guarantee the basic rights of everyone to "receive the goods and resources necessary for preserving" ourselves.[1] But beings have no such rights because to respect and protect these, others would lack the fundamental rights to their lives, liberty, and property. And the US Constitution thus far seems to have secured these rights with some measure of vigilance, although by no means adequately—which is why defending them requires "eternal vigilance." That, indeed, seems to have secured the unique fame of the United States of America, guided, largely, by tenets that critics consider fundamentally flawed. Such critics claim that various political outlooks would have to endorse these "rights." Thus, Sterba even contends that welfare rights follow from the essentially libertarian conception of rights found in the US Constitution itself.

Sterba summarizes his argument as follows:

The problem, as I see it, is that if we give Mary [her negative] liberty, it may well be at the cost of restricting George from doing the only thing he can do to meet his basic needs. In rich/poor conflict situations, as I see them, someone's liberty is going to be restricted. In this situation, either Mary's liberty to use some of the surplus she has produced (surplus here just means anything beyond what is required for meeting one's basic needs) is going to be restricted or George's liberty not to be interfered with in acquiring in the only way possible for him the goods he requires for meeting his basic needs is going to be restricted. Now if George could work for Mary, or anyone else, to earn those goods he needs, or if Mary, or someone else, would just generously give them to him, those alternatives would be preferable. But I am imagining a situation where such alternatives are unavailable, and for that situation I am asking whether Mary's liberty to use her surplus for meeting her luxury needs should be enforceable over George's liberty not to be interfered with in acquiring those resources (from Mary's surplus) that he requires for meeting his basic needs. My answer is that ought implies can favors enforcing George's liberty over Mary's. As I see it, the liberty that Mary would lose is far less significant than the liberty that George would otherwise lose.[2]

Immediately, Sterba reveals his nonlibertarian thinking about rights or liberty—they are, as he sees them, what "we give" people. This is not how individual human rights must be grounded. Instead, they're derived from one's human nature.

Next, Sterba uses neologism when he states that the liberty of the poor as they embark upon "acquiring in the only way possible for [them to obtain] the goods [they] require for meeting [their] basic needs" is "not to be interfered with." For Sterba, one's holding on to and protecting one's private property, either personally or by way of law enforcement, amounts to "restricting the liberty" of whoever might want to forcibly take it from one! There is, however, no right to a liberty to deprive another of his or her holdings. That is like claiming that when a would-be murderer is stopped from murdering, it is his or her liberty to take the life of the victim that's being restricted. Repelling thieves or murderers doesn't restrict their liberty—it protects their would-be victim's right to liberty, a right murderers or thieves lack when they attack another. Only if the would-be victim's life is deemed to belong to the would-be murderer—only if the victim is a justly held slave—would this hold up.

Then Sterba lacks any criteria by which to evaluate whether it is more significant that Mary versus George is interfered with in exercising the right to liberty. Is there some standard of significance that's available to tell which interference is just?

The central point of a theory of rights and its expression in a legal system is to identify what actions are justified and what actions aren't. If Mary's actions using her great wealth are justified because she has the right to private property vis-à-vis this wealth, then George's actions aren't—they are cases of theft, regardless of how desperate George happens to be. Such desperation may justify disregarding Mary's rights on very rare occasions—when peace is not possible, in lifeboat-type situations—but they do not warrant undermining a polity of individual (private property) rights. So no one may rob Bill Gates of his great wealth. He, instead, has the right to choose how it will be used. Consider, as a strong hint, that when other people do not kill, maim, kidnap, or rob someone, it isn't required for an individual to thank them for this. No gratitude is due to those who restrain themselves and act respectfully toward others' rights. In contrast, if we badly need help and others come to our aid, it is natural, routine, and right to thank them for this. Acts of generosity, charity, kindness, support, and compassion are not due us as is respect for our rights. We aren't entitled to such acts. When others perform them we are naturally appreciative instead of taking it all for granted, as we do with others' respect of our basic rights.

This may not be a universal datum, of course, and in some special communities there could be a practice different from what it suggests. Yet it seems that the way most people deal with the matter is at least indicative about basic human relationships.

Also, how could any kind of unchosen enforceable obligation arise from someone's having even the most desperate need for what another could provide, not if the other came by what he or she has without coercing another? It is a non sequitur to move from "A desperately needs B's wealth" to

"B may be coerced to provide his or her life/work to A." A, and no one else, has the right to A's life and works, and so with all human beings.

In a state of (wild) nature this may be overlooked, but the point of civilized society, with a legal order, is to forbid all coercion among people. If A has something B deems as extra but it is A's without the taint of having used another against his or her will—another who has an unalienable right to his life/liberty/property (the right being unalienable, not the goods obtained, which can be sold or given away at the owner's discretion)—then B needs to gain it by voluntary exchange. Otherwise B would own (part of) A. (When one of the Communist rulers of East Germany was asked why they shoot people who try to escape over the Berlin Wall, his answer was that they are thieves. What are they stealing? They are stealing labor, which belongs to the state [i.e., the whole society].)

STERBA'S ANTI-LIBERTARIAN POSITION

Sterba wishes to show that if libertarianism is correct and we do have the familiar basic rights to life, liberty, and property, then we all also have welfare rights, such as to health care, education, or basic support from others. I argue, in contrast, that if (and because) libertarianism is correct—that is, each of us is a sovereign individual and not a subject (of the will of others)—and because the rights to welfare and equal opportunity require the violation of fundamental libertarian rights, no one has welfare rights.

Arguably, the reason some people, including Sterba, believe otherwise is that they focus on rare instances in which some citizens could find themselves in circumstances that would require disregarding rights altogether, and their desperate aggressive—rights-violating—actions could suggest that they are entitled or have the moral authority to take such actions. It would be, Sterba argues, unreasonable to expect or demand that the desperately poor ought not take some of the resources of the very wealthy. It would violate "ought implies can," Sterba maintains. This would be in situations that cannot be characterized to be "where peace is possible," and every major libertarian thinker from John Locke to the present has treated these kinds of cases.[3]

So Sterba sets out to show that libertarians are philosophically unable to escape the alleged welfare statist implication of their commitment to negative liberty. Despite their belief that they are only supporting the enforceable right of every person not to be coerced by other persons, libertarians must accept, by the logic of their own position, that individuals also possess basic enforceable rights to the provision of various services and goods from others (such as, for example, another's "extra" work time or kidney or good eye).

He holds, then, that basic negative rights imply basic positive rights. Sure, in the middle of a hurricane or earthquake, people may act from panic or even instinct rather than based on moral principles. Yes, but that is not Sterba's point. Remarkably, he thinks such cases imply the political system of the welfare state.

NEGATIVE RIGHTS AND WELFARE "RIGHTS"

To libertarians, being free or at liberty means that we all, individually, have the right not to be constrained against our consent within our realm of authority—our belongings and ourselves. Sterba states that for such libertarians, "Liberty is being unconstrained by persons from doing what one has a right to do." Sterba adds, somewhat misleadingly, that for libertarians "a right to life [is] a right not to be killed unjustly and a right to property [is] a right to acquire goods and resources either by initial acquisition or voluntary agreement." Sterba does realize that these rights do not entitle one to receive from others the goods and resources necessary for preserving one's life—such goods and resources are what one is supposed to produce in one's life or acquire via voluntary exchange (or in some other peaceful way).

For libertarians, political justice—not the justice of Plato, which is best designated in our time as "perfect virtue"—presupposes individual rights. One cannot, then, explain rights in terms of justice but must explain justice in terms of rights.

For libertarians, any basic right to receive the goods and resources necessary for preserving one's life from nonconsenting others conflicts with the right to one's life, liberty, and property—the rights not to be killed, kidnapped, assaulted, or robbed. The latter are rights held by all individual human beings. To have and, normally, legally protect and maintain—that is, enforce—the former positive right would often require the violation of the latter. For example, A's right to keep and hold the food she has grown or purchased—even if she has, in Sterba's terms, a surplus thereof—is incompatible with B's right to take this same food from A. Both these rights could not be fundamental in an integrated legal system.

The situation of one having rights to welfare, and so on, and others having rights to life, liberty, and property is thus theoretically and practically intolerable. The point of a system of rights is the securing of mutually peaceful and consistent moral conduct on the part of human beings. As Ayn Rand observed, "'Rights' are . . . the link between the moral code of a man and the legal code of a society, between ethics and politics. Individual rights are the means of subordinating society to moral law."[4] Or, to use the terminology of Douglas Rasmussen and Douglas Den Uyl, rights are meta-norms that provide the proper framework within which members of society can engage in morally significant conduct.[5] Positive rights, if enforced, thwart such morally significant conduct—for example, generosity, compassion, charity, helpfulness, and so forth.[6]

In this respect, all rights theorists agree: Basic rights in a legal system serve to secure a moral order in society. But those advocating negative rights hold that this order is best secured when we provide people with reliable, ongoing, flexible but stable borders wherein they can choose their own conduct. And property rights are the concrete implementation of this purpose.

Those, however, who advocate positive rights see human beings as somehow naturally in a collective situation, as members of a natural team, owing each member support for some common purpose, even if it reduces the freedom of choice and prospect of success for some individuals.

To bolster his attempt to derive positive rights from (libertarian) negative rights, Sterba asks us—in another discussion of his views—to consider what he calls "a typical conflict situation between the rich and the poor." He says that in this conflict situation, "the rich, of course, have more than enough resources to satisfy their basic needs. By contrast, the poor lack the resources to meet their most basic needs . . . even though they have tried all the means available to them that libertarians regard as legitimate for acquiring such resources."[7]

The objective of a theory of rights would, of course, be defeated if rights were typically in conflict. Some bureaucratic group would have to keep applying its moral intuitions on the innumerable—typical—occasions when rights claims conflicted. A constitution is suited to the kind of beings—namely, moral agents—that human beings are if it helps to remove at least the largest proportion of such decisions from the realm of arbitrary (intuitive) choice and avails a society of men and women of objective guidelines that are reasonably integrated, not in relentless discord, and thus not in need of routine, typical, discretionary decisions by political authorities such as bureaucrats and even judges.

However, most critics of libertarianism assume some doctrine of basic unmet needs that they invoke to show that whenever some are not satisfied while others have "resources" that are not needed by them, the former have just claims against the latter. (The language of resources, of course, loads the argument in the critic's favor, because it suggests that the bulk of these goods simply comes into being and happens to be in the possession of some people, quite without rhyme or reason, arbitrarily.)

This doctrine is full of difficulties—for example, it lacks any foundation for why the needs of some persons must be claims upon the lives of others. Does this include body parts, for example, and if not, why not? And why are there such needs, anyway? To what end are they needs, and whose ends are these and why is the person or persons whose needs they are held responsible for not satisfying or supplying the needs? (Needs, as such, lack any decisive force in moral argument without the prior justification of the purposes or goals their satisfaction serves to fulfill. A thief has a basic need of skills and powers that are clearly not justified if theft is morally unjustified. If, however, the justification of basic needs, such as food and other resources, presupposes the value of human life, and if the value of human life justifies, as I would argue, the principle of the natural right to life, liberty, and property, then the fulfillment of basic needs for food may not involve the violation of these rights. Nevertheless, some ways of attaining such needs could—including forced redistribution of wealth.)

LIBERTARIANISM VERSUS "OUGHT" IMPLIES "CAN"

I will set these concerns aside for now and attend, instead, to the central criticism Sterba offers of libertarianism. He claims that without guaranteeing welfare and equal opportunity rights, libertarianism violates the most basic tenets of any morality, namely, that "ought" implies "can."

The thrust of "ought" implies "can" is that one ought to do that which one is free to do; that is, one is morally responsible for only those acts that one had the power either to choose to engage in or to choose not to engage in. This is not so different from the commonsense legal precept that if one is not sound of mind and uncoerced, one is not criminally culpable. Only free agents, capable of choosing between right and wrong, are open to moral evaluation. This, indeed, is the reason that many so-called moral theories fail to be anything more than value theories. They omit from consideration the issue of self-determination. If hard or soft determinism is true, morality is impossible, although values need not disappear.

If Sterba were correct about libertarianism typically contradicting "ought" implies "can," his argument would be decisive. (I know of few arguments against this principle, and they are not convincing.[8]) It is because Karl Marx's and Herbert Spencer's systems typically, normally, and indeed in every case violate this principle that they are not bona fide moral systems. And quite a few others may be open to a similar charge, despite the efforts by some philosophers to smuggle in a kind of moral theory while also embracing determinism, that is, denying that "ought" implies "can."

I am not, of course, certain "beyond a shadow of doubt" that libertarianism is not (conceivably, logically, possibly) flawed in the way Sterba claims. It would be dogmatic to hold a priori that it might not be. No system is so well established that one who agrees with it should regard it impossible that it could be flawed—one would need omniscience to possess such certainty. Political theories can be expected to be proven true only beyond reasonable doubt, and it is reasonable doubt that I find difficult to justify, concerning the merits of libertarianism. For the time being, I will concentrate on what could be wrong about Sterba's suggestion. I will do this by considering the cases he offers that he considers indicative of the problems he identifies in libertarianism. Before I turn to this, however, I wish to rebut a point Sterba has pressed against the position I defend. He has contended that I actually grant his views as a matter of theory, not, however, in practice. I do not, however, see such a dichotomy, especially in matters of political theory.

Sterba claims that I accept the "theoretical thrust" of his "argument that a libertarian ideal of liberty leads to a right to welfare."[9] This is wrong. What I have actually argued for, in this connection, quite independently of anything Sterba himself has said on the subject, is that there are rare cases when some innocent person who is in dire straits, for example, ought to disregard individual rights to property—from which it follows that such a person ought, on rare occasions, to take from another what he or she needs. Even this is confined to cases where no other alternative—say, offering something in trade—serves to fill his need. Along with other natural-rights libertarians, I have argued that when conditions make the respect and protection of rights impossible, morality can require one to disregard—but not to violate—rights. The point is that rights are not ethical primaries. They are derivative from other moral principles. If, as I have argued, a classical egoist or eudaimonist ethic is sound and it gives rise, in community life, to individual rights to life, liberty, and property, and if, in community life, peace is impossible, then emergency social ethics come into play.

This idea is not novel. John Stuart Mill, for example, argued that a person's liberty may be disregarded on rare occasions, as when he or she is about to step, unknowingly, on a collapsing bridge. Common sense also attests to this—it may be proper to restrain someone who is hysterical so as to prevent his harming himself or doing other wild things, in extraordinary circumstances. It may be proper, even, to slap the person so as to help in his recovery of mental focus. But none of this is carte blanche for rights-violating conduct—or for so-called welfare rights. As the saying goes, hard cases make bad law. A society would not be just for incorporating the ethics of emergency into its legal system.

It is true enough that if the world were such that the respect and protection of individual rights engendered general unhappiness, including
poverty, then libertarianism would be kaput. But that is akin to the saying that if pigs had wings, they could fly. It does not say that pigs can fly
or that libertarianism is wrong.

Furthermore, if, conceivably, libertarianism is wrong, it does not follow
that the welfare state would be right. The right to welfare is, in any case, a
right to involuntary servitude from other persons. Even if people are in
dire straits, let us say even in deadly straits, it does not follow that they acquire rights to the lives and labors of other persons, even if those are rich
lives and labors, involving what Sterba likes to call "surplus wealth." (As
noted already, one cannot simply borrow a concept from Marx and leave
off the rest of the Marxian edifice. Surplus wealth makes sense in the context of the rest of Marxian economics, with the theory of exploitation,
alienation, and so on all attached. Do we treat one's second eye as a surplus, or one's second kidney or other body part or organ? No.)

It seems to me that the welfare state—indeed, the claim that people
have a legally enforceable right to welfare that is to be legally protected
(that is, officially coerced provisions from others, ones who do not choose
to offer them)—needs a defense that does not piggyback on the theories
of socialism, feminism, libertarianism, or some other position in political
theory. This effort to derive welfare statism from other systems is, as far as
I can discern, a nonstarter.

None of this is to say, however, that a concern with how unfortunate
but decent people fare in a free society is misguided. It is vital that both
the rights of individuals to make their own significant choices in life and
their prospects for prosperity and happiness be addressed in any detailed
political treatise. Libertarianism rests on a conception of human nature
that suggests that people who are not coerced to "help" others will be generous, kind, charitable, compassionate, and so forth when the need for
these impulses arises. It also understands the right to private property as a
liberty right, meaning the right to peacefully acquire, hold, and trade valued things. What this right secures for them is a sphere of personal authority, to choose to do as they deem fit without having to ask for permission

from others, including governments. On those rare occasions that in a bona fide free society someone's right to private property stands in the way of another's liberty to pursue a meaningful life, the proper policy is to seek out peaceful ways to obtain assistance and not to violate another's rights. (Consider that if someone has a "surplus" kidney or "eye," no one else has a right to it, but in a rare situation it may be donated to another who is in dire need of it.)

WHAT IS OR IS NOT TYPICAL

Sterba offers his strongest argument when he observes that "ought" implies "can" is violated "when the rich prevent the poor from taking what they require to satisfy their basic needs, though they have tried all the means available to them that libertarians regard as legitimate for acquiring such resources." Is Sterba right that such cases would be typical in a fully free, libertarian society? Would the rich and poor, even admitting for the moment that there is some simple division of people into such economic groups, be at each other's throats all the time in a free country? Would the rich, who are often the producers and entrepreneurs in a free society and routinely create employment, prevent the poor from satisfying their basic needs? Even with homeless people, it is clear that many find help without having to resort to theft, mostly by seeking it from shelters the well-off have established. Clearly, in a system of justice that legally protects and preserves property rights, there can be cases where a rich person would personally (or by calling the police) prevent some poor person from taking what does not belong to that poor person but belongs, rather, to the rich one—for example, a chicken that the poor person might use to feed herself. Since, subsequent to such prevention, the poor person might starve or at least become seriously ill, Sterba asks the rhetorical question, "Have the rich, then, in contributing to this result, killed the poor, or simply let them die; and if they have killed the poor, have they done so unjustly?" His answer is that they have.

Sterba holds that a system that accords with the libertarian's idea that the rich person's preventive action is a just one "imposes an unreasonable sacrifice upon" the poor, one "that we could not blame them for trying to evade."[10] Not permitting the poor to act to satisfy their basic needs is to undermine the precept that "ought" implies "can," because, as Sterba claims, that precept implies, for the poor, that they ought to satisfy their basic needs by taking from the rich; otherwise they cannot act with dignity, as persons capable of significant choices in their lives, something that libertarianism assumes about us all or at least does so for the most part. They must, therefore, have the option or liberty—a welfare right—to take from the rich if they are to have a genuine choice about what they ought to do.

In fact, as I have already suggested, such cases are atypical in genuinely free—and thus also prosperous—societies populated by individuals assumed to be what libertarians assume about people, namely, that they are, on average, industrious and diligent, as well as generous, kind, and willing to help those in dire straits, in emergencies. And this is pretty much confirmed by the historical fact that it is the countries in the world that are more rather than less libertarian or capitalist that (1) achieve prosperity, (2) exhibit private generosity, and (3) reduce the number of those in dire straits. Yes, there is never any guarantee that such societies will achieve all these conditions, but neither is there any such guarantee with welfare states, which tend, on average, to be poorer and to have greater unemployment and less private charity than do the more rather than less libertarian ones in history.

LIBERTARIANISM VERSUS WELFARE STATISM

When people defend their property, what are they doing? They are responding to the acts of someone who would take something from them unjustly, something to which they and not others have a right. As such, these acts of prevention are preserving libertarian justice. They are making it possible for men and women in society to retain their own sphere of jurisdiction intact, to protect and preserve their own "moral space." Those who mount the attack, in turn, refuse to act in such a way that what they do does not encroach upon the moral space of their victims.

The point that cuts against the above scenario is that on some occasions, there can be people who, with no responsibility for their situation, cannot survive without disregarding the rights of others and taking from them what they need. This is indeed possible. But is it typical?

The argument that starts with this assumption about a society is already not comparable to libertarianism. That system concludes that "peace is possible," and so individual rights, which free men and women from those who would thwart their efforts at flourishing, are the best legal foundations for a good society. The underlying notion of human nature in such a theory rejects the description of the world implicit in Sterba's picture, whereby people are typically in conflict, so that some have and others must take from them in order to survive, with no other alternative available to them. The libertarian, in short, abates the worries of those rights theorists who would attempt to guarantee rights to service from others by having confidence in the willingness and general circumstances of virtually all persons to make headway in life. Once they are free of autocratic rule and tyranny, the rest will take care of itself as well as can be expected in an uncertain world and among beings who are capable of both good and evil.

The libertarian understands that private property rights are morally justified precisely as the concrete requirement for delineating the sphere of jurisdiction of each person's moral authority, where her own judgment is decisive. Once this basis for the right to property is recognized, and the argument is seen to presuppose a metaphysically hospitable universe where normally people need not suffer innocent misery and deprivation—so that such a condition is usually the result of (1) negligence or (2) the violation of Lockean rights (which has made self-development and commerce impossible)—the occasional departures from this typical circumstance of people will have to be seen as an emergency.

Normally, then, persons cannot be said to "lack the opportunities and resources to satisfy their own basic needs." Even if we grant that some poor persons could offer nothing to anyone that would merit adequate returns that would enable them to carry on with their lives and perhaps even flourish, there is still the other possibility to most actual, known hard cases, namely, seeking help. Yes, this is a recourse that libertarians consider legitimate, although most advocates of welfare rights forget about it. I am not speaking of the cases we know, namely, people who drop out of school, get an unskilled job, marry and have kids, only to find that their personal choice of inadequate preparation for life leaves them destitute. "Ought" implies "can" must not be treated ahistorically—some people's lack of current options is a function of their failure to have exercised previous options prudently and wisely. We are speaking here of the "truly needy," to use a shopworn but still useful phrase—those who have never been able to help themselves and are not now helpless from their own neglect. Are such people being treated unjustly, rather than uncharitably, ungenerously, indecently, or in some other respect immorally, when the rich who know about their plight prevent their efforts to take from them what they truly need if they refuse to seek help peacefully?

Contrary to what Sterba suggests, there is much that persons can and should do in those plausible, nonemergency situations that can be considered typical, apart from attempting to encroach upon, abridge, or violate the private property rights of the rich. The destitute should appeal for support, help, or assistance from all those rich who seem to have an inordinate amount of wealth that they allegedly do not need. Consider that when one's car breaks down on a remote roadway, it would be unreasonable to expect one not to seek some way of escaping one's problem. Clearly, one ought to at least obtain the use of a phone. Should one break into the home of a perfect stranger living nearby? Or ought one to ask to use the phone of such a person as a favor? "Ought" implies "can" is surely fully satisfied here—actual practice makes this quite evident. When someone is suffering from misfortune and there are plenty of others who are not, and the poor person has no other avenue for obtaining help than to obtain it from others, it would not be unreasonable to ask the poor to seek such help as might surely be forthcoming. We cannot assume here that the rich are all callous—supporting and gaining advantage from the institution of private property by no means implies that one lacks the virtue of generosity. The rich are no more immune from virtue than the poor are from vice—at least there is no reason to assume any such discriminatory outlook.

The poor typically have options other than to violate the rights of the rich. "Ought" implies "can" can be fully satisfied by the moral imperative that the poor ought to seek help, not to loot. There is, then, no injustice in the rich preventing the poor from seeking such loot by trying to violate the right to private property. "Ought" implies "can" is fully satisfied if the poor can take the kind of actions that could gain them the satisfaction of their basic needs, and the action in question could well be asking for help.

All along here I have been talking about the helplessly poor, those who through no neglect of their own—nor again through any rights violation of others who ought to be prosecuted and made to compensate for their criminal acts—are destitute. I am, in short, taking the hard cases seriously, where violation of "ought" implies "can" would appear to be most likely.

What I am not accepting, however, is that such cases are typical. I would consider them extremely rare in free societies. And even rarer would be those cases in which all avenues regarded as legitimate from the libertarian point of view have been exhausted, including appealing for help. We must remember that the bulk of poverty in the world is not the result of natural disaster or disease. Rather, it is political oppression, whereby people throughout many of the world's countries are legally not permitted to look out for themselves in production and trade. The famines in Africa and India, the poverty in the same countries and in Central and Latin America, as well as in China, Russia, Poland, Romania, and so forth, are not the result of lack of charity but of oppression, the kind that those who have the protection of the US Constitution, which does not guarantee welfare rights, are not experiencing. Critics of the document fail to realize that the first requirement of men and women to ameliorate their hardship is to be free of other people's oppression, not to be free to take from other people what they own.

THE JUST SELF-PROTECTION OF THE RICH

For the reasons discussed above, there is no injustice in the rich preventing the poor from violating their right to private property, nor any justice in the poor conducting themselves in a way that implies such encroachment.

"Ought" implies "can" is fully satisfied if the poor can typically take the kinds of action that could gain them the satisfaction of their basic needs, and this action could well be that of asking for help.

Of course, there would be immorality if the rich failed to help when this is clearly no sacrifice for them. However, even their refusal cannot be judged categorically immoral. Charity or generosity is not a categorical imperative, even for the rich. There are more basic moral principles that might require the rich to refuse to be charitable—for example, if they have embarked upon the protection of their freedom or of the just society in which they live by the use of most of their "extra" wealth. And certainly courage can be more important than charity, generosity, or compassion. But a discussion of the ranking of moral virtues would take us far along. Suffice it to note that one reason many critics of libertarianism find their own cases persuasive is that they think the libertarian can subscribe to only political principles or values. But this is wrong.

I wish to reiterate here that there can be emergency cases in which no alternative to disregarding the rights of others is available, but these are extremely rare, not at all the sort invoked by critics such as Sterba. I have in mind that typical "desert island" case where instantaneous action, with only one violent alternative, faces persons—the sort we know from the law books, in which the issue is one of virtually immediate life and death. These are not cases, to repeat the phrase quoted from Locke by H. L. A. Hart, "where peace is possible."[11] They are discussed in the libertarian literature, and considerable progress has been made in integrating them with the concerns of law and politics. Suffice it to note here that because we are discussing law and politics, which are general systematic approaches to how we normally ought to live with each other in human communities, these emergency situations do not aid us except as limiting cases: "Hard cases make bad law." And, not surprisingly, many famous court cases illustrate just this point as they confront these kinds of cases now and then after they have come to light within the framework of civilized society but do so in an exceptional fashion—for instance, by finding defendants guilty of murder but immediately pardoning them!

SUMMARY RESPONSE:
PROPERTY RIGHTS AND THE VERY BADLY OFF

So, then, is it reasonable to always demand respect for property rights? This is the question raised by some critics of the idea that human beings have the unalienable right to their lives, liberty, and property that may never be subject to violation with impunity within the legal system of a free society. Some claim that it is unreasonable to demand this of those in dire straits, the extremely poor, who would manage to survive and flourish only by violating these rights of the well-off. Thus, they argue, the welfare state—in which laws are passed that permit taxing the well-to-do so as to provide for those in dire straits—is just.

Of course, most of the welfare obtained via taxation doesn't serve to benefit people in dire straits, but rather owners, employees, customers, and trading partners of sizable business firms that seek support (e.g., bailouts) during economic downturns. The welfare state tends to support those weary of competition from foreign industry and farmers, not unwed mothers who cannot find work by which to support their children. But some of the recipients of welfare are in dire straits, through no evident fault of their own. And, so the argument goes, it would be unreasonable to demand of such people to refrain from taking from the well-to-do what they need.

As I have argued, because some of what those in dire need require would be the result of the labors of other people, this implies that it is unreasonable to demand of those in dire straits to abstain from coercing productive people to labor for them, to part with what they have produced, to even give up parts of their bodies if they can do without those parts. But that cannot be right—how could it be unreasonable to demand that people not be forced to labor for others? Does not forced labor violate the rights of those who are its victim? Does it not make of some the involuntary servants, even slaves, of others?

If one also adds that those in dire straits may very well have ample opportunity to obtain what they need by offering to work for the well-off, to engage in innovation, enterprise, and other efforts that can peacefully secure for them what they need to survive and flourish, the case that they may coerce others to work for them loses even the emotional appeal that at first inspection it possesses.

The most that this kind of reasoning advanced in support of the welfare state establishes, then, is that those who are well-off ought to be generous toward the very needy, that in emergencies those who can afford to should lend a hand to those who are genuinely helpless, through no fault of their own. Indeed, that is what the virtue of generosity amounts to: It inclines decent people of good character to come to the aid of deserving but badly off people. That would be the civilized solution rather than one that resorts to coercive means and treats those who are well-off as unwilling tools or instruments of the badly off, not as people who are ends in themselves and must give their consent whenever they are utilized by others, even the very hard up among us.

What does not follow from this is that the legal system of a society must be adjusted so as to accommodate emergencies, to require of well-enough-off citizens to be constant Good Samaritans. Relations among citizens in a free society, with a free market system, are not zero-sum games. Let me repeat, "Hard cases make bad law." One does not demand that a system of law change because of certain dire circumstances, especially because it would imply that some people get to place the rest under legal obligation to perform service that should come from goodwill, not at the point of a gun.

In *Science News,* the magazine that reports much of the pathbreaking scientific research around the globe, one short item noted that the degree of charity and philanthropy in societies with substantial free, unregimented markets is much greater than in top-down planned societies.[12] So not only is coercive welfare unjust, but it seems to discourage goodwill among citizens. And it is mostly such goodwill that takes the best care of the truly needy among us.

PART III

Responses to the Critiques

CHAPTER 9

FURTHER THOUGHTS ON ARGUING FROM RATIONALITY TO EQUALITY

James P. Sterba

There is a saying that you never see yourself as others see you. I suppose that has to hold true of philosophers, just like everyone else. I certainly can vouch for its truth with respect to many of the critical perspectives that the contributors to this volume have brought to bear on my essay. In what follows, I will take up their critical perspectives in detail in the same order that they were presented in the volume, hoping to show that with certain clarifications and refinements, my arguments can still survive their critiques. Of course, you will have to judge whether I have been able to do so without the usual self-deception that comes with failing to see ourselves as others see us.

CHARLES MILLS

The main thrust of Charles Mills's critique of my justification of morality was presented (I'm not kidding!) thirteen years ago at an American Philosophical Association, Pacific Division, Author Meets Critics Session on my

1998 book, *Justice for Here and Now*. Then as now, Mills was criticizing my argument from rationality to morality, and then as now, he was doing it by developing the contrasting notions of lexical and scalar egoism. I found out only fairly recently that Mills did not find my response to his critique at that time to be adequate. So I thought it would be good to return to the exchange we had at that the earlier Author Meets Critics Session, to a now-refurbished version of the exchange to be sure, and this time around to really put our disagreement to rest. In biblical terms, waiting seven years is sometimes appropriate, but waiting almost double that is just far too long to wait; we need a resolution.

At the heart of Mills's critique of my justification for morality is his claim to have discovered a new type of egoism, scalar egoism, that is immune from my rationality to morality argument. Or put another and even more damaging way, Mills claims to have discovered a form of egoism that on my account is inappropriately classified as a form of morality, a form of morality that I am defending. This would produce the unacceptable consequence that my defense of morality turns out to be a defense of at least one form of egoism as well.

Mills distinguishes his scalar egoist from a lexical egoist who always puts her interests first and gives no weight at all to the interests of others. Although the scalar egoist also puts his interests first, what distinguishes him from the lexical egoist is that he gives some weight, albeit considerably lesser weight, to the interests of others. Now, Mills thinks that whereas my appeal to a standard of non-question-beggingness may work against both the lexical egoist and her counterpart, the lexical altruist, it does not work against the scalar egoist, or for that matter his counterpart, the scalar altruist. In fact, Mills claims that scalar egoism, by taking others into account to some degree, turns out to be one of the forms of morality that I am, in fact, defending, which surely is a sign that something has gone wrong somewhere.

But let's take a closer look at Mills's scalar egoist. Although throughout his discussion, Mills draws comparisons between scalar egoism and racism, sexism, and the domination of nature, which we can call, following Karen Warren, naturism, scalar egoism is clearly different from these other forms of oppression and Mills recognizes this. At one point, referring to scalar egoism in that earlier version of his comments, he says, "the position in question is not racism, sexism, etc., but one of calculated and systematic *individual* privileging."[1] But if individual privileging is at issue here, as it is, and not group privileging, then we are dealing with egoism in the form of individual ethical egoism, a view that does not seem to have a coherent account. Its fundamental problem is that it seems impossible to come up with a feature about the scalar egoist himself that could justify privileging the egoist over all others to the degree to which he claims is justified. Virtually any feature that our scalar egoist could point to as justifying his degree of privileging himself over everyone else would also be shared by at least some persons, but not others, at least to some degree, and so, in consistency, our scalar egoist would have to grant that there is a comparable justification for privileging those other persons as well. This would make our scalar egoist a defender of some sort of objectionable group morality in the sense that racism, sexism, and naturism are objectionable group moralities favoring one group over others, whites over blacks, men over women, humans over nonhuman living beings. That is why in the debate over egoism, individual ethical egoism has been recognized to be an incoherent view, leading to the conclusion that the only viable form of egoism that needs to be dealt with is universal ethical egoism, the view that maintains that everyone ought to do what serves his or her own best interests. It is this form of egoism that I am addressing in my justification for morality. It is what Mills calls lexical egoism, but it is also a universal form of lexical egoism. Individual lexical egoism would be just as incoherent as scalar egoism. The individual lexical egoist could not point to any distinctive feature about herself that would justify totally privileging herself over others that would not be shared by at least some other persons, and so arguably support privileging them as well.

Nevertheless, even if scalar egoism cannot be coherently defended as a form of individual ethical egoism, it still has to be dealt with as an objectionable form of group morality similar to racism, sexism, or naturism. So it is here that Mills's challenge to my justification of morality can still be resurrected in a different form. The question is, how does my argument from rationality to morality work against objectionable group moralities like racism, sexism, and naturism?

The answer is simply that it doesn't, or at least that it didn't as I employed the argument in Chapter 2 of my 1998 book, *Justice for Here and Now*. In that chapter, I am simply targeting universal lexical egoism, the form of egoism that Mills allows my argument works against. Later, in Chapter 6 of that book and in later work, I use the same standard of non-question-beggingness against naturism that I employ against egoism in Chapter 2. In other chapters of that book, I argue against sexism, and I devote a section to arguing against racism. In 2000, when participating in a conference on the same book held here at the University of Notre Dame, Mills noted that most social and political philosophers in the United States today, all but a very small fraction of them being white, have had very little to say about racism in their work, and thus Mills welcomed what was then, in fact, in my judgment, my very meager contribution in this area. Since then, taking inspiration from Mills's remarks, I have tried to do better, first publishing a debate book on affirmative action with Carl Cohen and just last year, a single-authored book titled *Affirmative Action for the Future*, which I fittingly dedicated to Charles Mills. So all along, I have combined my defense of morality against egoism with a continuingly developing defense of an egalitarian morality against sexism, racism, and naturism.

However, in this essay, I have now developed a new and more general argument against objectionable group moralities, like racism, sexism, and naturism and all forms of immorality, that parallels the argument I employ against universal ethical egoism, a version of Mills's lexical egoism. I now argue with respect to these objectionable group moralities and other immoralities that there are no non-question-begging grounds for the way that those who are dominant favor their interests over the interests of those they dominate. More specifically, with respect to the group-based moralities of racism and sexism, there is a group-based epistemic failing—those who dominate use biased, that is, question-begging, information, to conceive of their interests as superior to the interests of those they dominate, which they then think entitles them to their privileged status. We can also generalize further and say that all immoralities involve an inappropriate (question-begging) favoring of the interests of self (or a particular group of selves) over the interests of others (or a particular group of others), and in this way run afoul of the defense of morality I have sketched in my essay.

In the revised version of his essay included in this volume, Mills seems to concede that my argument works against the egoist, both the individual and universal ethical egoist, but may not work more generally against just any kind of immoralist.[2] Now, while I grant that this was to some degree true of the justification of morality that Mills critiqued at that author-meets-critic session so many years ago, it definitely does not hold of the improved argument that I offer in this essay. In fact, it was Mills's initial critique, and the recent work of Anita Superson, that led me to see the need to generalize my argument against egoism into an argument against all forms of immorality, as I do in this essay. Mills rightly claims that to really defeat the immoralist one needs an argument based not on morality but on rationality.[3] Happily, my argument in this essay that all forms of immorality are question-begging does just that.

CANDACE VOGLER

I must say I didn't see Candace Vogler's critique coming. My expectation was that the author of *Reasonably Vicious* would try to counter my argument from rationality to morality with arguments from her book that attempt to show that vicious people, in fact, can be quite reasonable. But Vogler's comments take an entirely different approach to my justification for morality.

Vogler's main argument against my view is that there is no way to analyze or factor moral reasons into self-interested reasons and altruistic reasons. As she sees it, what is first required is a normative standard. Only by first using such a standard can we determine which self-interested reasons and which altruistic reasons are appropriately justified. What Vogler, I am sure, will be surprised to hear is that I completely agree with her view here. I, too, hold that a normative standard must be first employed in order to determine which self-interested and altruistic reasons are appropriately justified. I also think that John Rawls holds the same view.

Because Vogler tends to lump me together with Rawls and other neo-Kantians, let me first respond by explaining how Rawls holds Vogler's view and then explain how I hold it as well. In Rawls's theory of justice, the normative standard employed is clearly his original position decision procedure with its veil of ignorance. What serves as the analogue to self-interested and altruistic reasons in Rawls's theory are his primary social goods, various distributions of which would serve different self-interested and altruistic concerns. So in Rawls's theory, it is his original position decision procedure, itself embodying an ideal of fairness, that determines what is an appropriate distribution of primary social goods, and ultimately thereby determines the self-interested and altruistic reasons that are appropriately justified. In my more general approach, the principle of non-question-beggingness is the normative standard that determines the self-interested and altruistic reasons that are appropriately justified.

Whereas Rawls uses the explicitly moral standard of his original position to support principles of justice, I use what is a generally thought to be non-moral normative standard of non-question-beggingness to justify morality over egoism. Although Rawls and I are working toward different immediate ends, our arguments share a similar structure, and we both agree with Vogler that a normative standard must be first employed in order to determine the self-interested and altruistic reasons that are appropriately justified.

Moreover, I think it is important to note how the normative standards of which both Vogler and I approve seriously take both self-interested and altruistic concerns into account. Consider the example with which Vogler began her comments. She and a colleague were presented as having been locked into an agreement to meet for a discussion that, at the time the discussion was to occur, would serve the interests of neither of them. Vogler employs this example to show that it really is a normative standard and not the interests of the parties to a promise that determines what should be done.

Yet is this the conclusion we should draw here? Suppose that I, inveterate liberal do-gooder that I am, would have found out about the preferences of Vogler and her colleague with regard to their upcoming discussion. True to my liberal do-gooder nature, suppose I had tactfully let both of them know that the other really did not want to go forward with the meeting. Surely, there would have ensued a quick phone call from one to the other, the promise would have been undone, and the interests of both parties would have thereby been served. What this shows is that the practice of promising is justified because of the way that it serves the interests of those who engage in it. Although the practice does impose constraints on which self-interested and altruistic concerns are to be served, the justification for the practice is not independent of those concerns. All promises are not to be kept though the heavens fall. That is why in forms of contract law, there are general catastrophe clauses, stated or implicit, that allow the contracts to be canceled or renegotiated under certain conditions, so as to more appropriately serve the interests of the parties involved. And surely that understanding of contract law is morally defensible. So Vogler and I may not be disagreeing at all about the important role that both self-interested and altruistic concerns play in the justification for our practice of promising.

Where we seem to be disagreeing, however, is over the relative merits of a Kantian or neo-Kantian justification of morality compared to an Aristotelian one. Now, I have been concerned about this very issue for some time. In my 2005 book, *The Triumph of Practice over Theory in Ethics*, I tried to meet it by laying out an Aristotelian justification of morality that paralleled the admittedly Kantian-looking justification of morality that I had been employing up to that time—the one that is also developed in this essay. I know that endorsements don't count for much in philosophy, but when the ethics group here at Notre Dame discussed the manuscript for my 2005 book, I ran this idea of recasting my justification of morality into an Aristotelian framework by many of the neo-Aristotelian moral theorists in the group who are my colleagues here at Notre Dame, and they were generally content with this reframing of the justification.

But Vogler's objection here, more suggested than worked out, relies on a different philosophical authority—not my colleagues. It, in fact, relies on Michael Thompson's work, particularly on a fairly dense fifty-page article that he published in 2004. Even though Vogler just alludes to this article, let me briefly sketch Thompson's argument in favor of an Aristotelian over a Kantian justification of morality, and then indicate why I think it does not work.

Thompson distinguishes between two kinds of moral judgments. One has the form: X has a duty to Y to do A. Thompson calls moral judgments of this form bipolar because they imply that the parties are two poles in a relationship. The other kind of moral judgment has the form: X has a duty to do A. Thompson calls such moral judgments monadic because they are expressly nonrelational. Thompson also analogizes such bipolar moral judgments to civil law and monadic moral judgments to criminal law. He then argues both that bipolar moral judgments best capture the nature of morality because morality is relational at its core and that only Aristotelian ethics can best be construed as accommodating judgments of that form. By contrast, Kantian ethics, according to Thompson, is best construed as accommodating judgments that have the monadic form.

Now, Thompson's argument for the superiority of Aristotelian ethics over Kantian ethics is clearly contentious. As I see it, his interpretation cuts Aristotelian ethics a lot of slack, and Kantian ethics almost none at all. I just find it too hard to believe that an approach to ethics that perpetually wants us to ask, What if everyone did that? as Kantian ethics does, fails to have human relations at its core. Hence, I see no reason to prefer Aristotelian ethics to Kantian ethics on the basis of Thompson's argument. So here Vogler and I may well be disagreeing.

At the end of her comments, Vogler cautions that the long history of past injustices should make us wary of what reason-based arguments in ethics can do to improve the world in which we live. She may be right. But, of course, philosophers have been searching at least since the time of Plato, with little success, for an argument that shows that morality is rationally required.

But suppose that now a consensus began to emerge that we finally did have such an argument justifying morality, and suppose further that another consensus began to emerge that there is still another argument that could be joined with the previous argument that shows that morality leads to substantial equality. Suppose that neither argument is very complicated or difficult to understand. Would such arguments and the consensuses emerging around them do no good at all in our admittedly very unjust world? I find it hard not to be a bit optimistic about the possible positive impact of such arguments. Of course, it is for us to determine whether such arguments can be justifiably put forward. But if we do determine that they can be, why should we think that doing so would not help to improve the unjust world in which we live?

But I better stop here or my responses will no longer be just responses.

ANITA SUPERSON

Unlike the other contributors to this volume who also criticize the justification of morality that I develop in my essay, Anita Superson defends an alternative justification of morality of her own. Her justification relies on a principle of consistency rather than, like my own, on a principle of non-question-beggingness. Truth be known, when I first set out to try to provide a justification of morality in my book *The Demands of Justice,* I was also hoping to ground the justification on consistency alone. At the time, however, I couldn't figure out how to do it. And it was only a number of years later that I hit upon the strategy of using the principle of non-question-beggingness to ground the justification.[4] So I am intrigued by Superson's attempt in her recent book, *The Moral Skeptic,* to do what I thought could not be done. At the end of her essay in Chapter 4 here in response to my essay, Superson sketches her consistency-based justification of morality. But first she concerns herself with showing why my approach to justifying morality will not work.

Superson notes that I start my discussion with ethical egoism, not moral skepticism, although I claim that to defeat the one is to defeat the other. Ethical egoism, particularly in the form of universal ethical egoism, is characterized in terms of what the view is for (each person ought to do what best serves his or her own self-interest). By contrast, moral skepticism is characterized in terms of what the view denies or is agnostic about (that there are moral reasons).[5] Yet to simply assert either of these views against morality or altruism, I claim, is question-begging. Superson, however, rejects this.[6]

She begins by denying that to defeat egoism (by getting the egoist, or the "reformed" egoist, to recognize the prima facie status of altruism) would not lead to a defeat of moral skepticism. She claims this is because the moral skeptic denies or is agnostic about moral reasons and hence denies or is also agnostic about the altruistic reasons that are a significant component of such reasons. Thus, without the admission that altruistic reasons have or should have prima facie status, I would have to grant that the moral skeptic couldn't be similarly defeated.

Superson rightly anticipates that I would counter her argument by claiming that denial or agnosticism on the part of the moral skeptic is itself question-begging. Her response is that moral skepticism is understood in just this way "precisely because the position [so formulated] does not beg the question in favor of morality."

I grant that she is right about this. Nevertheless, not begging the question in favor of morality is certainly compatible with begging the question against it. And I claim that this is just what the moral skeptic does. To begin an argument by claiming that only self-interested reasons count is to beg the question against morality and in favor of moral skepticism. In order not to beg the question against *both* egoism/moral skepticism and morality, I claim, it is necessary to back off *both* from the general principle of egoism and from the general principle of altruism, thus granting the prima facie relevance of both self-interested and altruistic reasons to rational choice.[7] Here we have no non-question-begging justification for excluding either self-interested or altruistic reasons as relevant to rational choice. So we accept both kinds of reasons as prima facie relevant to rational choice. The conclusion of this step of my argument does not beg the question against either egoism or altruism because if defenders of either view had any hope of providing a good (that is, a non-question-begging) argument for their view, they, too, would have to grant this very conclusion as the only option open to them. In accepting this step of my argument, therefore, we are not begging the question against a possible defense of either of these other two perspectives, and that is all that should concern us.

If we were to begin simply with just self-interested reasons, there would be no way what we arrived at would have any of the self-sacrificial requirements that many of us think are characteristic of morality. At best, we would get a truncated morality of mutual benefit. But we cannot just assume that morality has such a truncated form and so not give prima facie status to altruistic reasons along with self-interested reasons at the initial stage of our argument. To do otherwise would beg the question against any conception of morality other than one of mutual benefit. What Superson fails to recognize here is that including prima facie altruistic reasons along with prima facie self-interested reasons at this stage of the argument is not the same as "importing morality" into the argument's premises. Rather, it is the only non-question-begging way for the argument to proceed.

In the second part of her essay, Superson turns to criticizing the content of the morality that I claim is rationally preferable to both egoism and altruism. She claims not to find in certain accounts of morality the moral reasons of self-regard that are part of the morality I defend, but then she seems to allow that these accounts may be defective, or at least less than ideal.

More significantly, she maintains that in preferring moral reasons over conflicting self-interested reasons, I am double counting moral reasons in just the way I find to be objectionable with respect to self-interested reasons. The double counting to which I object would result from "compromising" self-interested reasons with conflicting moral reasons by favoring high-ranking self-interested reasons over conflicting low-ranking moral reasons after first "compromising" self-interested reasons with altruistic reasons by favoring high-ranking self-interested reasons over conflicting low-ranking altruistic reasons. By contrast, I see preferring moral reasons over conflicting self-interested reasons as quite different from "compromising" those reasons with self-interested reasons.[8] Rather, such a preference, not a compromise of any sort, is grounded in the fact that the moral reasons have already taken self-interested reasons into account (through compromising), so there is no need to do that again at this juncture either through compromise or preference. To do otherwise, I claim, would constitute just that objectionable double counting or preference of self-interested reasons to which I object.

Superson wonders whether I provide any authority for my preference for high-ranking altruistic reasons over conflicting low-ranking self-interested reasons or my preference for high-ranking self-interested reasons over conflicting low-ranking altruistic reasons. The answer is that I do. That authority is provided by the principle of non-question-beggingness for contexts where we must act one way or the other.

Superson also questions my grounds for using rankings of self-interested and altruistic reasons and their interpersonal comparability. In my essay, however, I argue that the defender of egoism would not challenge these rankings or their interpersonal comparability. As I see it, egoism claims that each person ought to do what best serves his or her overall self-interest, and this clearly assumes that each person can know what that is. Nor is it plausible to interpret egoism as maintaining that although we can each know what best serves our own self-interest, we cannot know what best serves the interest of others, and that is why we should be egoists. Rather, the standard defense of egoism assumes that we can each know what is good for ourselves and what is good for others and then claims that even with this knowledge, we still always ought to do what is good for ourselves. Nor is the idea of providing a relatively precise ranking of one's self-interested reasons from an egoistic perspective or a relatively precise ranking of one's altruistic reasons from an altruistic perspective something to which an egoist would reasonably object. Nor would the egoist reasonably object to the interpersonal comparability of these rankings. Difficult though such rankings may be to arrive at in practice, the egoist's objection is that even when such relatively precise rankings of our self-interested and altruistic reasons are known, and even when it is known that acting on high-ranking altruistic reasons is comparably more beneficial to others than acting on conflicting low-ranking self-interested reasons is beneficial to ourselves, we should still always favor self-interested reasons over altruistic ones. What is at issue, therefore, is whether the egoist has any basis for making this claim.

At the end of her essay, Superson sketches her consistency-based argument for justifying morality. Now, I think her argument would work if she were allowed her preferred interpretation of consistency, what she calls consistency as impartiality, but, as I will show, there are good, that is, non-question-begging, reasons not to allow her this interpretation.

Superson begins by basically pointing out that the ethical egoist and the moral skeptic are not solipsists. They recognize that there are other people; they just regard them as having only instrumental value such that they never have to sacrifice their own good for the good of other people. Of course, the ethical egoist and moral skeptic allow that other people can take exactly the same stance vis-à-vis them. Other people can regard them in just the same way they regard other people. This is one way that Superson sees the ethical egoist and the moral skeptic embracing the principle of consistency. She calls consistency interpreted this way consistency as universalizability. It is also the way I regard the ethical egoist and the moral skeptical as consistent, and endorsing this interpretation of consistency does not lead to morality.

Yet Superson claims there is another way to think of the ethical egoist and the moral skeptic as being committed to consistency. She thinks the egoist and moral skeptic can and should also be committed to consistency as impartiality. To be impartial, I must regard other people's interests in particular contexts as having equal weight to my own, and so I cannot simply treat them as means to my own interests. In effect, I must treat them morally.

Superson recognizes that "morality requires impartiality." But it is also the case that impartiality implies morality. So if I require the ethical egoist or the moral skeptic to endorse "consistency as impartiality," I thereby guarantee that the ethical egoist and the moral skeptic will endorse morality as well. But surely this is question-begging. I have just imposed a moral requirement (impartiality) on the ethical egoist and the moral skeptic in order to secure their commitment to morality.

Compare the steps in Superson's argument here to those in my own. I argue that the ethical egoist in order not to beg the question against morality or altruism must grant prima facie status to altruistic reasons. And from this concession, with further argument, I then derive a commitment to morality. There is no lesser move I can make to avoid begging the question against morality or altruism other than granting that altruistic reasons have prima facie status. By contrast, there is a lesser move that Superson can make that would avoid begging the question against the egoist or moral skeptic. She can assume what she calls consistency as universalizability rather than consistency as impartiality. Of course, that will not get her to morality. Yet what this shows is that the only way Superson can use a principle of consistency to get to morality is by begging the question with respect to the account of consistency she employs, rejecting consistency minimally construed as universalizability in favor of consistency construed in an explicitly morally laden way as impartiality.[9] As it turns out, that was my conclusion in *The Demands of Justice*. There, I argued that the principle of consistency, when minimally and non-question-beggingly interpreted, would not get us to morality. To get to morality, I argued for the first time in "Justifying Morality: The Right and the Wrong Ways" and in subsequent publications that we need to go beyond a principle of consistency, minimally interpreted, to base the justification on the principle of non-question-beggingness, which, unlike impartiality, is not itself thought to be a moral principle.[10]

RUSS SHAFER-LANDAU

One rarely encounters a philosopher who engages one's view, as Russ Shafer-Landau has done, by sending you his essay four months in advance and affirming that he will not make any real changes in the interim. When I wrote him about a month after he sent his essay, indicating that I thought the paper represented a shift from the stance that he had taken in his 2005 book *Moral Realism*, I thought that he might want to back off from some of the criticisms he was making of my view in order to maintain more consistency with the view he had defended in his book. To my surprise, he responded that since writing his book, he has become less optimistic about offering a non-question-begging argument in favor of moral realism. So to my chagrin, he didn't propose making any changes with respect to his criticisms of my view.

Turning to Shafer-Landau's objections to my argument from rationality to morality. Shafer-Landau nicely restates my argument as having four premises, and he then objects to three of them. In objecting to the second premise, Shafer-Landau argues that by failing to explain how commitments and brute desires figure in an account of morality, I have failed to respond to the instrumentalist. Now, I agree that I need to give a response to the instrumentalist and that I have not done so in this essay. But I have already done so in two of my books.[11] However, although I do tend to repeat a lot, given limitations of space, I did not repeat that argument in this essay. Nevertheless, Shafer-Landau and I are definitely in agreement here that an adequate response has to be given to the instrumentalist, and the only defense I have is that I have already done so.

In further objecting to the second premise and to the fourth premise of my argument, Shafer-Landau maintains that morality as compromise, the conception of morality that I have argued is rationally preferably to egoism and altruism, is defective in various ways as an account of morality. To this objection, however, I think I can plead guilty without affecting the success of my argument for morality.

In the past, when this same objection was raised to my defense of morality, I have responded in two different ways. When Bernard Gert raised this objection in a journal article in 2004, I responded both then in the same journal and later in my 2005 book, *The Triumph of Practice over Theory in Ethics,* by first pointing out that morality as compromise is not intended to be useful as a general decision procedure for churning out particular requirements of morality, especially in troublesome cases. However, I went on to claim that even so, when we have reached a resolution of what is morally required in such a troublesome case, we may be able to read that resolution back into my account of morality. This may be possible to do by showing that the resolution implies that some particular altruistic reason is higher ranking than some particular self-interested reason, or vice versa, other things being equal. Yet I also allowed that this may not always be possible to do because it may not be the case that other things are equal. I went on to show how morality as compromise can be further tinkered with so that it gives morally defensible resolutions in more difficult cases. Nevertheless, I contend that morality as compromise is not designed to be a general decision procedure for churning out particular moral requirements, especially in troublesome cases. It is designed to show the rational preferability

of morality over egoism and altruism. For other purposes, other conceptions of morality may be more useful, and this should lead us into comparative evaluations of different conceptions of morality.

The other, and I think better, way I have of responding to objections
to morality as compromise as an account of morality of the sort that
Shafer-Landau raises here is found in my essay here in Chapter 1. What I
do there is ask my reader to suppose John Stuart Mill had given us a non-
question-begging argument that utilitarianism is rationally preferable to
egoism. I suggested that we would be happy to accept such an argument
as useful in our defense of morality, but then some of us would still want
to go on to indicate the ways that utilitarianism is an inadequate conception of morality, one that needs to be improved upon or reinterpreted in
various ways. Interestingly, many of the objections that Shafer-Landau
raises to morality as compromise as an account of morality match objections that have been raised to utilitarianism as an account of morality.

So that is the way I think about morality as compromise; it is a useful
way to think about morality for the purpose of showing the rational superiority of morality over egoism, but it is not as useful for other purposes.
That is why to settle the question of which moral requirements should be
enforced, in my essay and in my books, I have found it useful to shift discussion to a comparative evaluation of political-moral perspectives such as
libertarianism, welfare liberalism, and socialism. Nevertheless, once morality as compromise is completed with respect to the enforcement question,
as it is in the second part of my essay, then it can provide the appropriate
framework for determining more particular practical moral requirements.

Let me now consider the objections that Shafer-Landau raises to what
he calls the first premise of my argument from rationality to morality. His
first response to my claim that non-question-beggingness is required in a
fully adequate defense of morality is to claim that it is not required at all if
we are trying to rally the faithful to the cause of morality. Presumably, the
idea here is that by appealing to the right sort of moral premises or ideals we
may be able to shore up the commitment of the faithful to acting morally in
particular contexts. Shafer-Landau seems to see this as an acceptable way of

using question-begging arguments to defend morality, at least, particular moral requirements. But as I understand this form of argumentation, it is not question-begging at all. Non-question-begging arguments are always context dependent. So in a context in which we are trying to establish or shore up the commitment of the faithful to particular moral requirements, it does not beg the question to appeal to other moral requirements to which the faithful are already strongly committed in order to make our case.

With respect to the immoralist or egoist, however, Shafer-Landau does not think we can begin with morally laden premises and construct a non-question-begging argument for morality. Nor is the immoralist or the egoist any better off. As Shafer-Landau sees the possibilities for argument here, it is question-begging all around. As examples of where this happens in other contexts, Shafer-Landau offers us flat-earthers, skeptics, and those students who think *you* graded them poorly because *you* hate them.

Now, it is not part of my view that there is always a non-question-begging resolution to every disagreement. Whether there is one or not depends on a case-by-case analysis, although it is rather unfortunate to be in a situation where we face a very important issue and are not able to give a non-question-begging resolution. In general, however, as I argue in my essay, if one is committed to a standard of non-question-beggingness, one has to be concerned only with how one's claims and arguments stack up against others who are also committed to such a standard. If you yourself are committed to the standard of non-question-beggingness, you don't beg the question by simply coming into conflict with the requirements of other perspectives, unless those other perspectives (or better, their defenders) are also committed to the same standard of non-question-beggingness. In arguing for your view, when you come into conflict with those who are begging the question, you do not beg the question against them unless you are also begging the question yourself. I further argued that part of what is frequently involved in a commitment to a standard of non-question-beggingness is a willingness to back off from the most contentious premises of one's own view, especially if one's opponent is willing to do the same in order to pursue a resolution from more neutral premises.

Now, with this in mind, let us consider Shafer-Landau's examples of where he thinks that question-beggingness is unavoidable on all sides. Consider flat-earthers. My understanding is that all or most flat-earthers in recent times held to their view because they accepted the physical cosmology of the Bible on the authority of the Bible. Of course, that physical cosmology was once a near-universal view. But things have changed quite a bit in this regard. Even among those today who still want to give the Bible as much authority as possible, flat-earthism is not a very popular view. In fact, most of those who want to give the Bible as much authority as possible are convinced that there is non-question-begging empirical evidence for rejecting flat-earthism. But what about those remaining flat-earthers? What is so interesting about them is that, from time to time, they have actually been willing to subject their view to an empirical test, which I interpret to be an attempt to gather non-question-begging support for their view. Unfortunately, these tests—usually attempts to demonstrate that the earth shows no curvature between two distant points—did not go very well for the flat-earthers. Although I am not sure whether these test failures triggered a cosmological crisis for them, they do suggest that more modern-day flat-earthers, like so many before them, know how to non-question-beggingly proceed on the issue when they are interested in doing so.

By contrast, the pure skeptic, like the pure relativist, is a difficult case. Although we may be able to show that the pure skeptic or the pure relativist contradicts herself—a perfectly non-question-begging form of argument—it is not clear what it would mean for such a skeptic (or relativist) to back up to more neutral premises. This is why I think that the more interesting versions of skepticism and relativism are the limited versions of the views, particularly moral skepticism and moral relativism, because then, using the backup strategy to get to a more neutral standpoint becomes available if it is needed.

In any case, this strategy does make sense in the debate over morality, and it requires a stepping back from the principle of pure egoism and from the principle of pure altruism. From this more neutral standpoint, it is then possible to arrive at a non-question-begging resolution. Now, Shafer-Landau claims that when I do this stepping back, I guarantee altruists that their reasons will have pro tanto rather than just prima facie justificatory force, which is to say that I guarantee them that their reasons will definitely be felt in the final resolution. But this is just what I have denied in my essay. What I say there is that having done the backing up—from both the egoistic perspective and from the altruistic perspective—"it is still an open question whether either egoism or altruism will be rationally preferable, all things considered."[12]

To this claim, possibly with someone like Shafer-Landau in mind, I noted it in my essay:

> Now, it might be objected that neither the defender of egoism nor the defender of altruism would want to make this move if she were only to take into account where this argument is heading. But if the defender of egoism or altruism were to realize that if she takes a non-question-begging stance, her favored position would turn out to be indefensible and some other position would turn out to be defensible, doesn't that show that she already knows that her own position is indefensible? That is what I argue happens here. A non-question-begging stance requires giving both egoistic and altruistic reasons prima facie status, and this, I will argue, leads in a non-question-begging way to morality (as compromise). Knowing or coming to know this, both the defender of egoism and the defender of altruism either know or come to know that they will lose the argumentative game to the moralist.[13]

One last consideration, I ended my discussion of the modern-day flat-earthers with the hopeful observation that rather than just question-beggingly relying on the authority of the Bible in matters of physical cosmology, they from time to time are willing to carry out an empirical test of the curvature of the earth, and so, I surmised, they seemed to know what constituted a non-question-begging resolution of their group-defining issue. Now similarly, Shafer-Landau, who is very skeptical about the possibility of a non-question-begging justification for morality, does something that parallels the behavior of the flat-earthers. In seeking to establish the soundness of particular moral conclusions opposed to egoism,

Shafer-Landau in an earlier version of his essay appeals to the "convictions of those who do not already have a stake in the debate." Now, that may not be an appeal to a neutral, that is, non-question-begging, standpoint, but to me it begins to smell as sweet.

So there are my responses to Shafer-Landau's comments; hopefully, they will provide the basis of greater agreement between us.

ALLAN GIBBARD

When a philosopher both agrees and disagrees with your view, as Allan Gibbard has done, that can leave you in a bit of a moral quandary about how to proceed. Moreover, when the agreement is substantial, you can feel even more uneasy, maybe even ungrateful, trying to turn back the points of disagreement or criticism. As it turns out, I was able to resolve this quandary for myself only with the thought that if my responses work, then Gibbard and I will have reached that desirable state of affairs of agreeing upon even more than he had initially thought.

In his comments, Gibbard mentions that long ago he presented an internal critique of libertarianism, like the one that I develop in the second part of my essay. Truth be known, I was actually there at the APA Meeting when Gibbard presented that critique, which was subsequently published in *Nous*. So I have been well aware that Gibbard and I have been pushing libertarians in the same direction over the years. In Chapter 6 here, however, Gibbard contends that the internal argument against libertarians we share should take us further than I appear to be willing to go. He notes that I make a right to welfare conditional upon a requirement that the poor engage in mutually beneficial work if they can, and that they repay the aid they received to meet their basic needs once they can consistently do so while satisfying those needs. It is that second requirement to which Gibbard particularly objects. According to Gibbard, how the surplus over a basic needs minimum is to be distributed is to be determined by a hypothetical contract in which considerations of conflicting negative liberties and the possibilities for reciprocity are taken into account. The results of such a contract, Gibbard allows, could, drawing on the work of Hal Varian, still permit considerable inequality in individual societies. Gibbard does, however, endorse a 1 percent or greater surtax on the rich generally, in order to meet the needs of the poor internationally, even presumably where reciprocity does not obtain between the rich and the poor. Yet when considering obligations to future generations, Gibbard again sees the need for reciprocity or mutual benefit as limiting our obligations to just overlapping generations.

Well, how does this differ from my own view? In the first place, my view is not at all tilted in favor of the rich and productive as Gibbard seems to suggest. He is right that I say that those who receive assistance must repay the aid they have received once they can consistently do so while meeting their basic needs. But Gibbard wrongly assumes that the repayment will be made to the rich and productive in society. What I say when I first raised the issue and what I say later should have precluded that interpretation. When I first raise the issue, I say that what these former poor give back will not likely go to the rich, but rather to others who are still poor.[14] And near the end of my essay, I conclude that recognizing a universal libertarian-based right to welfare applicable to both existing and future people requires us to use up no more resources than are necessary for meeting our own basic needs, thus securing for ourselves a decent life but no more. So it should be clear that my view is not at all tilted in favor of the rich and productive.

Since both Gibbard and I share the argument from negative liberty, the only thing I see that keeps him from drawing the same conclusion that I do is his on-again, off-again requirement of reciprocity. He seems to see it as necessary for specifying obligations within societies, but not necessary for specifying an obligation to provide a guaranteed minimal welfare internationally, but then necessary again for there to be welfare obligations with respect to future generations. I don't see it as necessary in any of these domains. For me, the argument from negative liberty should suffice. Of course, the possibility of reciprocity can help, especially with enforceability. But here we are concerned not with what will or is likely to get enforced, but with what should be enforced. As I see it, even when no one tries to stop us, we can still be unjustifiably interfering with future genera-tions, when in order to satisfy our luxury needs, we deprive them of the nonrenewable resources they will require for meeting their basic needs.

However, Gibbard points out that if we use up nonrenewable re-sources for luxury purposes, "there is no way [future generations] could exercise a negative liberty to those resources." This is true. Yet it doesn't show that there hasn't been a rights violation. This is because the same thing can occur between presently existing people. For example, I could use up for luxury purposes resources that you require to meet your basic needs and then promptly die, leaving no useful resources that you or any-one else could use. Accordingly, there would then be no way you could exercise a negative liberty with respect to those now nonexistent resources or any other resources connected with me since there are none. Neverthe-less, it is still the case that your liberty rights were violated by me, and the same can hold true for future generations. Their rights can also be simi-larly violated. So my hope now is that on libertarian grounds alone, Gib-bard and I will come to find ourselves in even greater agreement.

Gibbard also expresses considerable agreement with the first part of my essay, where I develop my argument from rationality to morality. He allows that what my argument does here is "eliminate pure egoism and pure altru-ism from contention as accounts of how to live, by showing that they beg a question that a compromise between them doesn't beg." In other words, Gibbard allows that I have shown that morality as compromise, that is, morality conceived of as a compromise between self-interested and altruis-tic reasons, is rationally, that is, non-question-beggingly, preferable to pure egoism and pure altruism.[15]

Nevertheless, Gibbard goes on to raise an objection that, if not met, would surely undermine the ability of my argument to provide a rational justification of morality. Gibbard maintains that the same style of argu-ment that I use to justify morality over egoism can be used for including objectionable reasons, such as reasons for revenge, reasons that are ar-guably similarly basic, into an account of morality.

This objection, however, conflates two different uses of non-question-begging arguments. The use with which I am primarily concerned employs non-question-begging argument to show that morality is rationally preferable to egoism. The other use employs non-question-begging argument to determine what sorts of reasons should be included within a conception of morality. Thus, the question that is asked about reasons of revenge is whether such reasons should be included within a defensible conception of morality. The hope here is that we can construct non-question-begging arguments for excluding such reasons by showing that they conflict with other reasons that are central to a defensible conception of morality.

Nevertheless, constructing such arguments is not directly relevant to my defense of morality against egoism. To defend morality against egoism, it is not necessary to show that morality as compromise is beyond criticism. All that is necessary is to show that it is rationally preferable to egoism. Accordingly, providing a non-question-begging argument for morality as compromise over egoism is perfectly consistent with admitting that the conception is inadequate in certain respects. Such admission does not in any way affect the useful role that this conception plays in my overall defense of morality and its requirements.

I have always argued that morality as compromise is useful for one particular purpose—defeating egoism—but maybe not as useful for other purposes. With this in mind, when I am concerned with deriving practical moral requirements in my work, I shift to a comparative evaluation of Kantian, utilitarian, and Aristotelian views, or when my focus is more political, to a comparative evaluation of libertarian, welfare liberal, and socialist views.

Even so, while defending morality as compromise as useful for one particular purpose, defeating the egoist, and maybe not as useful for others, I do, here and there, attempt to defend it against particular attempts to show it to be inadequate. For example, in my essay, I try to show how morality as compromise can accommodate other reasons that might not be thought to be grounded in either self-interested or altruistic reasons, such as malevolent reasons seeking to bring about the suffering and death of other human beings, benevolent reasons concerned to promote nonhuman welfare even at the expense of human welfare, and aesthetic reasons concerned to preserve and promote objects of aesthetic value, even if those objects will not be appreciated by any living human being. With respect to malevolent reasons, I contend that they could be interpreted to be ultimately rooted in some conception of what is good for oneself or others, and as such they would have already been taken into account, and, in the best construal of both egoism and altruism, presumably outweighed by other relevant reasons in each case. And although benevolent reasons concerned to promote nonhuman welfare do need to be taken into account, I have found a way to non-question-beggingly do so in my work, something that few conceptions of morality that are defended today have managed to do. Finally, although aesthetic reasons concerned to preserve and promote aesthetic objects, even when those objects will not be appreciated by any living human being, might theoretically weigh against human interests, I contend that, for all practical purposes, the value of such objects will tend to correlate with the value of the aesthetic experiences they provide to humans. Even the famous prehistoric artwork in the cave at Lascaux, France, which has been closed to public viewing since 1963, seems to be valued because of the significance it has for us. Now, although my way of dealing with malevolent and aesthetic reasons may still be judged to be inadequate, as I see it, this in no way affects the usefulness of morality as compromise for defeating the egoist.

Another way I put my case is to suppose that John Stuart Mill had given us a non-question-begging argument that utilitarianism is rationally preferable to egoism. As I indicated before, I think that we would be happy to accept such an argument as useful in our defense of morality, but then some of us would still want to go on to indicate the ways that utilitarianism is an inadequate conception of morality, maybe for its inability to deal adequately with malevolent and aesthetic reasons. Similarly, even when we recognize that morality as compromise is useful for providing a non-question-begging justification of morality over egoism, we can still find it inadequate in other ways, for example, for deriving particular practical moral requirements, or for being able to deal adequately with other reasons deemed to be as fundamental.

So when Gibbard points out that it is not entirely clear how the rankings of reasons are to work in morality as compromise for the purpose of figuring out what we should do, I couldn't agree more. I contend that he should be justifiably concerned about the usefulness of morality as compromise for that purpose because the view was not designed to serve that purpose well at all. This is because the kind of precision in the ranking of reasons that I hypothetically assume holds in morality as compromise is not to be found in real life. The ranking assumptions I use in this account of morality do not translate into a practical moral decision-making procedure for real life, despite the temptation to think of them in this way. They are used in the discussion that leads to morality as compromise because all the discussants allow their use as a tool of representation so as to be able to focus attention on the issues that really divide them. Although they are useful for that purpose, if one wants a general decision procedure to determine what particular practical moral requirements people actually have, they may not be very useful at all. However, as I have indicated in my essay, once morality as compromise is completed in the way that I defend in the second half of my essay, it can then provide a proper social justice framework within which more particular practical moral requirements can be determined.

Gibbard raises two more objections, one more serious than the other. The less serious objection challenges my attempt to generalize my argument against egoism to cover group-based moralities such as racism and sexism. He allows that most forms of group-based immoralities do attempt to justify their requirements in question-begging ways and so can be defeated by a generalization of my argument against egoism. However, Gibbard points out that there can be groups that understand their requirements to be asymmetrically action-guiding, and hence, guiding only for themselves, just the way the egoist understands her requirements to be asymmetrically action-guiding, and hence, guiding only for herself.

This is a good point. Still, when we attempt to give these group-based interests a non-question-begging defense, we will need to rank them from highest-ranking group interests to lowest-ranking interests and then we will need to non-question-beggingly weigh those interests against a corresponding ranking of other-group-based interests from highest to lowest interests. I maintain that the priorities that would emerge from non-question-begging weighing of these conflicting interests would parallel the priorities that are found in morality as compromise. This is because just as the interests associated with meeting the basic needs of individual people trump the interests associated with meeting the nonbasic needs of others when they conflict, so too the liberties associated with meeting the basic needs of a particular group of people would trump the liberties associated with meeting the nonbasic needs of people belonging to other groups of people when they conflict. Hence, the overall effect would be roughly the same.

Gibbard's more serious objection concerns whom we should take to be the fundamental opponent of egoism for the purposes of providing a non-question-begging defense of morality. Gibbard, favoring Sidgwick's approach to the problem, opts for universal utilitarianism over altruism as the opponent of egoism. As Gibbard sees it, egoism should be opposed not to altruism but to a universal utilitarianism in which each person counts for one. However, Sidgwick recognized that he could not defend a straightforward compromise between egoism and universal utilitarianism, and so he claimed that the conflict can be "resolved" only as Kant had proposed, by hypothesizing a God who, through an appropriate allocation of rewards and punishments in an afterlife, makes universal utilitarianism in everyone's overall self-interest. In my discussion of Sidgwick, however, I point out that Sidgwick could have arrived at morality as compromise if he had taken a different route and recognized that the reason why universal utilitarianism could not be compromised with egoism is that it is already the result of a compromise between egoism and altruism. Hence, any additional compromise would result in an objectionable double counting of egoistic interests. Accordingly, the best way to avoid the problem, I claim, is to take the opponent of egoism to be altruism, not universal utilitarianism. Then a non-question-begging compromise between egoism and altruism would result in morality as compromise. In favoring a compromise between universal utilitarianism and egoism, Gibbard recognizes the need to avoid any double counting of self-interested reasons, but he fails to recognize that if this discounting is done effectively, it would transform his compromise between universal utilitarianism and egoism into my compromise between altruism and egoism.

Interestingly, in morality as compromise, one's own interests would be given greater weight than they would receive in a universal utilitarianism in which each person counts for one. This is because when faced with a choice between meeting one's own basic needs or meeting the basic needs of others, morality as compromise would arguably allow us to favor ourselves over others, whereas at least some versions of universal utilitarianism would not.

In conclusion, given that a great deal of common ground already exists between Allan Gibbard's views and my own, my hope is that my responses here, both with regard to my argument from rationality to morality and with regard to my argument from liberty to equality, will serve to still further increase that common ground.

GERALD GAUS

Gerald Gaus was one of those to whom I sent a very early version of my essay for comments, and although I tried to improve my argument in light of the suggestions that Gaus made at the time, it is clear from his contribution to this volume that he thinks that quite a few more improvements are still needed. In this response, I am going to try to make that number more manageable.

Let me begin with a point of agreement. Gaus claims that if you have only any two orderings of reasons or preferences from highest ranking to lowest ranking, there is no principle of rationality or logic that rules out the possibility that one of the two rankings could totally dominate the other. I definitely agree with this. Suppose one of the rankings is my preferences for different flavors of ice cream and the other is a ranking of my preferences for different kinds of chocolate bars. Now, I could still have these two sets of rankings, while one totally dominates the other. For example, I could always prefer ice cream to chocolate bars.

However, the situation is different when we are dealing with rankings of self-interested and altruistic reasons, respectively. Here, especially in cases of severe conflict, we must act on one reason or the other, and the resolution of such conflicts needs to be enforceable. That is why we need a non-question-begging resolution of such conflicts. Yet it is clear that we cannot give a non-question-begging defense of a dominance strategy of always favoring self-interested reasons or always favoring altruistic reasons. The only non-question-begging alternative is to favor high-ranking self-interested reasons over low-ranking altruistic reasons, as recommended by a self-interested perspective, and to favor high-ranking altruistic reasons over low-ranking self-interested reasons, as recommended by an altruistic perspective.

Gaus appears to concede that we need to sometimes favor self-interested reasons and sometimes favor altruistic reasons, but then he maintains that there is a variety of ways of doing this. Yet I argue that not just any resolution will do here. The resolution must be nonarbitrary, otherwise it will beg the question against either the egoistic or altruistic perspective. Accordingly, the resolution must be such that it requires that high-ranking altruistic reasons trump low-ranking self-interested reasons and high-ranking self-interested reasons trump low-ranking altruistic reasons. Unfortunately, none of Gaus's examples of compromises between self-interested and altruistic reasons fully display this required nonarbitrariness.

Nevertheless, Gaus's main worry about my view is that it demands too much altruism. Gaus maintains, and I agree, that a morality cannot demand "more altruism than, given her nature and character, our normal moral agent can deliver." Gaus thinks the demands of my view exceed this limit.

Gaus cites results from evolutionary biology as presumably offering a cautionary tale for any ethical theory that would consider coercively demanding significant altruism. What evolutionary biology maintains is that a considerable portion of altruism that is actually practiced can also be seen to serve to preserve the gene pool of those who practice it. This, however, does not show that such actions are not still altruistic as long as people who are so acting are intentionally acting to serve the good of others. That these actions serve to preserve their gene pool as well is just a known or unknown consequence of them. It is not why people so acting intentionally act as they do. Nor does it show that the altruism offered to those who just happened to be in one's gene pool should not be appropriately extended to those outside the group, particularly after that group's basic needs for a decent life have been met. To oppose that extension, we would need a good argument as to why the liberty of the poor should not be favored over the liberty of the rich in cases of severe conflict—an argument that I claim is unavailable to us.

Moreover, studies in the United States over decades have shown that the poor give a significantly higher percentage of their income to charity than do the rich, or relatively rich, while at the same time having significantly more children, and thus presumably doing more to preserve their gene pool.[16] So the idea that greater altruism, at least at the levels we are considering, endangers one's genotype is nowhere established.

Looking for an explanation of altruism toward strangers, Gaus cites the important role played in experimental games by punishing cooperators. Still, it is unclear what the relevance of these experiments is to the desirability and feasibility of the altruistic welfare transfer that I am arguing for in my essay. Even though a number of experiments that have been done show how cultural norms can lead to high levels of generosity, what we really would need is an experiment in which one party through no fault of her own is suffering from hardship and could not meet even her most basic needs and the other party has a considerable surplus that he is planning to use for luxury purposes. But I am pretty sure that such a relevant experiment would not get approved by most institutional review boards in the United States today. So it is difficult to see how current experiments in cooperation would give us reason to oppose a resolution of the conflict between the rich and the poor that is non-question-beggingly justified.

But there is a more general problem with Gaus's recommendation of caution with respect to coercively demanding significant altruism. Its supposition is that most societies have not demanded that much altruism with respect to the poor, and so we should hesitate to even entertain the possibility of doing so. What I want to suggest, however, is that this supposition is false, and so in no way limits the possibility of institutionalizing the political arrangements I am recommending. The reason this supposition is false is that most societies have illegitimately demanded a high level of altruism from their poor members; they have frequently forced the poor to do without the minimum of resources they need for a decent life. And the poor, believing that they have no alternative, have generally reconciled themselves to living lives of forced altruism toward the rich. This is because the poor have not generally attempted to take from the surplus possessions of the rich those very resources to which they are entitled and that they need for a decent life.

So when we raise a question about the level of altruism we can demand of people, what we really should be asking is whether it is possible to replace the high degree of altruism that we socially and legally have almost always expected of the poor with a lesser degree of altruism that we could come to expect of the rich. Surely, there is no reason to think that *by nature* the rich and the poor have fundamentally different capacities for altruism in this regard. Accordingly, it should not be all that difficult to shift from a social arrangement in which we unjustifiably expect a significantly higher degree of altruism from the poor to a social arrangement in which we justifiably expect a significantly lower degree of altruism from the rich. Clearly, then, my view cannot be faulted for the degree of altruism it requires if it would legitimately require less altruism from the rich than most contemporary societies illegitimately require from the poor.

Now, Gaus acknowledges that people do face a choice of altruisms. As he sees it, there is the typically voluntary altruism directed at close relatives and there is the typically forced altruism that benefits the poor. What Gaus does not include here, of course, is the forced altruism directed at the rich that has such an important role in most societies. Gaus also rightly points out that if we are going to build a political program for change, we will have to look at the particular institutions and circumstances in existing societies. Nevertheless, it does not hurt when attempting to bring about particular reforms to keep in mind that the overall goal should be to replace an unjustified system that requires significant altruism from the poor with one that justifiably requires a lesser altruism from the rich.

In a just-published book, *The Order of Public Reason*, Gaus considers what should be the constraints on proposals for how a society should be governed, and he mentions "a modest common good requirement" that provides each person with "control over basic resources needed to live a life." This seems to me to be virtually equivalent to a right to welfare. So understood, I couldn't agree more with Gaus. Further, a good part of my argument in my essay is simply an attempt to show that it is just this right to welfare extended to distant peoples and future generations that leads to the substantial equality that I endorse.

Hopefully, then, my responses have shown that the argument in my essay needs a little less refurbishing than Gaus's comments might have initially indicated.

TIBOR MACHAN

Tibor Machan and I have been discussing each other's work on the topic of the practical implications of libertarian morality for many years now. I have always found the discussions interesting and illuminating, but you would think that by now we should be reaching some sort of a resolution. I think that may well be the case. Here is why.

Tibor begins by noting what he claims is an oddity about my account. He says: For Sterba, someone's holding on to his or her property, either personally or by way of law enforcement, amounts to "restricting the liberty" of a would-be thief!

But Machan knows that if we are talking about justified holdings of property, then this is true in his view as well as in mine. Under the specified conditions, we both hope to be "justifiably" restricting the liberty of would-be thieves.

Machan then goes on to point out commonsense phenomena that suggest why there are no welfare rights. He notes that when other people do not kill, maim, kidnap, or rob us, we do not thank them for their abstinence. By contrast, if we are in dire straits, and others come to our aid, we are naturally appreciative. Yet Machan is well aware that if we were living under a vicious tyranny, we may well thank our masters, and express our gratitude to them for not killing, maiming, or doing some other horrible thing to us. And as for the natural appreciation we show when people come to our aid when we are in dire straits, this is surely compatible with thinking we have a right to such aid. Alternatively, we might think that in our society such aid is not regarded as a right, and so for the time being such behavior should still be encouraged by an expression of appreciation. At the same time, we may look forward to the time when such behavior is appropriately regarded as a matter of right, and, hence, to when no such response is needed. So there is nothing here that Machan and I are currently disagreeing about.

Where we are still disagreeing concerns how to think about serious conflicts of liberty between the rich and the poor. The first thing that Machan wants to say about such conflicts is that they are untypical. Now, whether such conflicts are untypical or not, and in what sense, is an important question, and we will come back to it later. But at the moment let's for the sake of argument go along with Machan here and regard such conflicts as untypical. On that supposition, how, then, does he want us to deal with them?

What Machan claims is that the poor in such conflict situations ought simply to disregard the rights to property of the rich and take from them whatever they need. Surprisingly, Machan appears to be making an even stronger claim on behalf of the poor for these conflict situations than I am making. Where I claim that those in need should not be interfered with in taking from those with a surplus (which is simply more than one requires to meet one's basic needs), Machan claims that the poor ought to take from the rich who have a surplus in such situations.

Yet appearances are deceiving here. We need to take into account that Machan's libertarian view is ultimately based on what he calls classical egoism, which holds that each person ought to do what best serves his or her overall interest. And though classical egoism does maintain that the needy in severe conflict situations ought to take from the rich in order to meet their basic needs, it also holds that the rich ought to try to stop the poor from doing just that. Thus, Machan's claim is not stronger than mine here because my claim implies that the rich ought not to interfere with the poor's doing what they are permitted to do, whereas Machan's egoistic ought claim has no such implication. By contrast, Machan's solution for severe conflict of interest situations between the rich and the poor allows the rich to use their wealth and power to deny the poor access to their surplus. The poor are morally free to try to access the surplus of the rich to meet their basic needs, but the rich are also morally free to try to prevent the poor from doing just that.

Moreover, given that the rich are likely to have paid supporters on their side, they are also more likely to come out on top in such struggles. Of course, nothing is guaranteed and sometimes such struggles do go in favor of the poor, but what is important to recognize is that Machan regards the rich and the poor to be on an equal moral footing in such struggles. When the rich win out and the poor starve or are debilitated as a result, nothing morally wrong has been done, as he sees it.

Now, sometimes, Machan allows that the rich ought to help the poor in such conflict situations. Even so, it is not exactly clear what the grounds are for such an ought in his view, given his commitment to classical egoism. In any case, Machan is adamant that helping the poor cannot be coercively *required* of the rich. Helping the poor is not something that the rich can't justifiably resist. No matter how badly off the poor happen to be, the poor could never justifiably have the right to welfare in Machan's account.

Yet how can this be? Why wouldn't it be morally justified in situations of severe conflict of interest to have laws that justifiably require the rich to transfer (or not to resist the transferring of) some of their resources to the deserving poor in order to meet their basic needs? How can Machan think that by just allowing the poor to do what they can and by allowing the rich to respond as they wish, he has provided a defensible resolution of such conflicts between the rich and the poor?

At the heart of Machan's defense of his resolution of these severe conflicts of interest is his claim that such conflicts are untypical or rare. Taken to be untypical, Machan thinks that like hard legal cases, they would make bad law, and so a legal resolution of them is not appropriate. Hence, no coercively supported right to welfare is justified for such cases. Nevertheless, this implies that if they were typical and not rare, then it would be appropriate to use the law to deal with them. If such conflicts were typical and not rare, then there would be grounds for a right to welfare.

Obviously, it is important here is to understand the sense in which Machan takes these cases of severe conflict of interest to be untypical or rare. Now, at different times in our debate over the years, I took Machan to be making an empirical claim.[17] This led me to cite data about various existing societies to show that such conflicts were not, in fact, untypical.

Machan himself entered into this discussion, objecting to some of the data that I offered and citing opposing data of his own.[18] Recently, however, it became abundantly clear that Machan's claim about whether severe conflicts of interest between the rich and the poor are typical or not is not to be settled empirically.[19] Rather, Machan is making a claim about what would obtain in yet nonexistent ideal libertarian societies. His claim is that in such yet nonexistent libertarian societies, cases of severe conflict of interest between the rich and the poor would be untypical or rare.

Still, it is hard to see how Machan can make this untypical claim even about yet nonexistent ideal libertarian societies. Surely, whether it would be untypical or rare for people to lack the opportunities and resources to meet their basic needs in yet nonexistent ideal libertarian societies would depend on the availability and distribution of resources in such societies. Even in wealthy societies, that would surely depend on whether resources are appropriately distributed to meet the basic needs of all their members. In less wealthy societies, it is even less clear how yet nonexistent libertarian legal framework could, independently of the availability and distribution of resources, guarantee that it was rare for people to lack the resources and opportunities for meeting their basic needs. Moreover, if we take into account the needs of distant peoples and future generations as well, it is almost inconceivable how it would be untypical or rare for the people anywhere and at any time under ideal libertarian institutions to lack the resources and opportunities to meet their basic needs. And if it is not untypical or rare for the people to lack the resources and opportunities to satisfy their basic needs in these circumstances, then Machan's reason for not having an established, coercively supported right (hard legal cases make bad law) would not hold. Given, then, that severe conflict of interest would not be untypical or rare even under nonexistent yet ideal libertarian institutions, we would have every reason to want to set a legal resolution of such conflicts, one that guaranteed the poor the resources and opportunities to meet their basic needs.

Furthermore, under the non-ideal societies in which we live, where the basic needs of large groups of people are typically not being met, in any transition to greater justice either nationally, internationally, or intergenerationally, a right to welfare should be similarly enforced whenever sufficient resources for meeting people's basic needs obtain and they are not being allocated to do so. In fact, in all circumstances except in those extremely rare circumstances when it turned out that sufficient resources were being voluntarily and regularly made available for meeting people's basic needs nationally, internationally, and intergenerationally, a right to welfare would be normatively grounded. In this way, a right to welfare that when extended to distant peoples and especially future generations leads to substantial equality would almost always be supported by the libertarian premises that Machan endorses. This looks to me like the debate resolution that Machan and I have been looking for.

ABOUT THE AUTHORS

Gerald F. Gaus is the James E. Rogers Professor of Philosophy at the University of Arizona, where he directs the program in philosophy, politics, economics, and law. Among his books are *On Philosophy, Politics, and Economics* (2008), *Justificatory Liberalism* (1996), and *Value and Justification* (1990). His most recent book is *The Order of Public Reason: A Theory of Freedom and Morality in a Diverse and Bounded World* (2011). With Fred D'Agostino, he is currently editing the *Routledge Companion to Political and Social Philosophy*.

Allan F. Gibbard is the Richard B. Brandt Distinguished University Professor at the University of Michigan. His two books, *Wise Choices, Apt Feelings* (1990) and *Thinking How to Live* (2003), develop a general theory of moral judgments and judgments of rationality. He has been elected fellow of the American Academy of Arts and Sciences, member of the American Philosophical Society, fellow of the Econometric Society, and member of the National Academy of Sciences. He has been president of the Central Division of the American Philosophical Association.

Tibor R. Machan, professor emeritus at the Department of Philosophy, Auburn University, Alabama, holds the R. C. Hoiles Chair in Free Enterprise and Business Ethics at the Argyros School of Business and Economics, Chapman University, California. He is a research fellow at the Hoover

Institution, Stanford University, California. He edited *Reason* magazine for two years and *Reason Papers*, an annual journal of interdisciplinary normative studies, for its first twenty-five years. His memoir, titled *A Man Without a Hobby*, was published in 2004.

Charles W. Mills is John Evans Professor of Moral and Intellectual Philosophy at Northwestern University. He works in the general area of oppositional political theory and is the author of five books: *The Racial Contract* (1997), *Blackness Visible: Essays on Philosophy and Race* (1998), *From Class to Race: Essays in White Marxism and Black Radicalism* (2003), *Contract and Domination* (with Carole Pateman) (2007), and *Radical Theory, Caribbean Reality: Race, Class, and Social Domination* (2010).

Russ Shafer-Landau is professor and chair of the Department of Philosophy at the University of Wisconsin–Madison. He is the author of *Moral Realism: A Defence* (2005), *Whatever Happened to Good and Evil?* (2004), and *The Fundamentals of Ethics* (2009). He has edited numerous collections in ethics and is the editor of *Oxford Studies in Metaethics*.

James P. Sterba, professor of philosophy at the University of Notre Dame, has published twenty-seven books, including the award-winning *Justice for Here and Now* (1998), *Three Challenges to Ethics* (2001), *The Triumph of Practice over Theory in Ethics* (2005), and *Are Liberty and Equality Compatible?* (with Jan Narveson, 2010). He is past president of the American Section of International Society for Social and Legal Philosophy, Concerned Philosophers for Peace, the North American Society for Social Philosophy, and the Central Division of the American Philosophical Association.

Anita M. Superson is professor of philosophy at the University of Kentucky. She is the author of *The Moral Skeptic* (2009) and co-editor (with Sharon Crasnow) of *Out from the Shadows: Analytical Feminist Contributions to Traditional Philosophy* (2005). She specializes in ethics and feminism, and is interested in moral skepticism, moral psychology, and autonomy. Her current interests are in moral bindingness and bodily autonomy.

Candace A. Vogler is the David B. and Clara E. Stern Professor of Philosophy at the University of Chicago. She has written two books, *John Stuart Mill's Deliberative Landscape: An Essay in Moral Psychology* (2001) and *Reasonably Vicious* (2002), and essays in ethics, social and political philosophy, philosophy and literature, cinema, psychoanalysis, gender studies, sexuality studies, and other areas. Her research interests are in practical philosophy (particularly the strand of work in moral philosophy indebted to Elizabeth Anscombe), practical reason, Kant's ethics, Marx, and neo-Aristotelian naturalism.

NOTES

CHAPTER 1

1. Although I mention egoism and immorality separately here, egoism, for me, is still one particular type of immorality. I further understand the moral-immoral classification (where moral includes morally permissible as well as morally required) to be exhaustive. Accordingly, I take the amoralist to be just a particular kind of immoralist, not too different, if different at all, from the egoist.

2. Although egoism is an ethical perspective because it provides norms about how one should behave, it is not what I would regard as a moral perspective because it never requires a person to sacrifice her overall interest for the sake of others. Yet even when egoism is seen in this way as an ethical, not a moral, perspective, the egoist can still be regarded as immoral when she fails to conform to requirements of morality.

3. John Rawls is typical here, as is Thomas Nagel. See Rawls's *A Theory of Justice* (Cambridge, MA: Harvard University Press, 1971), p. 136, and Nagel's *The View from Nowhere* (New York: Oxford University Press), p. 200ff.

4. Ibid.

5. Alan Gewirth, *Reason and Morality* (Chicago: University of Chicago, 1978).

6. Another way to put the problem for Kant is that both the general principle of egoism and the categorical imperative are "unconditional" in that the acceptance of neither principle is conditional upon the acceptance of some more ultimate principle. In addition, both principles are universal and thus have the "form of law." This means that we do not have here a Kantian argument that favors morality over egoism. See Immanuel Kant, *Groundwork for a Metaphysics of Morals*, trans. H. D. Paton (New York: Harper and Row, 1956), pp. 420–421.

7. Christine Korsgaard, "The Sources of Normativity," in *The Tanner Lectures on Human Values* (Salt Lake City: University of Utah Press, 1992), pp. 20–112. In her e-mail comments on an earlier version of this argument (February 3, 2008), Korsgaard says that she does not intend her argument here to be an appeal to consistency as I characterize it, but rather argues that egoism fails a publicity requirement for reasons analogous to the way "private languages" fail a publicity requirement for languages. But in "The Sources of Normativity," Korsgaard does say, "The idea of a private language is inconsistent with the normativity of meaning" (p. 95), and I take this to also mean "inconsistent with the publicity of meaning." So I would have thought she is also claiming that just as private languages are inconsistent with the publicity of meaning, so egoism is inconsistent with the publicity of reasons. And, of course, what I am arguing here is that objectionable though the egoism may be on other grounds, the view is not inconsistent with a publicity requirement because its reasons are public, analogous to the way that languages are public, or to the way that the "oughts" or reasons of competitive games are public, even though they are not public in exactly the same way that moral reasons are public. But, of course, Korsgaard wasn't arguing that egoistic reasons fail a publicity requirement because they are not public in exactly the same way that moral reasons are public!

8. The universal ethical egoist has to see himself as having the same legitimate goals as everyone else. If the egoist is going to give his own self-interest complete priority, in consistency, he has to say that others can legitimately do the same. Of course, the claims he makes about himself and the claims he makes about others are asymmetrically action-guiding in contrary ways.

9. Those committed to morality, however, may want to hide their reasons from those who are not similarly committed in order to avoid being taken advantage of by such individuals.

10. Meeting the stronger publicity requirement of morality would render the practice of egoism self-defeating in just the same way that it would render the practice of many competitive games self-defeating. But this fact could only count against the practice of egoism if it also counts against the practice of competitive games, and it does not count against the practice of competitive games.

11. "Ought" presupposes "can" here. So unless people have the capacity to entertain and follow both self-interested and moral reasons for acting, it does not make any sense to ask whether they ought or ought not to do so. Moreover, as I will make clear later, moral reasons are understood here to include some altruistic reasons and some self-interested reasons. So the question of whether it is rational for us to follow self-interested reasons rather than moral reasons should be understood as the question of

whether it is rational for us to follow self-interested reasons exclusively rather than some appropriate set of self-interested reasons and altruistic reasons.

12. I understand the pure altruist to be the mirror image of the pure egoist. Whereas the pure egoist thinks that the interests of others do not count for herself, except instrumentally, the pure altruist thinks that her own interests do not count for herself, except instrumentally.

13. Of course, some philosophers have used the second strategy with the egoist and tried to derive morality from purely egoistic premises. David Gauthier's work *Morals by Agreement* (Oxford: Oxford University Press, 1986) takes this approach. However, I have argued elsewhere (*How to Make People Just* [Totowa, NJ: Rowman and Littlefield, 1988]) that the use of this particular strategy is unsuccessful, justifying at best a truncated morality. Moreover, altruists or those endorsing the altruistic side of morality have little or no reason to accept what results from using this strategy.

14. I will argue that the compromise view does provide a non-question-begging resolution to the particular debate between the egoist and the altruist. This is because neither the egoist nor the altruist has any non-question-begging grounds for not allowing both sorts of reasons to have prima facie status. So the debate between these views is not about the existence of self-interested or altruistic reasons but about which reasons should have priority (egoists say self-interested reasons always have priority, whereas altruists say that altruistic reasons always have priority). They are really not contesting the existence of the reasons they oppose. However, once both sorts of reasons are allowed prima facie status, we do have non-question-begging grounds for favoring high-ranking over low-ranking reasons, or so I argue. In that way, I claim, we get morality as compromise.

15. Nel Noddings, *Caring: A Feminine Approach to Ethics and Moral Education* (Berkeley: University of California Press, 1984); Joyce Trebilcot, ed., *Mothering* (Totowa, NJ: Rowman and Littlefield, 1983); Susan Brownmiller, *Femininity* (New York: Ballantine Books, 1984).

16. James Doyle, *The Male Experience* (Dubuque, IA: W. C. Brown and Co., 1983); Marie Richmond-Abbot, ed., *Masculine and Feminine,* 2nd ed. (New York: Random House, 1991). Of course, men often do behave altruistically as well, especially when there is a need to defend their families or their countries.

17. Victor Seidler, *Rediscovering Masculinity* (New York: Routledge, 1989); Larry May and Robert Strikwerda, *Rethinking Masculinity* (Lanham, MD: Rowman and Littlefield, 1992).

18. Some might want to question Mother Teresa's reputation as a paradigm of altruism. See Christopher Hitchens, *The Missionary Position: Mother Teresa in Theory*

and Practice (London: Verso, 1995). Others have suggested that I should cite a real-life paradigm of egoism here to match my reputed real-life paradigm of altruism. The problem is that successful real-life egoists tend to present themselves as being committed to morality. For this reason, even Thrasymachus is not really the best fictional paradigm of egoism because he is too public about his views, despite the fact that he has long played that role in philosophical discussion.

19. Notice, too, here that moral reasons and altruistic reasons are not equivalent sets of reasons. For example, altruistic reasons could recommend greater sacrifice of self-interest than morality permits.

20. This is because, as I shall argue, morality itself already represents a compromise between egoism and altruism.

21. William P. Barrett, "United Way's New Way," *Forbes*, January 16, 2006, at http://www.forbes.com/2006/01/13/united-way-philanthropy-cz_wb_0117unitedway.html.

22. As quoted in the *Outlook* 56 (1949): 1059. The original story used "selfishness" in each place that I have inserted "self-interest." But I think my usage captures the intent of the original story better than its own usage. This is because "selfishness" conveys the sense of "an excessive concern for oneself." But the original story did not intend to convey that meaning at all by its use of the term. By its use of "selfishness," the story just meant to convey "self-interest."

23. Notice that by "egoistic perspective" here I mean the view that grants the prima facie relevance of both egoistic and altruistic reasons to rational choice and then tries to argue for the superiority of egoistic reasons. Similarly, by "altruistic perspective" I mean the view that grants the prima facie relevance of both egoistic and altruistic reasons to rational choice and then tries to argue for the superiority of altruistic reasons.

24. I owe this objection to Michael Smith, and a later version of it to Martin Carrier.

25. We are imagining that we are getting a true and accurate ranking of a person's self-interested reasons from an egoistic perspective—one that may be different from what a person thinks is his or her true and accurate ranking of such reasons—and the same holds true of a person's altruistic reasons as seen from an altruistic perspective.

26. Of course, a defender of moral relativism, such as Gilbert Harman (see his *Moral Relativism and Moral Objectivity*, with Judith Jarvis Thomson [Oxford: Blackwell, 1996]), would not see the relativist as a foe of morality. However, for a critique of moral relativism, see my *Justice for Here and Now* (New York: Cambridge University Press, 1998), pp. 14–17. As far as the moral skeptic is concerned, she cannot be denying what the egoist grants for the sake of argument. Rather, what the moral skeptic must be claiming is that we do not know what I am trying to non-question-beggingly establish: that morality is justified over egoism and altruism. So to defeat the egoist, as I claim to do, really is to defeat the moral skeptic as well.

27. Appearances can be somewhat deceiving here, however. See the last section of this essay for an explanation of how there can be relatively deep conflicts between ourselves and members of future generations.

28. When we consider conflicts between humans and nonhumans, there appear to be even more "lifeboat situations" because, for one thing, humans need to eat something in order to live, and there are good reasons for them to generally avoid eating fellow humans.

29. Even high-ranking morally acceptable, but not morally required, self-interested reasons would have priority over low-ranking altruistic reasons with which they conflict.

30. See R. Duncan Luce and Howard Raiffa, *Games and Decisions* (New York: John Wiley and Sons, 1967), chap. 13. The analogy here is only partial because in decision theory, the equal probability assumption is applied under conditions of either imagined ignorance or existing, but not necessarily nonremedial, ignorance. In the egoism-altruism case, however, the choice situation is different because we are pretty confident we know, and are not just assuming, that neither egoism nor altruism provides a non-question-begging starting point.

31. See Bernard Gert, *Common Morality* (New York: Oxford University Press, 2006), pp. 86–88, 91–95.

32. The egoist does not appeal to any particular feature about himself that could provide a non-question-begging justification for his exclusive preference for his own interests. By contrast, the group-based immoralist does appeal to some shared feature of the group as a justification for her group-based preference. But that appeal is question-begging.

33. One interesting difference between these immoralities is that whereas the oughts of egoism, like the oughts of competitive games, are claimed to be asymmetrically action-guiding, the oughts of group-based moralities, like the oughts of morality, are claimed to be symmetrically action-guiding, and, unfortunately, even those who are oppressed by group-based immoralities sometimes accept them as such.

34. See Christine Korsgaard, *The Sources of Normativity* (Cambridge, UK: Cambridge University Press, 1996), p. 250.

35. Henry Sidgwick, *The Methods of Ethics*, 7th ed. (London: Macmillan, 1907), concluding chapter.

36. Thomas Nagel, *Equality and Partiality* (Oxford: Oxford University Press, 1991).

37. Samuel Scheffler, *Human Morality* (New York: Oxford University Press, 1992).

38. The justification for blaming and censuring such persons would not be based on any possibility for reforming them because we were assuming that they were incapable of reform. Rather, the justification would be based on what the persons in question deserve because of their past behavior and on whatever usefulness blaming and censuring them would have in deterring others.

39. Surely, the most defensible externalist and internalist views would hold that in order to appropriately blame people for not acting on certain reasons, it must be the case that they are, or were, at least capable of acting on those reasons. Internalists can further agree with externalists that moral reasons do not motivate under all conditions, just as externalists can further agree with internalists that moral reasons do, and must, motivate at least under some conditions.

40. Jeffrey Reiman, "What Ought 'Ought' Implies 'Can' Imply?" *Journal of Social Philosophy* 22 (1991): 73–80.

41. Ibid.

42. This objection I owe to Charles Pigden.

43. Here I am referring to right libertarians, such as John Hospers and Robert Nozick, not left libertarians, such as Hillel Steiner and Peter Vallentyne. Left libertarians, unlike right libertarians, assume that each person has an equal right to, or common ownership of, the earth's natural resources. And from this assumption, they do derive a right to welfare, but one that is not as robust as the one that I defend because it does not require the rich and talented to sacrifice any of the products of their labor to support it. Moreover, left libertarians usually fail to see future generations as having welfare rights against existing generations (Steiner explicitly argues against such rights), and so they do not end up endorsing the substantial equality that I defend.

Even among right libertarians, however, there are a few who endorse a minimal right to welfare, for example, Loren Lomasky, *Persons, Rights and the Moral Community* (New York: Oxford University Press, 1987), pp. 125–129. In this essay, however, I will be primarily addressing the overwhelming majority of right-wing libertarians who reject any right to welfare, starting from the premises of their view and arguing that these premises support both a right to welfare and substantial equality. Using this strategy here is appropriate, as I indicated earlier, because it is possible to work internally within the libertarian view to readjust its weighing of self-interested and altruistic reasons in order to bring it more in line with views to which it is seemingly opposed. Nor would the "backup" strategy work well for this particular debate, for the reasons I gave earlier.

44. F. A. Hayek, *The Constitution of Liberty* (Chicago: University of Chicago Press, 1960), p. 11.

45. John Hospers, *Libertarianism* (Los Angeles: Nash Publishing, 1971).

46. Ibid.

47. Isaiah Berlin, *Four Essays on Liberty* (New York: Oxford University Press, 1969), pp. xxxviii–xl.

48. On this point, see Maurice Cranston, *Freedom* (New York: Basic Books, 1953), pp. 52–53; C. B. Macpherson, *Democratic Theory* (Oxford: Oxford University Press,

1973), p. 95; Joel Feinberg, *Rights, Justice and the Bounds of Liberty* (Princeton, NJ: Princeton University Press, 1980), chap. 1.

49. I have earlier referred in a shorthand and somewhat imprecise way to "people doing what they want or are able to do," where I understood the first disjunct to include "and are able," as was clearly implied by the surrounding discussion.

50. Hospers, chap. 7, and Tibor Machan, *Human Rights and Human Liberties* (Chicago: Nelson-Hall, 1975), p. 231ff. We should think about the libertarian ideal of liberty as securing for each person the largest morally defensible bundle of liberties possible.

51. In the libertarian view, property can also be legitimately acquired by producing it out of what one already owns or legitimately possesses.

52. See Milton Friedman, *Capitalism and Freedom* (Chicago: University of Chicago Press, 1962), pp. 161–172; Robert Nozick, *Anarchy, State, and Utopia* (New York: Basic Books, 1974), pp. 160–164.

53. Basic needs, if not satisfied, lead to significant lacks or deficiencies with respect to a standard of mental and physical well-being. Thus, a person's needs for food, shelter, medical care, protection, companionship, and self-development are, at least in part, needs of this sort. For a discussion of basic needs, see my *How to Make People Just,* pp. 45–48.

54. Tibor Machan, *Libertarianism Defended* (Burlington, VT: Ashgate, 2006), chap. 20; Eric Mack, "Libertarianism Untamed," *Journal of Social Philosophy* 22 (1991): 64–72; Jan Narveson, "Comments on Sterba's *Ethics* Article," unpublished circulated paper (1994) and Narveson's *Libertarian Idea* (Peterborough, CA: Broadview Press, 2001), p. 35.

55. Libertarians have never rejected the need for enforcement when important liberties are at stake.

56. The combined predicate "unreasonable/contrary to reason" in my version of the "ought" implies "can" principle is meant to suggest that the unreasonableness of the sacrifice or restriction being assessed here is not to be determined simply by an assessment of the magnitude of the burden imposed on the agent in and of itself, but rather also requires an assessment of the reasonableness of imposing this burden in light of related burdens and obligations imposed on others.

Moreover, there are moral requirements, such as love your neighbor as yourself (if it is a moral requirement), that violate the "ought" implies "can" principle, except when they are interpreted in an aspirational way. There are also moral requirements that give rise to residual obligations when they cannot be straightforwardly fulfilled, such as a promise to return a borrowed item one has just lost, and on that account do not really violate the "ought" implies "can" principle. There are still other requirements that violate the "ought" implies "can" principle but do not appear to be moral requirements, such as that kleptomaniacs ought not to steal, unless they are interpreted as giving rise to indirect requirements, such as that kleptomaniacs ought to seek psychological help, in which case these requirements do not violate the "ought" implies "can" principle. See Charles Pigden, "Ought-Implies-Can: Erasmus, Luther and R. M. Hare," *Sophia* (1990): 2–30; Steve Sapontzis, "'Ought' Does Imply 'Can,'" *Southern Journal of Philosophy* (1991): 383–393; Terrance McConnell, "'Ought' Implies 'Can,'" and the Scope of Moral Requirements," *Philosophia* (1989): 437–454; Alan Montefiore, "'Ought' and 'Can,'" *Philosophical Quarterly* (1954): 24–40.

57. It should be pointed out that the "ought" implies "can" principle primarily ranges over that part of morality that we can justifiably enforce against others because we can reasonably expect that its requirements are accessible to those to whom they apply.

58. Here again we should think about the libertarian ideal of liberty as securing for each person the largest morally defensible bundle of liberties possible.

59. As I state in the text, this requirement "that moral resolutions must resolve conflicts of interest in ways that it is reasonable and not contrary to reason to require everyone affected to accept" is actually the contrapositive of the "ought" implies "can" principle, as I stated it in the text. Whereas the "ought" implies "can" principle claims that if any action is not reasonable or is contrary to reason to ask or require a person to do, all things considered, that action is not morally required or a moral resolution for that person, all things considered [–R/C(A v Req)–> –MReq/MRes], the above requirement claims that if any action is morally required or a moral resolution for a person to do, all things considered, that action is reasonable and not contrary to reason to ask or require that person to do, all things considered [MReq/MRes–> R/C(A v Re)].

60. The basis for this understanding is the priority of high-ranking altruistic reasons over conflicting low-ranking self-interested reasons that is non-question-beggingly justified in morality as compromise, combined with the further realization (following from our discussion of the libertarian ideal of liberty) that since we must coercively support one or the other of these reasons, we should support (require) the reason that has moral priority, in this case, the high-ranking altruistic reason that corresponds to the negative liberty of the poor not to be interfered with in taking from the surplus of the rich what they require to meet their basic needs.

61. By the liberty of the rich to meet their luxury needs, I continue to mean the liberty of the rich not to be interfered with when using their surplus possessions for luxury purposes. Similarly, by the liberty of the poor to meet their basic needs, I continue to mean the liberty of the poor not to be interfered with when taking what they require to meet their basic needs from the surplus possessions of the rich.

62. The employment opportunities offered to the poor must be honorable and supportive of self-respect. To do otherwise would be to offer the poor the opportunity to meet some of their basic needs at the cost of denying some of their other basic needs.

63. What these "former" poor give back, however, will not likely go to the rich but to others who are still poor.

64. For a time, I thought so myself. See my *Justice for Here and Now*, chap. 3.

65. Working for one's fellow citizens is somewhat analogous to fighting for them, but libertarians are unlikely to see it that way.

66. See John Hospers, "The Libertarian Manifesto," in James P. Sterba, ed., *Morality in Practice*, 7th ed. (Belmont, CA: Wadsworth Publishing Co., 2004), especially p. 32.

67. Sometimes advocates of libertarianism inconsistently contend that the duty to help others is supererogatory but that a majority of a society could justifiably enforce such a duty on everyone. See Theodore Benditt, "The Demands of Justice," in *Economic Justice*, ed. Diana Meyers and Kenneth Kipnis (Lanham, MD: Rowman and Littlefield, 1985).

68. Sometimes advocates of libertarianism focus on the coordination problems that arise in welfare states concerning the provision of welfare and ignore the far more serious coordination problems that would arise in a night watchman state. See Burton Leiser, "Vagrancy, Loitering and Economic Justice," in *Economic Justice* (1985).

69. It is true, of course, that if the rich could retain the resources that are used in a welfare state for meeting the basic needs of the poor, they might have the option of using those resources to increase employment opportunities beyond what exists in any given welfare state, but this particular way of increasing employment opportunities does not seem to be the most effective way of meeting the basic needs of the poor, and it would not at all serve to meet the basic needs of those who cannot work.

70. Again, libertarians have never rejected the need for enforcement when important liberties are at stake.

71. This result, in turn, correlates with the moral priority of high-ranking altruistic reasons over conflicting low-ranking self-interested reasons.

72. When the poor are acting collectively in conjunction with their agents and allies to exercise their negative welfare rights, they will want, in turn, to institute adequate positive welfare rights to secure a proper distribution of the goods and resources they are acquiring.

73. Rex Martin, *Rawls and Rights* (Lawrence: University of Kansas, 1984), chap. 2.

74. Anita Gordon and David Suzuki, *It's a Matter of Survival* (Cambridge, MA: Harvard University Press, 1990). See also Donella H. Meadows, Dennis L. Meadows, Jorgen Randers, and William W. Behrens III, *The Limits to Growth,* 2nd ed. (New York: New American Library, 1974), chaps. 3 and 4.

75. Actually, I argued earlier only that the poor must take advantage of whatever opportunities are available to them to engage in mutually beneficial work, but it is this broader claim that I am making here that is required.

76. See http://www.worldhunger.org/articles/Learn/world%20hunger%20facts% 202002.

77. Thomas Pogge, *World Poverty and Human Rights* (Cambridge, MA: Polity, 2002), p. 204ff.

78. Peter Singer, "What Should a Billionaire Give—and What Should You?" *New York Times,* December 17, 2006.

79. Ibid.

80. See http://www.balance.org/articles/factsheet2001.html.

81. Ibid.

82. Ibid.

83. Ibid.

84. Lester Brown, *Plan B 2.0* (New York: W. W. Norton and Co., 2006), pp. 84–91. See also Lester Brown, *Outgrowing the Earth* (New York: W. W. Norton and Co., 2004), especially chap. 5.

85. Linda Starke, ed., *State of the World, 2004* (New York: W. W. Norton and Co., 2004), p. 9. For a lower comparative consumption comparison that still supports the same conclusion, see Jared Diamond, "What's Your Consumption Factor?" *International Herald Tribune,* January 3, 2008.

86. See ibid. There is no way that the resource consumption of the United States can be matched by developing and underdeveloped countries, and even if it could be matched, doing so would clearly lead to ecological disaster. See Constance Mungall and Digby McLaren, eds., *Planet Under Stress* (Oxford: Oxford University Press, 1990) and Frances Lappe and Joseph Collins, *World Hunger: Twelve Myths* (New York: Grove Press, 1986).

87. To say, then, that future generations have rights against existing generations, we can simply mean that there are enforceable requirements against existing generations that would benefit or prevent harm to future generations.

88. Of course, there is always the problem of others not doing their fair share. Nevertheless, as long as your sacrifice would avoid some basic harm to others, either now or in the future, it would still seem reasonable to claim that you would remain under an obligation to make that sacrifice, regardless of what others are doing.

89. See, for example, Jared Diamond, *Collapse* (New York: Penguin, 2005) and Ronald Wright, *A Short History of Progress* (New York: Carroll and Graf, 2004).

90. Derek Parfit, *Persons and Reasons* (Oxford: Clarendon Press, 1984).

91. A similar example was used by James Woodward in "The Non-Identity Problem," *Ethics* 96 (1986): 804–831. Woodward also provides the example of Viktor Frankl, who suggests that his imprisonment in a Nazi concentration camp enabled him to develop "certain resources of character, insights into the human condition and capacities for appreciation" that he would not otherwise have had. At the same time, we clearly want to say that the Nazis unjustifiably violated Frankl's rights by so imprisoning him (Woodward, p. 809). See also Norman Daniels, "Intergenerational Justice," *Stanford Encyclopedia* (2003).

92. Again, to appeal here to premises acceptable to libertarians, giving up or sacrificing the satisfaction of basic or nonbasic needs can be taken to imply merely noninterference for the sake of the satisfaction of such needs.

CHAPTER 2

1. H. A. Prichard, "Duty and Interest" (1928), reprinted in Wilfrid Sellars and John Hospers, eds., *Readings in Ethical Theory,* 2nd ed. (Englewood Cliffs, NJ: Prentice-Hall, 1970), pp. 690–703.

2. Rawls, *A Theory of Justice.*

3. My thanks to Tyler Zimmer for the computer graphics.

4. In his reply to me, Sterba draws on the distinction between individual and universal ethical egoism. But to begin with, I think the lexical-scalar differentiation I am introducing cuts across this familiar distinction, so that either version could be put forward in lexical or scalar form. More important, though, I am not representing my counterexample to Sterba as a modified version of egoistic morality but as a policy of immorality. In that respect, adopting Sterba's vocabulary might have been a mistake, insofar as egoism is often interpreted as representing a competing ethic. So perhaps I should just have spoken of the "immoralist" throughout. As I interpret the classic challenge, then, it is to prove to the immoralist that morality is rationally required, and that is what I took Sterba to be trying to do. Demonstrating that egoism, whether individual or universal, is problematic as a moral theory does not, it seems to me, answer this challenge, since the immoralist is not trying to put forward a moral theory in the first place but rather a prudential policy of how best to operate. One refutes him by showing that this policy is irrational, not that it's immoral (though it is). What I have tried to illustrate above is that Sterba's particular attempt to show the immoralist that rationality demands morality does not work, since even by Sterba's "rational compromise" criterion, the immoralist could take others' interests into account in a noninstrumental way, but give them far lesser weight than his own, thereby continuing to act immorally.

CHAPTER 3

1. G. E. M. Anscombe, "On Promising and Its Justice, and Whether It Need Be Respected in Foro Interno," in *The Collected Philosophical Papers of G. E. M. Anscombe,* vol. 3, *Ethics, Religion and Politics* (Oxford: Basil Blackwell, 1981), p. 19.

2. For an excellent account of the rational structure of moral conduct, see Michael Thompson, "What Is It to Wrong Someone? A Puzzle About Justice," in R. Jay Wallace, Philip Pettit, Samuel Scheffler, and Michael Smith, eds., *Reason and Value: Themes from the Moral Philosophy of Joseph Raz* (Oxford: Oxford University Press, 2004), pp. 333–384.

3. G. E. M. Anscombe, "Modern Moral Philosophy," *Philosophy* 33 (1958): 1–19; reprinted in *The Collected Philosophical Papers of G. E. M. Anscombe,* vol. 3, *Ethics, Religion and Politics,* pp. 26–42; more recently reprinted in Mary Geach and Luke Gormally, eds., *Human Life, Action, and Ethics: Essays by G. E. M. Anscombe* (Essex, UK: Imprint Academic, 2005), pp. 169–194. Page references in the notes will be to the 1981, *Collected Papers,* 3rd ed., hereafter MMP. For this reference, see MMP, p. 40.

4. I use "source" to mark what is in the will and can be expressed in intentional action as such—partly captured in sentences like "Promises are to be kept," but also involving skills, attention to salient aspects of circumstances, and patterns of judgment.

5. John Rawls, "Two Concepts of Rules," reprinted in Philippa Foot, ed., *Theories of Ethics* (Oxford: Oxford University Press, 1967), pp. 144–170.

6. Again, not just the rules of the game, but also the skills, patterns of attention, a sense for play, and so on.

7. Anscombe, "On Promising and Its Justice," pp. 10–21. The essay begins with a paradox: It would seem that a man cannot do such things as marry, enter into a contract, swear an oath, or make a gift, because in order to do so, he must think that he is doing so, but, "If thinking that you are getting married is essential to getting married, then mention of thinking that you are getting married belongs to the explanation of what getting married is; but then won't an explanation of what getting married is be required if we are to give the content of the thought that one is getting married? Hence it will be impossible to say what is the thought of the man who thinks he is getting married; and so generally for all cases of this type" (p. 10).

8. Language-games are more diverse than full-blown social practices in the relevant sense of "practice." Full-blown social practices require an institutional context (for Anscombe and her followers). Language-games are conventional tools or techniques but are more various than social practices.

9. See G. E. M. Anscombe, "On the Source of the Authority of the State," *Ethics, Religion and Politics,* pp. 134–135. For extensive discussion of this point in Rawls, David Gauthier, and Philippa Foot, see Michael Thompson, "Some Remarks on the Role of Generality in Practice," PhD dissertation, UCLA, 1992. For extensive criticism of neo-Kantian attempts to make sense of the singular source, see Michael Thompson, "What Is It to Wrong Someone?" pp. 334–384.

10. Anscombe, "On Promising and Its Justice," p. 17.

11. Anscombe's own forays into responding to the objection are to be found in the late lectures "Knowledge and Reverence for Human Life," reprinted in Geach and Gormally, eds., *Human Life, Action, and Ethics,* pp. 59–66, and "The Dignity of the Human Being," ibid., pp. 67–73, as well as an earlier essay, "Authority in Morals," reprinted in *The Collected Philosophical Papers of G. E. M. Anscombe,* vol. 3, pp. 43–50. All involve some reliance upon divine law ethics (in the lecture on reverence, for example, she urges that the Holy Spirit has given us the light by which we can apprehend the intrinsic value of human life), but the essay on authority argues that some moral knowledge could not be primarily revealed, for example, fundamental precepts of justice.

12. MMP, p. 36.

CHAPTER 4

1. Plato, *Republic,* in *The Collected Dialogues of Plato,* ed. Edith Hamilton and Huntington Cairns, trans. Paul Shorey (Princeton, NJ: Princeton University Press, 1980), pp. 575–844.

2. Thomas Hobbes, *Leviathan,* ed. Michael Oakeshott (New York: Collier Books, 1962).

3. David Hume, *An Enquiry Concerning the Principles of Morals,* ed. J. B. Schneewind (Indianapolis: Hackett, 1983). See Hume's discussion of the sensible knave.

4. Immanuel Kant, *Groundwork for the Metaphysics of Morals,* trans. and ed. Mary J. Gregor (New York: Cambridge University Press, 1996), pp. 370–540.

5. Henry Sidgwick, *The Methods of Ethics,* 7th ed. (Indianapolis: Hackett, 1981).

6. David Gauthier, *Morals by Agreement* (New York: Oxford University Press, 1986).

7. David Gauthier, Jean Hampton, Gregory Kavka, and others favor this reading of Hobbes, who arguably takes the goal of defeating the skeptic to shape the contractarian moral theory he defends. Whereas Hobbes speaks in terms of desires and interests, Gauthier favors the language of preferences.

8. See Gauthier, *Morals by Agreement,* pp. 87, 100–104.

9. I understand egoism to be a moral theory, according to which one always ought (in a moral sense of "ought") to act in ways that best promote one's self-interest. Here, Sterba must mean that egoism gives us a rational ought: One ought, rationally speaking, always to act in ways that best promote one's self-interest. This reading I understand to be the traditional position of the skeptic.

10. But acting in ways that best promote one's overall self-interest need not entail acting immorally, since it might be the case that acting morally is in one's overall self-interest.

11. This I take to be the assumption made in the traditional view of the skeptic, that one can have any desires but moral ones, that is, an intrinsic interest in the interests of others.

12. Traditionally, no distinction is drawn between moral reasons and altruistic reasons. Moral reasons are taken to include altruistic reasons, as Sterba defines them. A moral theory might require altruism, and it might not.

13. I discuss problems with Hobbes's and Gauthier's attempts to defeat the skeptic in my book, *The Moral Skeptic* (New York: Oxford University Press, 2009).

14. Gauthier, *Morals by Agreement,* p. 1. This was one of Gauthier's objections to Hobbes's strategy, and one reason he favors attempting to show that being morally disposed is rationally required because it is in one's self-interest, but that every instance of acting on one's moral disposition is rational but in some other sense than self-interested.

15. Hampton states: "If you ask me why I should treat you morally, and I respond by saying that it is in my interest to do so, I am telling you that my regard for you is something that is merely instrumentally valuable to me; I do not give you that regard because there is something about you that merits it, regardless of the usefulness of that regard to me." See Jean Hampton, "Feminist Contractarianism," in Louise M. Antony and Charlotte E. Witt, eds., *A Mind of One's Own: Feminist Essays on Reason and Objectivity,* 2nd ed., pp. 337–368, at 234.

16. I offer my own criticisms of it in *The Moral Skeptic.* These include: that it unnecessarily constrains the kind of answer we can give to the skeptic by grounding it in self-interest, that its formal version does not exclude as irrational desires deformed by patriarchy, and that it is consistent with psychopathy because it does not require that the agent have desires and interests in the full sense, seeing their connection to reasons for action.

17. See Jean Hampton, *The Authority of Reason* (New York: Cambridge University Press, 1998), p. 238, and the discussion at pp. 234–241, for the justification of expected utility theory.

18. See, for example, Elizabeth Anderson, *Values in Ethics and Economics* (Cambridge, MA: Harvard University Press, 1995), especially chap. 6.

19. Sterba notes that even utilitarianism represents a nonarbitrary compromise between self-interested and altruistic reasons, but he does not explain why.

20. This point is debated thoroughly by many of the contributors to the anthology *Self-Interest,* ed. Ellen Frankel Paul, Fred D. Miller Jr., and Jeffrey Paul (New York: Cambridge University Press, 1997).

21. David Gauthier, "Morality and Advantage," *Philosophical Review* 76: 460–475.

22. The difference, of course, is that for Kant, being an interest-bearer warrants one's having intrinsic value, but for Hobbes, it warrants one's having only instrumental value.

23. See *The Moral Skeptic.*

24. See my discussion in *The Moral Skeptic* at pp. 123–125.

25. Jon Elster calls consistency a "thin theory of rationality." See Jon Elster, *Sour Grapes: Studies in the Subversion of Rationality* (New York: Cambridge University Press, 1983), p. 1.

26. More specifically, I argue for invoking consistency as coherence (rather than noncontradiction) existing between an agent's reasons for adopting a moral disposition, the argument for the moral theory or set of principles that the agent adopts (this invokes the Kantian notion of intrinsic value of persons), the agent's reasons for acting, and the agent's desire to be a moral person as reflected in the maxim the agent adopts. See *The Moral Skeptic.*

CHAPTER 5

1. Midway through his essay in Chap. 1, Sterba claims that egoists and altruists "are really not contesting the existence of the reasons they oppose." Their dispute is only about the relative importance of such reasons. But this seems mistaken. The reasons that altruists endorse are nonderivative altruistic reasons—reasons to do things because they serve the interests of others, and not because they serve self-interest. Rational egoists do reject such reasons. Of course, they allow that we sometimes have reason to help others. But there are such reasons only insofar as acting on them helps oneself. Egoists insist that any altruistic reason is wholly derivative—every genuine altruistic reason is also, and more important, an egoistic reason—so, if egoists are right, there can be no question of how to rank altruistic versus egoistic reasons. For the rational egoist, all reasons are really egoistic ones, so there are not two relevant scales, but only one.

CHAPTER 6

1. See my "Morality as Consistency in Living: Korsgaard's Kantian Lectures," *Ethics* 110 (1999): 140–164.

2. Robert Audi, "Acting for Reasons," *Philosophical Review* 95 (1986): 513.

3. See my *Wise Choices, Apt Feelings: A Theory of Normative Judgment* (Cambridge: Harvard University Press, 1990) and *Thinking How to Live* (Cambridge, MA: Harvard University Press, 2003).

4. See the early portion of Sterba's essay in Chapter 2 here.

5. Sterba says early in his essay here that many different compromises between egoism and altruism are possible.

6. Motives of self-regard for altruism, though, can't be dismissed, I would agree. The Judaic tradition includes: "If I am not for myself, who will be for me? If I am not for others, what am I?" The first could be a universalistic vindication of a nonfundamental ground for looking after one's interests. The second, favoring strictly altruistic motives, is an appeal to self-regard.

7. See the early part Sterba's essay in this volume.

8. Rawls, *A Theory of Justice*.

9. Henry Sidgwick, *Methods of Ethics*, Book 3, 7th ed. (London: Macmillan, 1907); W. D. Ross, *The Right and the Good* (Oxford: Clarendon Press, 1930); my "Why Theorize How to Live with Each Other?" *Philosophy and Phenomenological Research* 55 (1995): 323–342.

10. R. M. Hare, "Could Kant Have Been a Utilitarian?" *Utilitas* 5 (1) (May 1993): 243–264.

11. See my "Natural Property Rights," *Nous* 10 (1976): 77–88.

12. Alan Page Fiske, "The Four Elementary Forms of Sociality: Framework for a Unified Theory of Social Relations," *Psychological Review* 99 (1992): 689–723. Some of the labeling here is mine.

13. My best recollection from 1966.

14. For these arguments, see John Broome, *Weighing Goods: Equality, Uncertainty, and Time* (Oxford: Basil Blackwell, 1991); and my *Reconciling Our Aims: In Search for Bases in Ethics* (Oxford: Oxford University Press, 2008), with Broome commentary and my reply.

15. See my "What's Morally Special About Free Exchange?" *Social Philosophy and Policy* 2 (1985): 20–28.

16. This kind of thinking is central to Rawls's *A Theory of Justice*.

17. I investigate how such arguments work in *Reconciling Our Aims*.

18. Hal R. Varian, "Redistributive Taxation as Social Insurance," *Journal of Public Economics* 14 (1980): 49–68.

19. *The Economist*, September 12, 2009.

20. Amartya Sen, *Poverty and Famines: An Essay on Entitlement and Deprivation* (Oxford: Clarendon Press, 1981).

CHAPTER 7

1. Sterba does not employ the notation I use in the text. For the moment I will accept that reasons can be simply ordered. See below, §2.

2. For example, his invocation of the analogy with the principle of insufficient reason suggests that in the absence of further information, the two sets of considerations should be treated as equally important. Cf. also his remark that "it may also be objected that my argument for favoring morality over egoism and altruism would be analogous to naturalists and supernaturalists splitting the difference between their views and counting supernaturalist reasons as valid half of the time, and naturalist reasons as valid the other half of the time." I try to show in this essay that any equal weighing of self-regarding and altruistic considerations would be deeply implausible.

3. Rawls, *A Theory of Justice*, p. 153ff.

4. W. D. Hamilton, "The Genetical Evolution of Social Behaviour, I," *Journal of Theoretical Biology* 7 (1964): 1–16. For a very helpful discussion, see Natalie Henrich and Joseph Henrich, *Why Humans Cooperate* (Oxford: Oxford University Press, 2007), p. 45ff.

5. See Elliot Sober and David Sloan Wilson, *Unto Others: The Evolution and Psychology of Unselfish Behavior* (Cambridge, MA: Harvard University Press, 1998), p. 18ff.

6. According to one way of formalizing this idea, S is an evolutionarily stable strategy if and only if, with respect to a mutant strategy S^* that might arise, either (1) the expected payoff of S against itself is higher than the expected payoff of the mutant S^* against S or (2) while the expected payoff of S against itself is equal to the expected payoff of S^* against S, the expected payoff of S against S^* is higher than the expected payoff of S^* against itself. The idea is this. Suppose that we have an S population in which one or a few S^* types are introduced. Because of the predominance of S types, both S and S^* will play most of their games against S. According to the first rule, if S does better against itself than S^* does against S, S^* will not get a foothold in the population. Suppose instead that S^* does just as well against S as S does against itself. Then S^* will begin to grow in the population, until there are enough S^* so that both S and S^* play against S^* reasonably often. According to the second rule, once this

happens, if S does better against S* than S* does against itself, S will again grow at a more rapid rate. To say, then, that S is an ESS is to say that an invading strategy will, over time, do less well than will S. There are other ways of formulating the basic idea of an evolutionarily stable strategy, but that need not detain us here.

7. Henrich and Henrich, *Why Humans Cooperate,* p. 45.

8. In which a female has two alleles but a male only one.

9. For a very helpful survey, see Henrich and Henrich, *Why Humans Cooperate,* chap. 3; Sober and Wilson present the case for the importance of genetic group selection in *Unto Others.*

10. See Robert Axelrod, *The Evolution of Cooperation* (New York: Basic Books, 1974).

11. See, for example, Brian Skyrms, *The Evolution of the Social Contract* (Cambridge, UK: Cambridge University Press, 1996), chaps. 3 and 4.

12. See Henrich and Henrich, *Why Humans Cooperate,* p. 42.

13. See Robert Boyd and Peter J. Richerson, "The Evolution of Reciprocity in Sizable Groups," in their *The Origin and Evolution of Cultures* (Oxford: Oxford University Press, 2005), chap. 8. See also Peter J. Richerson and Robert Boyd, *Not by Genes Alone: How Culture Transformed Human Evolution* (Chicago: University of Chicago Press, 2006), p. 197ff.

14. But cf. Skyrms, *The Evolution of the Social Contract,* pp. 61–62.

15. I am following Robert Boyd, Herbert Gintis, Samuel Bowles, and Peter J. Richerson, "The Evolution of Altruistic Punishment," in Herbert Gintis, Samuel Bowles, Robert Boyd, and Ernst Fehr, eds., *Moral Sentiments and Material Interests: The Foundations of Cooperation in Economic Life* (Cambridge: MIT Press, 2005), pp. 215–227.

16. See ibid.; Boyd and Richerson, "Why People Punish Defectors," in their *The Origin and Evolution of Cultures,* chap. 10.

17. See Boyd and Richerson, "Punishment Allows the Evolution of Cooperation (or Anything Else) in Sizable Groups," in their *The Origin and Evolution of Cultures,* chap. 9.

18. Armin Falk, Ernst Fehr, and Urs Fischbacher, "Driving Forces Behind Informal Sanctions," IZA Discussion Paper No. 1635 (June 2005). Available at SSRN: http://ssrn.com/abstract=756366.

19. Ibid., p. 15. This is not to deny that there is disagreement on the best interpretation of the data. For more egalitarian interpretations, see Christopher T. Dawes, James H. Fowler, Tim Johnson, Richard McElreath, and Oleg Smirnov, "Egalitarian Motives in Humans," *Nature* 446 (April 12, 2007): 794–96; James Fowler, Tim

Johnson, and Oleg Smirnov, "Egalitarian Motive and Altruistic Punishment," *Nature* 433 (January 6, 2004): E1.

20. I develop this idea in *The Order of Public Reason: A Theory of Freedom and Morality in a Diverse and Bounded World* (Cambridge, UK: Cambridge University Press, 2011), chap. 3.

21. Evidence supports the hypothesis that norms about fairness to strangers develop along with markets. Ibid., chap. 8.

22. Sober and Wilson, *Unto Others*, p. 240. Emphasis in original.

23. Ibid.

24. See Cristina Bicchieri and Erte Xiao, "Do the Right Thing: But Only If Others Do So," *Journal of Behavioral Decision Making* 22 (2009): 191–208. In their experimental work on public goods games among the Machiguenga and the Mapuche, Joseph Henrich and Natalie Smith also found that "the primary indicator of what a subject will do is what the subject thinks the rest of the group will do." "Comparative Evidence from Machi-guenga, Mapuche, and American Populations," in J. Henrich, R. Boyd, S. Bowles, et al., eds., *Foundations of Human Sociality: Economic Experiments and Ethnographic Evidence from Fifteen Small-Scale Societies* (Oxford: Oxford University Press, 2004), pp. 125–167 at p. 153.

25. Perhaps there are certain wild-eyed libertarians who, regardless of the background institutions and the norms in play, will always respond "Let them eat cake!" (though we should remember that Marie Antoinette does not have a place in the libertarian pantheon). If some libertarians think that claims to property need not be justified in terms of norms, rules, and institutions that give reasonable benefits to all participants, and which all as free and equal moral persons can endorse, then Sterba is entirely right to dismiss such views. But, as I have been stressing, the serious and difficult issue is what background norms and institutions satisfy these conditions.

CHAPTER 8

1. See, for example, James Sterba, "A Libertarian Justification for a Welfare State," *Social Theory and Practice* 2 (1) (Fall 1985): 285–306.

2. This passage is taken from an extensive e-mail exchange between Sterba and me conducted in the spring of 2008.

3. For how Locke handled such a case, see H. L. A. Hart, "Are There Any Natural Rights?" *Philosophical Review* 64 (1955): 175.

4. Ayn Rand, "Value and Rights," in J. Hospers, ed., *Readings in Introductory Philosophical Analysis* (Englewood Cliffs, NJ: Prentice-Hall, 1968), p. 382.

5. Douglas B. Rasmussen and Douglas J. Den Uyl, *Norms of Liberty: A Perfectionist Basis for Non-Perfectionist Politics* (University Park: Penn State University Press, 2005).

6. Ibid.

7. See Sterba, "A Libertarian Justification for a Welfare State."

8. See, for example, John Kekes, "'Ought Implies Can' and Kinds of Morality," *Philosophical Quarterly* 34 (1984): 460–467. See also Kekes, *Facing Evil* (Princeton, NJ: Princeton University Press, 1991), which includes the bulk of the discussion from the aforementioned paper as well as others, such as "Freedom," *Pacific Philosophical Quarterly* 61 (1980): 368–385. I address Kekes's case in Tibor R. Machan, *Initiative— Human Agency and Society* (Stanford, CA: Hoover Institution Press, 2000).

9. James P. Sterba, "Progress in Reconciliation: Evidence from the Right and the Left," *Journal of Social Philosophy* 28 (Fall 1997): 102.

10. Sterba, "A Libertarian Justification for a Welfare State," pp. 295–296.

11. Hart, "Are There Any Natural Rights?"

12. See http://esciencenews.com/articles/2008/05/01/researchers.explore.altruisms .unexpected.ally.selfishness.

CHAPTER 9

1. In the most recent version of his comments, Mills, to the same effect, still talks about the scalar egoist subordinating everyone but himself.

2. See Mills's essay, note 4, in Chapter 2 of this volume.

3. Ibid. In this note, Mills makes the additional claim that his lexical/scalar distinction cuts across the individual/universal egoism distinction. So what is at issue here is whether scalar egoism can take on both individual and universal forms. I claim that scalar egoism, given that it involves individual privileging, can be only a form of individual ethical egoism, thereby subject to the insurmountable difficulties that form of egoism faces. Scalar egoism treats people differently, depending on where they fall on a scale. By contrast, universal ethical egoism generates the same (asymmetrical) oughts of self-interest for everyone. So the two forms of egoism are quite different.

4. I think I got the idea for this strategy from Paul Taylor's use of it against anthropocentrism in his *Respect for Nature* (Princeton, NJ: Princeton University Press, 1987).

5. Superson mistakenly claims that I think the moral skeptic is agnostic between egoistic and moral reasons. In fact, I hold the standard view that the moral skeptic

claims to be agnostic only about moral reasons. As I put it, the moral skeptic claims not to know that morality is justified over egoism and altruism (see my essay in Chapter 1, note 26).

6. Superson cites Judith Thomson's argument in favor of abortion as paralleling her preferred way of arguing with the moral skeptic. And it does parallel Superson's argument. Thomson assumes in her argument that the fetus is a person and with this assumption still claims to derive a right to abortion in cases of rape and maybe in cases where all precautions have been taken to avoid conception. But this is not even the right to abortion guaranteed by *Roe v. Wade.* Accordingly, Thomson would surely have to allow that her argument justifies only a truncated right to abortion, and that it also begs the question against the prochoice side of the debate by assuming that the fetus is a person. So just as Thomson's argument in favor of abortion begs the question against the pro-choice side of the abortion debate, Superson's way of arguing with the moral skeptic also begs the question against morality or altruism.

7. I shift the discussion here from one of self-interested reasons and moral reasons to one of self-interested reasons and altruistic reasons because I regard altruistic reasons as more fundamental and because I understand moral reasons as themselves constituting an approved set of both self-interested reasons and altruistic reasons.

8. Compromising here would involve favoring high-ranking moral reasons over conflicting low-ranking self-interested reasons and favoring high-ranking self-interested reasons over conflicting low-ranking moral reasons.

9. Nor can Superson claim that there is need to endorse consistency as impartiality in order to avoid the distortions of deformed desires. In my account, simply requiring that people's self-interested reasons truly represent what is in the best interest of the individual and that their altruistic reasons truly represent what is in the best interest of others achieves the same effect without employing an explicitly moral-laden standard to get there.

In her book, Superson appeals to a requirement to acknowledge each individual's intrinsic worth to eliminate deformed desires, but this well-known Kantian requirement is also explicitly morally laden, and, hence, question-begging against egoism (see Superson, *The Moral Skeptic,* p. 84ff). Later, not surprisingly, Superson connects this morally laden requirement with what we have regarded as the similarly morally laden requirement of consistency as impartiality. See Superson, p. 124ff. What is surprising, however, is that Superson claims that both these requirements—requirements that are widely regarded to be moral requirements—are, in fact, as stated, requirements of rationality and so not explicitly morally laden at all! Superson, p. 84ff and p. 124ff.

10. See my essay in Chap. 1.

11. James P. Sterba, *How to Make People Just* (Lanham, MD: Rowman and Little-field, 1988), chap. 9, and *Justice for Here and Now*, chap. 2.

12. In a lengthy endnote, Shafer-Landau criticizes my claim that egoists and altruists "are really not contesting the existence of the reasons they oppose." But he fails to note the circumstances under which I think this claim holds. First, the claim presupposes that egoists and altruists are arguing non-question-beggingly with each other. Second, it presupposes that they are just beginning their debate, given that each hopes to conclude the debate by showing that their reasons always override all other reasons—which is sort of the equivalent of there really not being other sorts of reasons after all.

13. See my essay, Chapter 1.

14. See ibid., note 63.

15. Citing an endnote, Gibbard claims I allow for different resolutions to the conflict between self-interested and altruistic reasons, but all that I claim in that endnote is that there are different strategies for seeking a non-question-begging resolution of such conflicts, some more useful in certain contexts, and others more useful in other contexts.

16. Judith Warner, "The Way We Live Now: The Charitable-Giving Divide," *New York Times*, August 22, 2010.

17. Tibor Machan, "The Nonexistence of Welfare Rights" (new expanded version), in Tibor Machan and Douglas Rasmussen, eds., *Liberty for the Twenty-first Century*, in the Social, Political, and Legal Philosophy Series, ed. James P. Sterba (Lanham, MD: Rowman and Littlefield, 1995), pp. 218–220.

18. Sterba, *Justice for Here and Now*, pp. 66–67.

19. E-mail from Tibor Machan, May 16, 2008: "Since we have no fully free libertarian society, any more than some full blown welfare state or socialist polity—indeed virtually all but the most authoritarian systems (e.g., Saudi Arabia) are a political-economic smorgasbord—there is no way to test this result purely empirically. Thought experiments are what we can use because we have no way to set up controlled ones. And that is what we do in political philosophy and theory."

INDEX